Tell This Silence

Asian American Women Writers
and the Politics of Speech

Patti Duncan

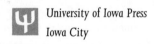 University of Iowa Press
Iowa City

University of Iowa Press, Iowa City 52242

Design by April Leidig-Higgins

http://www.uiowa.edu/uiowapress

The publication of this book was generously supported
by the University of Iowa Foundation.

Printed on acid-free paper

Library of Congress Cataloging-in-Publication Data
Duncan, Patti, 1970–
Tell this silence: Asian American women writers and the politics of speech /
by Patti Duncan.
   p.   cm.
Includes bibliographical references and index.
   Contents: The uses of silence and the will to unsay—What makes an Ameri-
can?: histories of immigration and exclusion of Asians in the United States in
Maxine Hong Kingston's China Men—White sound and silences from stone: discursive silences in the internment writings of Mitsuye Yamada and Joy Kogawa—
Cartographies of silence: language and nation in Theresa Hak Kyung Cha's Dictée—
Silence and public discourse: interventions into dominant national and sexual
narratives in Nora Okja Keller's Comfort Woman and Anchee Min's Red Azalea—Tell
this silence: Asian American women's narratives, gender, nation, and history.
   ISBN 0-87745-856-1 (cloth)
   1. American literature—Asian American authors—History and criticism.
2. American literature—Women authors—History and criticism.   3. Asian
American women—Intellectual life.   4. Politics and literature—United States.
5. Women and literature—United States.   6. Asian American women in literature.   7. Asian Americans in literature.   8. Sex role in literature.   9. Silence
in literature.   I. Title.
PS153.A84D86 2004
810.9'895—dc21   2003050739

04   05   06   07   08   C   5   4   3   2   1

contents

The mainstream [American] culture doesn't know the history of Chinese Americans, which has been written and written well. That ignorance makes a tension for me, and in [*China Men*] I just couldn't take it anymore. So all of a sudden, right in the middle of the stories, plunk—there is an eight-page section of pure history. . . . It really affects the shape of my book, and it might look quite clumsy. But on the other hand, maybe it will affect the shape of the novel in the future. Now maybe another Chinese American writer won't have to write that history.—Maxine Hong Kingston

preface

The above quotation, excerpted from Timothy Pfaff's interview with Maxine Hong Kingston about her book *China Men*, illustrates a tension within Asian American studies regarding the relationship between history and literature. I open with this quotation as a way to self-consciously note my own "clumsiness" in *Tell This Silence*, most notably demonstrated by the awkward and at times jarring juxtaposition of historical and literary themes and analyses. However, drawing together history and literature has long been a critical objective among scholars of Asian American studies. Asian Americans, so long excluded from the dominant history of the United States and written out of literary narratives that assume our nonexistence, continue to trouble the boundaries between these categories in search of new ways to tell our stories. Of such boundaries, we might ask, What is or should be the relationship between history and literature? What constitutes the "pure" history of which Kingston writes in the above quotation? How are the historical narratives of Asian American scholars and writers distinct from the dominant "official" histories of the United States? And in what ways do these histories both resist and risk reinscribing hegemonic relations in our search for some "truth" about the past?

In *Tell This Silence*, I rely on this disjuncture between history and literature, which comprises my method and strategy to trouble other boundaries and open up central questions crucial to Asian American, American, and women's studies, as well as the fields of history and literature. Having had little access to history—that dominant account of the past—or rendered invisible by historical silences, Asian Americans have written alternative histories, often through literary forms that explicitly challenge notions of authenticity. Sometimes such resistant narratives have functioned as attempts to offer a more complete version of the past, to fill in the gaps, to tell the "truth" about what happened. More often, however, recent writers and historians have suggested that we pay attention to the silences themselves, to what is considered unknown or unknowable, in order to learn why such elisions occurred in the first place and what political agendas serve and have been served by them.

Leslie Bow, in her conclusion to *Betrayal and Other Acts of Subversion*, writes: "I want not merely to replace what was previously unknown with empirical knowledge, but to question the very ways in which language produces meaning and how positionality and context are intrinsic to that production" (177). An interrogation of the dynamics of language, then, is critical to any understanding of how histories are produced, represented, and disseminated and the strategies, politics, and contexts that inform such processes. In *Tell This Silence*, I problematize language and its production of meaning by building on the groundbreaking work of King-Kok Cheung (1993) in order to explore historical and literary silences in the writings of Asian American women. While silence has operated as a significant trope in multiple social-justice movements within the Western world, the writers discussed in *Tell This Silence* implicitly critique the notion that breaking silence necessarily leads to freedom or empowerment. As recent events have clearly demonstrated, "free speech" is not a right enjoyed by all members of U.S. society.

For Asian Americans in general, and Asian American women in particular, the price of assimilation into and acceptance within U.S. culture has often been enforced silence. Asian American women are then both praised and blamed for their perceived silence. However, even breaking such silence has effected few and limited changes in the sociopolitical landscape for Asian American women. Because even when speaking out,

Asian American women have rarely been heard or taken seriously, and because speech is neither guaranteed nor necessarily liberating, Asian American women and members of other marginalized communities have often been forced to develop alternative strategies of resistance. To suggest that silence is one such strategy is not to suggest any simplistic celebration of silence. Neither is it to assert an easy conflation between silence and empowerment. Rather, emphasizing the forms of discourse engaged and enacted by silence breaks down the binary opposition so often posited between speech and silence. As Trinh T. Minh-ha suggests, silence, too, operates as a form of discourse and as a will to "unsay." Representing both a refusal to participate in the dominant narrativizing apparatuses that have excluded them and a form of resistance to the official historical record of the United States, silence for the writers in this book operates as a significant means to juxtapose their unofficial narratives against such totalizing histories.

In *Tell This Silence*, I discuss multiple meanings of silence in various texts by Asian American women writers, focusing on writers of Chinese, Japanese, and Korean descent. By doing so, I explore the ways in which silence is articulated or expressed by these writers, and I discuss the meanings and significance of such articulations. I rely on an interdisciplinary approach that revolves around historical and literary forms of analysis in order to adequately interrogate the many forms of silence deployed by the Asian American women writers in this text. I characterize this approach by turning to what Judith Halberstam calls a "queer methodology," in which she argues for a combination of multiple forms of analysis (including literary analysis, textual criticism, historical survey, etc.) that "betrays a certain disloyalty to conventional disciplinary methods" (10). Such a methodology, in Halberstam's words, is "a scavenger methodology that uses different methods to collect and produce information on subjects who have been deliberately or accidentally excluded from traditional studies" (13). Even though my focus in *Tell This Silence* is not exclusively queer subjects and themes, I feel that an analysis of the writings of Asian American women, who have been misrepresented or excluded altogether from traditional historical narratives, benefits from such a method.

While I take silence as my central theme, using it to interrogate the relationship between history and literature for Asian American women writers, I also map its relationship to conceptualizations and representations of nation and nationalism. In other words, silence operates as the trope around which multiple themes and questions revolve—relationships among race, gender, sexuality, and nation; between history and literature; between official and unofficial histories; and between feminist and nationalist positionings within Asian America. Thus, *Tell This Silence* also explores history's relationship to themes of nation and nationalism, considering the ways in which contemporary historicization is always bound up with representations of national identity and belonging. Even as I attempt to contest the truth of dominant history through literature, I am aware of the fact that no such "truths" can exist. Herein lies one of the methodological crises of *Tell This Silence*, which simultaneously represents an attempt to provide an alternative history and a disavowal of the promises of history altogether. Yet, for the time being, this contradictory space of contestation opens up a range of new possibilities for reconceptualizing the resistant narratives and strategies of Asian American women writers, who occupy a critical position in relation to history and literature, marked by gendered and racialized discursive practices that continually both reinscribe and subvert the terms of their positioning and subjectivity.

The first chapter of *Tell This Silence* offers an introduction to the multiple meanings of silence for Asian American women writers, suggesting the uses of silence as a method of confrontation and resistance. To place my discussion, I rely on readings of Kingston's *The Woman Warrior*. In the second chapter of this project, "What Makes an American?" I provide a historical overview of Asian immigration to the United States in order to broadly contextualize the entire project and the specific writings I discuss in subsequent chapters. To illustrate some of the historical immigration practices and early experiences of Asians in the United States, I rely on textual examples from Kingston's autobiographical work, *China Men*. Also in this chapter, I discuss processes of racialization in the United States in order to examine the ways in which American identities are constructed through processes of exclusion, including racism and anti-immigrant sentiments, especially in relation to dominant historical narratives.

In chapter 3, I include a discussion of what is one of the most talked about yet simultaneously most silenced event in Asian American history, the internment of persons of Japanese ancestry during World War II. I examine two internment narratives, Mitsuye Yamada's collection of poems, *Camp Notes*, and Joy Kogawa's novel, *Obasan*, in order to demonstrate the ways in which the "unofficial histories" of these two writers directly conflict with the official histories of the United States and Canada, questioning the realities of experience, history, and memory through language and silence. Chapter 4 continues my discussion of history and the politics surrounding the narration of histories of nation and national belonging through an examination of Theresa Hak Kyung Cha's experimental work, Dictée. Cha's text represents a significant attempt to unsay a particular history while also reinscribing a history of resistance. Dictée in many ways functions as a unidirectional letter, waiting for a response. Through various literary and visual strategies, Cha problematizes notions of history—what counts as history—as well as language, speech, silence, and translation. In this chapter, I interrogate both the silences surrounding the central themes of this text and the textual silences deployed by Cha.

In the final chapter, I turn to the issue of sexuality in writings by Asian American women, emphasizing the sexual silences in Nora Okja Keller's novel, Comfort Woman, and Anchee Min's autobiographical Red Azalea. Both writers force readers to rethink sexuality, sexual desire, sexual violence, and same-sex eroticism, especially within non-Western cultural contexts. Both texts rely on specific understandings of history, allowing each of the writers to reconceptualize language and silence in unique ways, especially in relation to national subjectivity. Finally, in the conclusion to this manuscript, I discuss the value of silence, in particular, to interventions into contemporary feminist theorizing. By demonstrating the multiple meanings of silence as well as the uses of silence, I envision this project, too, as an intervention into Anglo-American feminist analyses that valorize speech and equate voice with subjectivity, reducing silence to nonsubjectivity and therefore equating Asian American women's silences, in specific circumstances, with a lack of subjectivity. Such discussions have tended to overlook the involvement of Asian Pacific American women in the history of feminist movements in the United States, as well as the existence and cultural participation of Asian American people. Yet such exclusions and misrepresentations have not gone without question or challenge. In fact, the Asian American women writers whose work I explore in this project directly confront such practices and ideologies, and the reinscribing of silence as a strategy of resistance has been one significant means of doing so. While far from complete or definitive, I hope Tell This Silence engages other scholars of Asian American and women's studies to take up the questions posed in these chapters, aware of the values and meanings of multiple discursive practices and strategies.

acknowledgments

This work was inspired by the writings and scholarship of many Asian American women, in particular Theresa Hak Kyung Cha, Trinh T. Minh-ha, Mitsuye Yamada, King-Kok Cheung, and Elaine H. Kim. The title of this work comes from Theresa Hak Kyung Cha's *Chronology* (1977), published in *The Dream of the Audience: Theresa Hak Kyung Cha* (1951–1982), ed. Constance M. Lewallen (Berkeley: University of California Press, 2001), 110–127. I am indebted to these writers, whose creative risks and critical visions created the possibility for me to write this book. For support during the early stages of this work, I thank the Civil Liberties Public Education Fund, the Woodrow Wilson National Fellowship Foundation, the National Women's Studies Association Scholarship Fund, and Emory University's Institute for Women's Studies and Graduate School of Arts and Sciences. I also gratefully acknowledge Stephanie Cannizzo, curator of the Theresa Hak Kyung Cha Archive at the University of California–Berkeley Art Museum and Pacific Film Archive, who not only allowed me access to the writings and art of Cha but also engaged me in wonderfully stimulating discussions about Cha and about my own work.

I know I would never have begun to write *Tell This Silence* without the support and insight of Ami Mattison, who carefully read the very first drafts of this manuscript. For her willingness to envision this project with me, I am grateful. At Emory University, I was fortunate to find supportive mentors who encouraged me to think critically about the world around me. Mary Odem, Angelika Bammer, Kate Nickerson, Wendy Simonds, Beverly Guy-Sheftall, and especially Julie Abraham all gave generously of their time; they taught me important lessons about the concepts of gender, race, class, and sexuality in relation to feminism and women of color and pushed me to deepen my own analyses of these themes. And, from California, Elaine H. Kim generously offered her vision and enthusiasm for this project when it was most desperately needed. Her willingness to engage and mentor emerging scholars such as myself never ceases to amaze and inspire me.

This work has benefited from the comments and astute insights of many colleagues and friends. In particular, I thank Patti Sakurai, who has provided me with a sense of continuity. I feel fortunate to call her both a colleague and dear friend. Patricia Schechter warmly welcomed me to Portland, Oregon, consistently offering inspiration and companionship. I could not have found a better mentor or friend. And in Marie Lo I have found another rare friend and colleague whose humor and insightful reflection about our work sustained me through the final stages of completing this manuscript. Other friends and colleagues who influenced and/or sustained me in different ways and at various times during the long years of graduate school include Tiya Miles, Angie Cotten, Meredith Raimondo, Kimberly Springer, 'Becca Cragin, Lauraine LeBlanc, Namita Goswami, and Frances Wood. At Portland State University, I am indebted to Johanna Brenner and Ann Mussey for creating an environment in which research and writing about Asian American women and feminism can be taken seriously.

For their unconditional support, loving friendship, and willingness to engage with my endless discussions about the themes of this book, I also thank Svati Shah, Janet Guerrero, Patricia Kensel Hammes, Trishala Deb, Abbie Illenberger, Danielle Sansone, Sanford Posner, Tanya Pluth, Mitra Rahnema, Jeannie LaFrance, Brooks Nelson, Maude Hines, Sandra Harada, Emily Newmann, Jennifer Haejin Kim, Jacqueline Francis, Erin O'Briant, Estelle Green, Melissa Kulik, Zisca Burton, Sheri Davidowitz, Renee Gladman, Carol McElroy, Brooke McElroy, Allison McElroy, and especially Misty McElroy, who helped guide this project toward completion. Throughout the course of writing this book, a number of students have inspired me: Son Ah Yun, Mike Kim, Helena Kim, Lamya Chidiac, Lisa Davila, Asako Chihaya, Zack Menasche, Ismoon Hunter-Morton, Cheryl Wilson, and Leslie Bull. I especially thank my student and research assistant, Mashinda Hedgmon, from whom I have learned a great deal. And for administrative (and many other kinds of) support, I thank Kristin Engelbretson. I am also grateful to Prasenjit Gupta, my editor at University of Iowa Press, who believed in this project from the beginning, and who has offered extreme patience and many thoughtful insights. I thank the anonymous reviewers and the entire staff of the University of Iowa Press for the time and care they have taken to strengthen this book. My parents, Stanton Duncan and Sung Hee So Duncan, provided me with the tools to undertake such a project in the first place, and my sister, Susan Duncan, offered her consistency and faith in my ability to achieve my goals.

Finally, for her friendship and inspiration, I thank Akko Nishimura—a woman warrior in her own right—whose tragic, untimely passing on February 17, 2000, made me determine more than ever to gain a hearing for our many ways of "saying" and "unsaying." I dedicate this book to her and to other Asian American women fighting to find new ways to tell our stories and transform the world.

Grateful acknowledgment is given to Mitsuye Yamada and Rutgers University Press for permission to quote the following copyrighted works by Mitsuye Yamada: "Dialogue," "Evacuation," "Mess Hall Discipline," "The Night Before Goodbye," "Thirty Years Under," "Here," "There," "The Speech," and portions of "Enryo," "In the Outhouse," "Inside News," "Cincinnati," "Mirror Mirror," and "To the Lady," all from *Camp Notes and Other Poems*, copyright © 1976, 1980, 1986, 1988, 1992 by Mitsuye Yamada, reprinted by permission of Rutgers University Press. Also, I thank Janice Mirikitani for permission to quote the following copyrighted works: "We, the Dangerous," "Breaking Silence," and "Prisons of Silence," all of which appear in *We, the Dangerous: New and Selected Poems*, copyright © 1995 by Janice Mirikitani. I thank Greenwood Press for permission to reprint "The Uses of Silence: Notes on the 'Will to Unsay'" in *Women of Color: Defining the Issues, Hearing the Voices*, ed. Diane Long Hoeveler and Janet K. Boles, Greenwood Press, 2001. Finally, I gratefully acknowledge the U.C.-

Berkeley Art Museum and Pacific Film Archive for permission to reprint quotations from the following works by Theresa Hak Kyung Cha: "Artist's Statement" (presumed 1978), "It Is Almost That," and "Audience, Distant Relative," reprinted by permission of the Regents of the University of California.

Tell This Silence

Literary history and the present are dark with silences: some the silences for years by our acknowledged great; some silences hidden; some the ceasing to publish after one work appears; some the never coming to book form at all.

These are not natural silences, that necessary time for renewal, lying fallow, gestation, in the natural cycle of creation. The silences I speak of here are unnatural; the unnatural thwarting of what struggles to come into being, but cannot. In the old, the obvious parallels: when the seed strikes stone; the soil will not sustain; the spring is false; the time is drought or blight or infestation; the frost comes premature. — Tillie Olsen, *Silences*

one

Introduction.
The Uses of Silence and
the Will to Unsay

By calling this introductory chapter "The Uses of Silence," I invoke Audre Lorde's essay "The Uses of Anger: Women Responding to Racism," in which she discusses anger as an appropriate, viable, and useful response to racism. Anger, she writes, when "expressed and translated in the service of our vision and our future is a liberating and strengthening act of clarification. . . . [It] is loaded with information and energy" (127). Lorde compares anger to other, less useful responses to racism, such as reactionary defensiveness, hatred, and guilt. She suggests that guilt "is not a response to anger; it is a response to one's own actions or lack of action. . . . It becomes a device to protect ignorance and the continuation of things the way they are, the ultimate protection for changelessness" (130). Thus, Lorde effectively reclaims an emotion previously regarded as negative, even harmful. She examines the ways in which anger, within specific contexts, is "loaded with information and energy" and, when used as a means of social and personal transformation, can liberate and clarify.

Lorde's analysis of anger in relation to racism also serves to expand and complicate definitions and understandings of both race and racism. Her focus on women's racism links race to gender, suggesting the ways in which such categories of identity are inextricably intertwined and must be examined synchronously. In *Tell This Silence*, I recognize and acknowledge the many complex ways in which race and gender are structured in our culture, as well as the different forms that racism and sexism enact at various societal levels, from interpersonal interactions to larger sociostructural relationships. Also, I seek to expand the very concept of racism, as contemporary understandings of racism in the United States commonly fail to account for the cultural discrimination faced by Asian Americans, as well as other people of color and immigrants. Upon careful review, however, there seem to be multiple silences at work in relation to race, gender, sexuality, and national identity. Such silences are suggestive of the various social and political possibilities and processes inherent to discussions of the critical intersections of categories of identity. Hence, I look to the silences within writings by Asian American women in order to interrogate their meanings to contemporary discourse about the relationships among race, gender, sexuality, and national belonging.[1]

An examination of silence, in relation to Asian American women's experiences in the United States, opens questions regarding history, authenticity, and resistance to subjugation. As a critical reconceptualization and, at times, reclamation of silence, *Tell This Silence* attempts to reinscribe its potential as a strategy of resistance. I suggest that an exploration of the uses of silence offers new insights into the ways in which silence operates as a form of discourse and as a means of resistance to hegemonic power, particularly the forms of power structuring the lives of contemporary Asian American women. Interrogating and historicizing representations of silence within feminist and postcolonial writings and theories provide one significant site for reconsidering notions of language, translation, memory, and history—processes that remain crucial to political and social-justice agendas. Thus, I analyze the notion of silence within several Asian American women's narratives. I focus on this particular group for numerous reasons, not the least of which are the negative stereotypes (e.g., silence, passivity, deceptiveness, and inscrutability) often associated with women, with women of color in the United States, and with Asian American women in particular.

Along with silence, I also explore the cultural meanings of speech in the United States, often conceptualized as the opposite of silence. In fact the two are not binarily opposed but have most often been understood through such a framework within Western culture. *Tell This Silence* suggests that both speech and silence must be examined for their implicit meanings, the assumptions that underlie our understandings of them, and the complicated associations they have for and with marginalized groups of people in the United States. To demonstrate these points, I include in this introductory chapter a discussion of the multiple implications of speech and silence in Maxine Hong Kingston's *The Woman Warrior*.[2]

The Politics of Naming and Terminology

I use the terms "Asian American" and "Asian Pacific American" cautiously and rather self-consciously. While I use these terms interchangeably in some instances, I also recognize the specificity implied by each term. Like Chandra Talpade Mohanty's statements about her decision to use the problematic term "Third World woman," I recognize that while "[this] is the only terminology available to us at the moment," we must continue to question such designations. Mohanty suggests that she employs the term in order to designate a common context of struggle and to link women from various social and geographical locations (52–54). In fact, and most notably, she pushes the term beyond geography to demarcate a space that is social and political. Thus, "Third World," in this context, suggests those women often defined outside of current mainstream notions of feminism—women of "developing" countries, including those of radically disparate regions and economies; women of color in the Western world; and in some cases any and all women who choose to align themselves with "minority" women, who are situated within contexts of struggle and/or who imagine themselves as part of a community committed to exploring the relationships among race, gender, class, sexual identity, and national belonging. Thus, "Third World women" implies a political definition—not an essentialist one.[3] Similarly, Beverly Guy-Sheftall also advocates use of the term "Third World women" rather than or in addition to "women of color" in some contexts. Guy-Sheftall suggests that while problematic, "Third World women" may be more useful in moving out of the binary black/white framework so often implied by the term "women of color" and also situates feminist struggle within a global context.[4]

Other writers debate the political usefulness of terms such as "women of color" and "minority women." No simple exercise in semantics, such debates actually frame the interests and agendas of various social, economic, and political constituencies, highlighting the ways in which language is extremely political, especially for marginalized groups of people. For example, Nancy Naples discusses the political implications, within feminist organizing, of terms such as "Third World," "postcolonial," "international," "global," and "transnational." Underscoring each term are issues surrounding these politics of naming. "Postcolonial," for instance, while "typically applied to nations like India where a former colonial power has been removed . . . [may actually] mask continuing colonial relations that shape the lives of people in these nations" (5). Any attempt to apply singular definitions to diverse groups of women in relation to feminist struggle, Naples suggests, requires asking, "Who gets to define issues to be brought to the transnational political stage, who gets to participate in this form of activism, and whose voices are left out of the dialogue?" (8).

I use the term "Asian American" in the broadest sense to refer to individuals of Asian descent living in the United States. While my discussion also includes a work by an Asian Canadian writer, Joy Kogawa, I recognize that doing so, in the words of Laura Hyun Yi Kang, "risks reasserting the hegemony of the United States in claiming the identification of 'American' as a nationality" (2002, 216).[5] However, given that "Asian American" is itself a construction, produced through various sociopolitical transnational processes and diasporic movements, including Western intervention into Asian nations, the inclusion of Kogawa's text enables some consideration of the specific forms racialization of Asians has taken in both the United States and Canada. Many activists in the United States have preferred "Asian American" since the 1960s, when the word "Oriental" was critiqued and then discarded as a derogatory term connoting exoticism and inferiority. Also in the 1960s, the hyphen between "Asian" and "American" was eliminated by some writers and activists in order to affirm Asian Americans' sense of being American by avoiding the inference of split identities and not-quite-American status, as well as stereotypes of conflicted and tragically bifurcated Asian American identities. Other women of color, such as Gloria Anzaldúa, offer critiques of terms for ethnic groups that place ethnicity first, as adjectives, before the noun "American" (1987, 53–64). To Anzaldúa such a practice not only conveys that, for example, "Mexican Americans" are neither Mexican nor American, but when push comes to shove they must identify more as "American" than "Mexican"; to her this is a form of "copping out." Yet other members of ethnic minority groups have suggested that by claiming "American" for ourselves, we assert our status as belonging, and we intervene into preconceived ideas about what "American," after all, means.

"Asian American" as a term comes with its own set of problems. For instance, it masks differences among people of Asian descent based on national origin and national identity, region, class, generation, religion, etc. It seems to imply some sort of unity among all Asian countries, when this is not the case (in fact, there are long and complicated histories of colonization, war, and partitions among and within Asian countries). "Asian American" does not specify immigration and generational differences, though a great deal has been written about, for instance, the Issei, Nisei, and Sansei generations within Japanese American communities.[6] Furthermore, while the project of "claiming America," according to Shu-Mei Shih, was once the hallmark of Asian American identity politics, it has come under scrutiny in recent years by both Asian Americanists and new immigrants, who locate themselves in the spaces between two or more nations (144). Asians and Asian Americans are often conflated, taken to signify two interchangeable groups, thus equating national and racial identifications. However, many first-generation Asians in the United States may not identify themselves as Americans, and, as JeeYeun Lee states, "many people of all generations who originate from nations that have endured colonial subjugation in the past and/or neocolonial relationships in the present, such as the Philippines, reject Americanness: to a certain extent, these people have already been forcibly made 'American' in their own homelands" (116).

Finally, use of the terms "Asian American" and "Asian Pacific American" tends to marginalize certain groups and individuals that, at various historical moments, may or may not fall into this category legally, politically, or culturally. At the same time, the term "Asian American" seems to center other groups. For example, "Asian Pacific American" supposedly denotes those of Chinese, Japanese, Okinawan, Korean, Taiwanese,

Filipino, Indian, Bangladeshi, Bhutanese, Pakistani, Sri Lankan, Vietnamese, Indonesian, Thai, Burmese, Cambodian, Laotian, Malaysian, Singaporean, Nepalese, Hmong, native Hawai'ian, Guamanian, and Samoan descent, among others. However, at various historical moments, people of South Asian descent have been considered other than Asian or Asian American, or the term "South Asian" has been conflated with Indian, at the exclusion of "other" South Asians.[7] Pacific Islanders currently face exclusion, marginalization, or simply being engulfed into the classification of Asian American—"swallowed whole and remaining ever invisible among (East) Asian Americans" (Kauanui and Han 377). People of mixed heritage fail to live up to the standard image implied by the term "Asian American."[8] In fact, according to Lisa Lowe, anyone who is not male, heterosexual, middle-class, of East Asian descent, and English-speaking, does not qualify as "Asian American" in the sense that the term is often coded. Similarly, Elaine H. Kim writes that historically, there have not been many ways to be Asian American: "The ideal was male, heterosexual, Chinese or Japanese American and English-speaking. The center of Chinese America was San Francisco or New York Chinatown, and the heart of Japanese America was in Hawaii or along Highway 99. . . . Asian American history was about railroads, 'bachelor societies,' and internment" (1995, 12–13).

Asian Americans, then, have been homogenized by mainstream American culture and by those who comprise the so-called norm within Asian American communities. Members of dominant groups within the United States who have argued for the exclusion of Asians from this nation have viewed Asians as an expendable workforce and as interchangeable ("they all look alike"). Some members of dominant groups within Asian America (e.g., East Asians, men, the affluent and middle-class, the English-speaking), in their attempts to assimilate into Western capitalist paradigms of "success," have also homogenized Asian Americans, ignoring and erasing differences in gender, class, language, ethnicity, and even region and history.[9] It is this homogenization of Asian Americans that in some cases contributes to the oppression and cultural discrimination Asian Americans face in the United States. Lowe suggests that we acknowledge the ways in which cultural definitions must change along with social and economic realities. She writes, "The boundaries and definitions of Asian American culture are continually shifting and being contested from pressures both 'inside' and 'outside' the Asian-origin community"

(1996, 66). She urges us to recognize the ways in which Asian America constitutes heterogeneous, hybrid, and multiple social locations.

I employ the term "Asian American," then, with full awareness of its problematic political and social implications. As a strategic term and group identification, it lends itself to the illusion of unity, masking differences that, some argue, threaten the already precarious position of Asians in the United States. As *Tell This Silence* suggests, however, our recognition of such differences, with careful consideration of the historical, social, and political trajectories of the distinct experiences of Asian Americans, will ultimately strengthen Asian American communities.

The Transformation of Silence

The notion of silence has long been a trope in liberation and social-justice movements in the United States, including feminist, lesbian/gay/bisexual/transgender, and civil rights and antiracist struggles and movements of people of color.[10] Since the late 1960s and early 1970s, feminist and African American, Asian and Pacific Islander American, Native American, and Latino/a and Chicano/a activist leaders have advocated to their constituencies the importance of "finding a voice," of "speaking out" against oppression and injustice, and of moving away from the silences that may imply consent to subjugation, as well as to the maintenance of dominant power.[11] The liberatory rhetoric of U.S. gay and lesbian—and queer—movements have also utilized notions of "speaking out" and "breaking silence" by linking those acts with the process of coming out. Similarly, AIDS activists proclaim "silence = death" and demand that we "break the silence" imposed upon our lives. This rhetoric, its common appeal to "speaking out," "finding a voice," and "breaking silence," places its liberatory aspirations precisely within the very discourses of speech, suggesting that speech itself represents liberation, while in opposition to speech, silence represents both the precondition and the very foundations of oppression.

Invisibility, loss, absence, repression, oppression, the unspoken, the unknown—these concepts continue to be equated with silence, while visibility, gain, presence, liberation, and "truth" are equated with the act of speech itself. As such, silence becomes antithetical to liberatory agendas and practices in the realm of political activism and in fields of scholarship. In these contexts, certain Eurocentric premises regarding social norms about speech and silence prevail. Free speech is supposedly one of the few protected rights of citizens. However, as Kyo Maclear suggests, the idea that all speech is "free" is open to critique. She notes the frequent operations of censorship and oppression, and she questions the notion that democratic participation and representation are ensured through "speech." This speech is located in a Western philosophical tradition that posits, in the words of Maclear, "speech = agency = freedom" (8). Thus, subjectivity is defined in opposition to silence. Concurrently, speech is conceived to be a necessary condition for subjectivity.

Speech and silence are themes that continue to recur among feminist writings and in the writings of people of color in the United States. Adrienne Rich, in her influential essay, "Taking Women Students Seriously" (1978), writes about women's silences in the classroom. She urges readers to consciously explore the actions and behaviors of women students, especially women's relationships to language, speech, and silence.

> Look at the many kinds of women's faces, postures, expressions. Listen to the women's voices. Listen to the silences, the unasked questions, the blanks. Listen to the small, soft voices, often courageously trying to speak up, voices of women taught early that tones of confidence, challenge, anger, or assertiveness, are strident and unfeminine. Listen to the voices of the women and the voices of the men; observe the space men allow themselves, physically and verbally, the male assumption that people will listen, even when the majority of the group is female. Look at the faces of the silent, and of those who speak. Listen to a woman groping for language in which to express what is on her mind, sensing that the terms of academic discourse are not her language, trying to cut down her thought to the dimensions of a discourse not intended for her. . . . (243–244)

To Rich, then, speech, assertiveness, even confidence, are discouraged in women during processes of socialization because such qualities are assumed to be unfeminine and therefore threatening to the status quo. For a woman to break free from such constraints requires grappling with and overcoming socialization and societal expectations of gender roles and language, since the very language that surrounds us is a male-dominated discourse, a language of male domination over women. Similarly, Gloria Anzaldúa, nearly ten years later, writes, "language is a male discourse" (1987, 54). Recounting an experience of the first time she overheard two Spanish-speaking women use the word *nosotras* (a feminine rewriting of the generally masculine plural form, *nosotros*), she writes, "I was shocked. I had not known the word existed. We are robbed of our female being by the masculine plural" (54). Silences, in these two examples, result from gender socialization and cultural domination.[12]

bell hooks also urges women, especially women of color, to start "talking back," to challenge silences, in order to resist objectification and become active subjects of our experiences and lives. Underlying her analysis of women's silences is a complex understanding of various differences speech and silence may represent for members of different societal groups. "Within feminist circles," she writes, "silence is often seen as the sexist 'right speech of womanhood'—the sign of woman's submission to patriarchal authority" (1989, 6). However, while it might be accurate to suggest that white women have been silent (and silenced), hooks argues, women in black communities have not. The struggle for black women, she suggests, "has not been to emerge from silence into speech but to change the nature and direction of our speech, to make a speech that compels listeners, one that is heard" (6). Thus, it is not simply that silence can and must be replaced with speech (any silence, any speech). Rather, as stated earlier, both speech and silence must be continually interrogated for their meanings, both explicit and implicit. As modes of discourse, they suggest certain assumptions about and associations for people of color in the United States.

Other writers, including Darlene Clark Hine, Paula Giddings, Evelyn Brooks Higginbotham, and Patricia Hill Collins, have discussed the politics of silence in the history of African American women, where sexuality in particular represents an unspoken/unknown realm for a variety of historical reasons.[13] These silences of black women, while protective devices, have also had physical, psychological, and emotional consequences. Hine suggests that rape and/or the threat of rape influenced the development of a "culture of dissemblance" among black women, within a context of institutionalized sexual violence against black women. Defining dissemblance as "the behavior and attitudes of Black women that created the appearance of openness and disclosure [while] actually shield[ing] the truth of their inner lives and selves from their oppressors" (292), Hine argues that this culture was an effect and "ideological consequence" of the consolidation of links between black women and illicit sexuality during the antebellum years. Thus, in the face of multiple attacks upon all aspects of black women's sexuality, dissemblance became a strategy of self-protection and a means of retaining some sense of self and control over their own bodies, sexualities, reproduction, and children (293–294). While this culture of dissemblance became an effective tool for protection and enabled black women to assert agency over their own bodies and lives, Hine argues that one major consequence of such a culture has been the "absence of sophisticated historical discussion of the impact of rape (or threat of rape) and incidences of domestic violence on the shape of Black women's experiences" (295). In addition, many black women, she argues, have felt "compelled to downplay, even deny, sexual expression" (295) in order to counter negative stereotypes. The silences, in this case, while strategic and useful, have had very real consequences.

Similarly, Traise Yamamoto discusses the ways in which Japanese American women have donned the "mask" as a form of self-protection and strategy for survival. Yamamoto suggests that masking, much like silence, has been one of the few strategies available for Japanese American women, especially contextualized within the history of internment and a general reluctance to speak about Japanese Americans' experiences in the camps during World War II. She writes: "Inaugurated by the trauma of the racially marked, gendered, and sexualized body's positioning in the social economy of the United States, masking is a resistant strategy by which the body and, through the body, subjectivity may be claimed" (100–101). Masking, then, has enabled some Japanese American women writers to engage themes of internment, violence, and degrading sexualized representations, yet at what costs?[14]

Abdul JanMohamed refers to the institution of slavery in the United States as an "open secret," where racialized sexuality functioned historically as a peculiar *silence*—a will to conceal, rather than a will to knowledge, in the Foucaultian sense. In JanMohamed's analysis, silence remains a force of oppression whereby certain groups have not only been silenced historically but are effectively written out of history itself. He argues for an "equal historical articulation" for African Americans in particular (116). Such an articulation must do more than simply insert African Americans into history, it must also critically revise the methods and tools of historicization. Thus, he seems to suggest, it is only through articulation—an act of speech—that we can address the silences surrounding the historical oppression of African Americans.

Audre Lorde asserts the necessity, for oppressed groups of people, to find ways to transform our silences into actions that may be part of various struggles to end domination. In her essay "The Transformation of Silence into Language and Action," she writes, "My silences have not protected me. Your silence will not protect you. . . . What are the words you do not have yet? What do you need to say?" (41). In describing the discovery of her breast cancer and her subsequent feelings about the possibility of death, Lorde states that she was "forcibly and essentially aware of [her] mortality . . . and what [she] most regretted were [her] silences" (41). It was "learning to put fear into a perspective," she writes, that gave her the strength to break those silences (41). That Lorde mentions fear is significant to her analysis of silence, for she suggests that fear is commonplace for marginalized and oppressed groups of people who, in fact, were "never meant to survive" (42). Breaking silences, to Lorde, does not mean living without fear but simply speaking out despite the fears of censure, of contempt, of judgment, of challenge, of visibility, and even of annihilation. She argues that because of distorted and stereotypical images and interlocking systems of racism and sexism in this country, visibility is simultaneously the greatest source of vulnerability and the greatest source of strength for women of color (42).

Other writers also link speaking and silence to notions of visibility and invisibility. Mitsuye Yamada exhorts Asian Pacific American women to "make ourselves more visible by speaking out on the condition of our sex and race and on certain political issues which concern us" (1981, 71). Yet she cautions against the kind of visibility that is reducible to stereotypes and one-dimensional representations of "the passive, sweet . . . 'Oriental woman'" (1981, 71). Likewise, Yamamoto observes that Asian American women, when not invisible, have often been most visible only as sexually exotic objects. Writing by Asian American women, she notes, "suggests that feelings of invisibility compete with feelings of being all too visible, resulting in images of fragmentation, splitting and corrosion" (74). Thus, it is not that any visibility—or any act of speech, for that matter—will do. Rather, speaking out and being seen must occur in very particular ways to be of any value to the kinds of societal transformations these writers advocate. In other words, language and visibility that can be reduced to stereotypical representations only contribute to the oppression of women of color. Anzaldúa, in her "Letter to Third World Women Writers," writes, "[the] woman of color is invisible both in the white male mainstream world and in the white women's feminist world. . . . [T]he lesbian of color is not only invisible, she doesn't even exist. Our speech, too, is inaudible. We speak in tongues like the out-cast and the insane" (1981, 165). In Anzaldúa's example, speech is not absent but misunderstood, incomprehensible, or unnoticed altogether.

And, too, entire fields of study seem intimately bound to the issues of speech and silence, visibility and invisibility. Historians of sexuality and queer studies rely on these themes and frameworks to discuss a history of sexual oppression in the United States.[15] For example, the editors of *Hidden from History*, an anthology that purports to "reclaim the gay and lesbian past," suggest that the first phase of this sort of history involves what they refer to as biographical reclamation.[16] In other words, first we must find and restore to history those gay and lesbian lives that heretofore have been missing, absent, invisible. Yet this notion of invisible, silent, isolated individuals living in shame and secrecy has been called into question in recent years. John D'Emilio and George Chauncey, among others, have attempted to dispel the myths of what Chauncey calls "isolation," "invisibility," and "internalization."[17] Chauncey, for one, seeks not to uncover previously hidden lives but to restore to history a whole social world—"highly visible, remarkably complex, and continually changing" (1)—a gay male world with a distinctive culture and language in New York City between the years 1890 and 1940. Others such as Jennifer Terry argue instead for an "effective history" that might be attentive to "the ruptures and discontinuities in history" and useful as "an interventionist strategy . . . necessary to those positioned in the margins of dominant accounts" (56). She writes:

> [This paradigm] involves what Foucault calls "historical sense"—a strategic awareness of points of emergence or "possibilities" existing at particular historical moments in the formation of particular discourses. . . . Effective history allows us to theorize a counterdiscursive position of history-telling which neither fashions a new coherence, nor provides a more inclusive resolution of contradicting "events." . . . Effective history exposes not the events and actors elided by traditional history, but instead lays bare the processes and operations by which these elisions occurred. (56)

In other words, Terry emphasizes discursive "silences," those historical gaps or elisions, as the very sites upon which to interrogate history.

Queer theorists and film critics search novels, films, and other cultural texts for any indication of lesbian or gay themes, "the love that dare not speak its name." For example, Deborah McDowell, Bonnie Zimmerman, and Teresa de Lauretis, to name a few, have attempted to re-read familiar narratives for lesbian content, asserting the notion of "coding" as a significant representational strategy for lesbian and gay texts.[18] However, the assertion of "coded" representations relies on assumptions of silence, secrecy, and repression as an implicit and overarching framework for the production of lesbian, gay, bisexual, and transgender images and narratives. Thus, the reliance on notions of "coded" representations tends to relocate queer subjectivities within dominant discourses that associate sexuality in general and homosexuality in particular with the unspoken and unspeakable. Also, as Julie Abraham suggests, certain texts (and lives) can be read as "coded" or silenced "only if the lesbian novel is understood as the lesbian text" (24).[19] She writes:

> The repression hypothesis from which coding derives implies that there were other, more direct ways for saying what was being said, of writing "about lesbianism," that the writer avoided because of social pressure. It implies, moreover, that we know the forms lesbian writing would take were it not for social hostility. . . .
>
> "Coding" implies that heterosexual and lesbian writers occupied different literary worlds, and that public and private speech can be clearly differentiated. (25)[20]

Thus, as Abraham's analysis suggests, the notion of coding precludes a more critical analysis of the roles and functions of silence in more than simple causal relationships or easy binaries between speech/silence, visibility/invisibility, public/private, repression/liberation, and a host of other relationships that imply implicit vs. explicit "truths" to be known and that tend to homogenize marginalized persons.

Silence, conceptualized as antithetical to the liberation of oppressed groups of people, has most often been viewed as yet another method and symbol of oppression. However, such interpretations fail to recognize the different forms and meanings silence may take, as well as the ways in which speech acts, too, are limited and constrained. There are qualitative distinctions between being silent and being *silenced*. Similarly, as I have suggested, it is a quite different process to be silent than it is to be unheard. One may speak and simply not be listened to, understood, or taken seriously. Thus, even speech is structured by always already existent relations of power. As Maclear states, freedom of speech in the

United States is not necessarily a protected right enjoyed by all members of society. Not all silences are the same; likewise, speech acts may also be distinct from one another in their meanings, implications, and effects. Hence, we might ask, How effective are "speaking out," "finding a voice," "breaking silence," and "coming out" as liberatory rhetoric and political acts when such notions rely on the very discursive practices through which social and political domination occurs? How might silence also represent a means of political resistance to domination, rather than a means of compliance? And how might silence signify political and social agency rather than solely the loss or lack of such agency?

Gendered Subjectivity and the Uses of Silence

Silence is not simply the absence of speech. In his influential *History of Sexuality*, Michel Foucault questions the Western myth of sexual repression. Foucault interprets the act of confession as part of a will to knowledge, a form of seeking "truth" whereby speaking is both demanded by and a demand for power. Power is both productive and prohibitive; in fact prohibition, or not speaking, is part of the production of power. Foucault's theory suggests that silence, too, is productive, and it is not to be understood in opposition to speech but as a part of discourse; silence in such a model may operate as a different way of saying.

In her essay "Not You/Like You," Trinh T. Minh-ha identifies the uses of silence as a form of difference that "undermines the very idea of identity" (372). She writes: "Within the context of women's speech silence has many faces. . . . Silence is commonly set in opposition with speech. Silence as a will not to say or a will to unsay and as a language of its own has barely been explored" (1990, 372–373). And in *Woman, Native, Other*, Trinh suggests that "silence as a refusal to partake in the story does sometimes provide us with a means to gain a hearing. It is a voice, a mode of uttering, and a response in its own right" (83). Silence, rather than being outside of discourse, is very much within it, functioning along with and in relation to what is said. However, silence may also be misconstrued. Trinh goes on to suggest that without other silences, "[her] silence goes unheard, unnoticed; it is simply one voice less, or more point given to the silencers" (1989, 83). Thus, silence functions as a way of saying (and of unsaying) and is related to ways of seeing (unseeing) and knowing (unknowing), but it is useful only in contexts of other silences, whereby it signifies resistance rather than voicelessness.

The relationship between speech and silence represents a site of power wherein subjectivities may be created, destroyed, or otherwise transformed. Yet, this site is highly unstable, and those processes of subjectivity, implied by speech/silence, are all the more tenuous. As Trinh highlights, the meanings of speech and silence are always open to (mis)-interpretation. And Foucault suggests that the act of speaking, or confessing, does not necessarily lead to liberation from power; rather, it acts as the very process by which power is produced. Also, as noted earlier, within specific historical and cultural contexts, the production of "free" speech remains regulated and controlled.[21] Finally, notions of speaking tend to posit specific conceptions of subjectivity. For instance, Sagri Dhairyam describes the binary established in the field of queer theory between the "silent closeted native" and the articulate (speaking) white queer (32). Her assertion suggests that breaking silence and coming out for people of color may involve moving away from specific cultural traditions —and spaces—and into (white) lesbian or gay subjecthood.

More than simply a trope, then, silence for marginalized groups of people in the United States and elsewhere is also a history, a reality, and a lived experience. Silencing is a means of domination, and access to free speech is often limited. Control of language is a constant and powerful tool in the acts of domination and colonization. Within such political contexts, speaking and its association with writing become crucial for the centering of previously marginalized subjectivities. For instance, associated with the speech so central to feminism is the de-centering of the neutral, unmarked (read: male) subject. For women, subjectivity, demarcated by the "I" who speaks and writes, has always been disturbed by silence(s), gaps, and elisions: the unrepresented, the unseen, the unsaid. Dichotomous thinking within Western culture implies binaries such as man/woman, Western/Eastern, mind/body, culture/nature, and subject/object.[22] Such oppositions generally privilege one part of the dichotomy over the other, holding up, for example, men, the West, the mind, culture, and the subject as superior. These terms, Collins states, gain meaning only in relation to their counterparts. Those who occupy inferior subject positions are often viewed in opposition to the "norms" of our culture—male, white, Western, middle-class, heterosexual, able-bodied, etc.—and are therefore viewed as society's "others" and accordingly objectified. Feminist writers have explored the consequences of being rendered "other," in terms of language and the struggle for subjectivity, since at least the early part of the twentieth century.

My analyses are influenced by other feminist writings on the theme of silence, attributed by many to the early work of Tillie Olsen, both her talks at the Radcliffe Institute in the early 1960s and her text, *Silences*, published in 1978. In their introduction to the anthology *Listening to Silences*, Elaine Hedges and Shelley Fisher Fishkin identify the theme of silence as not only "central to feminist literary inquiry" but also a means to understand women's experiences on a multitude of levels (3). Citing works by Marge Piercy, Adrienne Rich, Joanna Russ, and Audre Lorde, Hedges and Fishkin document a recent history of feminist writings about silence. They suggest that while Olsen originally relied on the notion of silence in order to emphasize external impediments to and constraints on women's writing (related to "their more limited access to education, cultural pressures that dissuaded them from taking themselves seriously as artists, the fragmentation of their time amidst the duties and distractions of motherhood, or the workings of a male literary establishment that excluded them" [5]), a new critical perspective, influenced by poststructuralist and postmodern theories, stresses as well the silences within—and "intrinsic to"—texts. Silences, according to this critical perspective, "might reveal reticences culturally imposed upon women, the workings of a repressed ideology, or, alternatively, women's deployment of silence as a form of resistance to the dominant discourse" (5).

In *A Room of One's Own* (1929), Virginia Woolf comments on the great "I" of literature and history:

> It was delightful to read a man's writing again. It was so direct, so straightforward after the writing of women. It indicated such freedom of mind, such liberty of person. . . . All this was admirable. But after reading a chapter or two a shadow seemed to lie across the page. It was a straight dark bar, a shadow shaped something like the letter "I." One began dodging this way and that to catch a glimpse of the landscape behind it. Whether that was indeed a tree or a woman walking I was not quite sure. Back one was always hailed to the letter "I" . . . the worst of it is that in the shadow of the letter "I" all is shapeless as mist. Is that a tree? No, it is a woman. But . . . she has not a bone in her body. (103–104)

Woolf highlights the gender politics of writing and language. The traditional "I" of Western literature and history, according to Woolf, represents (white) male subjectivity. This "I" looms large over our cultural landscape, blurring and overshadowing the subjectivities of woman/women. Yet Woolf's solution asserts not a challenge to, or an undoing of, the assumed normativity of this "I" but rather a lack of sex-consciousness, an unmarking, a disavowal.

More recently, debates within feminist criticism have engaged issues of reading and writing "as" or "like" a woman or a man.[23] These dialogues raise questions about the relationship between speaking and writing. Significantly, they also introduce issues of language, subject position, and subjectivity. For example, in *The Lesbian Body* (1973), Monique Wittig suggests that language is always political: to say "I" [Je] one must be a subject. She proposes "j/e" to symbolize the impossibility of speech for the divided nonsubject.

> The "I" [Je] who writes is alien to her own writing at every word because this "I" [Je] uses a language alien to her; this "I" [Je] experiences what is alien to her since this "I" [Je] cannot be "un ecrivain." . . . J/e is the symbol of the lived, rending experience which is m/y writing, of this cutting in two which throughout literature is the exercise of a language which does not constitute m/e as subject. J/e poses the ideological and historic questions of feminine subjects. . . . If I [J/e] examine m/y specific situation as subject in the language, I [J/e] am physically incapable of writing "I" [Je]. I [J/e] have no desire to do so. (10–11)

According to Wittig, in order to signify a *subject*, "I" cannot be partial or relative. "I" cannot be silent; "I" must speak.

It is precisely this "I," so troubling to white, Western feminists, that also presents problems (related yet significantly different) for Asian American women writers. For instance, young Maxine,[24] narrator of Maxine Hong Kingston's autobiographical *The Woman Warrior*, cannot understand this English—this *American*—"I." "The Chinese 'I' has seven strokes—intricacies. How could the American 'I,' assuredly wearing a hat like the Chinese, have only three strokes, the middle so straight?" (166). And Maxine's confusion over the "I" is underscored by her silence, by her inability to speak in school. "It was when I found out I had to talk that school became a misery, that the silence became a misery. I did not speak and felt bad each time I did not speak. . . . I knew the silence had to do with being a Chinese girl" (166). And this silence, she writes, was "thickest—total—during the three years that [she] covered [her] school paintings with black paint" (165).[25] This silence causes her misery and shame. Her "broken" voice, when she forces it out, is even worse— "weak," "frozen," and "ugly," described by a Chinese woman from her family's village as the quack of a duck (165, 192). Her mouth, she writes, "went permanently crooked with effort, turned down on the left side and straight on the right" (171). Interestingly enough, the silence noted here is imagined as already existent, problematic only in the context of enforced speech in the American educational system of school. What is it about "being a Chinese girl" that colludes with and even produces silence and makes speech so difficult? Kingston seems to suggest such possibilities as U.S. school systems, processes of remembering, "Americanization," and standards of femininity as underlying the production of silence for the narrator.

Indeed, critics have suggested that the Chinese "I" is strikingly distinct from the American "I," marking a cultural difference in experiences of subjectivity. In Judy Yung's analysis of Jade Snow Wong's autobiography, *Fifth Chinese Daughter* (1950), deference to parents and elders was ingrained in Wong and signified "her understanding of her proper place in the Confucian hierarchical order" (117). While autobiographical, the book is written in the third person, identified by Wong as "Chinese habit." In fact, according to Wong, "in written Chinese, prose or poetry, the word 'I' almost never appears, but is understood. . . . Even written in English, an 'I' book by a Chinese would seem outrageously immodest to anyone raised in the spirit of Chinese propriety" (Yung 117). However, as Yung points out, Wong does not follow such a practice in her second autobiography, *No Chinese Stranger* (1975), in which Wong begins in the third person singular but changes to first-person midway through the text. Resonating with Virginia Woolf's experience, the change occurs after her account of her father's death, suggesting that in Wong's case, it was only after his death that she was able to assert her identity through first-person narration.[26] Such an example suggests the consequences of patriarchal oppression for women's subjectivity. Also of significance, however, in a Chinese American woman's refusal to employ the first-person "I" in a narrative is its equation with subjugation. Kingston writes, "There is a Chinese word for the female I—which is 'slave.'

Break the women with their own tongues!" (47). Thus, in questioning this "I," a symbol of subjectivity for American women, writers such as Kingston and Wong signify their refusal to be participants in their own victimization.

In educational institutions as well as other locations of mainstream U.S. culture, a high premium is placed on speech and language. Pedagogical discussions of race and classroom dynamics often focus on the silence of Asian American students and other students of color, generally chalked up to "their cultures" as though culture is static and atemporal. In her essay "Not in So Many Words," Maclear discusses her own silence in the classroom and her experiences as an Asian Pacific American student. She writes that she was silenced by being made to feel that she, as a woman of color, had nothing of value to contribute to class discussions. Silences in the classroom, however, may also relate to the content of what is studied (particularly the lack of subject materials about women and people of color in the United States), as well as the absence of instructors or other students of similar racial, cultural, or class backgrounds.[27] Maclear states that in her case, "racialized and gendered constructions of Asian women had functioned to serve up my silence as 'good 'n' natural'—as emblematic of my docility and obedience" (6). Her silence was perceived, then, as natural to Asian American women, buttressing stereotypes of Asian American women as obedient, passive, and lacking in subjectivity. Yet in her analysis, Maclear states that she was not being "silenced" as much as she was unheard—"a more subtle and insidious form of exclusion" (7). Her statement suggests, once again, the distinct ways in which language and silence may be structured in society for members of various groups according to subject position.

In her work *Articulate Silences*, King-Kok Cheung discusses the multiple meanings of silences in works by Hisaye Yamamoto, Maxine Hong Kingston, and Joy Kogawa. She questions the placement of verbal and nonverbal forms of communication into hierarchical terms, suggesting that the meanings of silence must be culturally contextualized. Through her discussion of distinct forms of silence, including "rhetorical," "provocative," and "attentive" silences, she argues that the Asian American women writers under consideration employ strategies of silence to engage directly with history, offering critiques of the histories that have homogenized and excluded them or effaced their subjectivities.

For Wittig, speech is related to memory. She urges women to remember, and, if unable to remember, then to *rewrite* the past: "You say you have lost all recollection of it, remember. . . . You say there are no words to describe this time, you say it does not exist. But remember. Make an effort to remember. Or, failing that, *invent*" (1969, 89; emphasis added).[28] Wittig links the absence of memory to an absence of language, resonant of Rich's assertion that the language available to us is a male-dominated language incapable of the full expression of women's ideas and thoughts. And for young Maxine as well, the problem of memory is not simply a matter of forgetting. Rather, memory and history are themselves marked by peculiar silences. She writes: "How could I have that memory when I couldn't talk? My mother says that we, like the ghosts, have no memories" (167). Indeed, the narrator's mother links her children's lack of memory to their lack of feelings and interprets both in relation to her inability to effectively communicate with them (115). Here in the United States among the "barbarians,"[29] where the children speak English, Kingston's parents do not seem to hear them (123). She cannot remember because she cannot speak; she cannot speak because she cannot remember. Moreover, there are reasons why she is not *supposed* to remember. "We had so many secrets to hold in. . . . There were secrets never to be said in front of the ghosts, immigration secrets whose telling could get us sent back to China" (182–183). Maxine's parents tell lies on a regular basis—they give false names, addresses, birthdates, and former jobs. Significantly, as I discuss in the following chapter, exclusionary U.S. immigration procedures actually encouraged and even facilitated such "lies." Because of changing restrictions and injustices, Asian immigrants in particular often had little recourse but to falsify information and documents in order to enter the country or to bring family members to the United States. One major exempt status of the Chinese Exclusion Act, for example, resulted in the emigration of large numbers of "paper sons" and "paper daughters" to the United States. In such cases, young people could claim derivative citizenship in order to enter the country by purchasing the name and family status of Chinese men already living in America (Yung 106). In addition, those immigrants who had already entered the United States often created slots for new immigrants by falsely documenting children who did not exist, thereby further complicating familial histories and relationships.[30]

Also, in *The Woman Warrior*, parents keep truths about their lives and histories from their children: "They would not tell us because we had been born among ghosts, were taught by ghosts, and were ourselves ghost-like" (183). This "ghostliness" of which Kingston speaks represents generational differences, linguistic differences, and contextualized against the very real threat of immigration authorities and deportation, the possible betrayals of parents by children. Kingston writes that for her parents, America was "full of machines and ghosts" (96). To her mother, Brave Orchid, the country represents a "terrible ghost country, where a human being works her life away" (104). Both her mother and father mythologize China as "home," and in so doing, "they suspended America. They suspended enjoyment" (99).[31] However, though her parents fear America, they fear deportation and an enforced return to China even more, thereby justifying the many lies and secrets that must be maintained.

On the one hand, Maxine's parents keep secrets because the differences between the generations and the "Americanization" of their children are disturbing to them: "They called us a kind of ghost. Ghosts are noisy and full of air; they talk during meals. They talk about anything" (183–184). The children's "ghostliness" comes to signify their "Americanness," their "noisy . . . talk[ing] during meals." On the other hand, as I have pointed out, there are valid reasons to lie to authorities:

> Lie to Americans. Tell them you were born during the San Francisco earthquake. Tell them your birth certificate and your parents were burned up in the fire. Don't report crimes; tell them we have no crimes and no poverty. Give a new name every time you get arrested; the ghosts won't recognize you. Pay the new immigrants twenty-five cents an hour and say we have no unemployment. And, of course, tell them we're against Communism. Ghosts have no memories anyway and poor eyesight. (184–185)

Kingston relates memory to vision and sight, connecting what is known to what is seen (or cannot be seen, as the case may be). "There were secrets never to be said in front of the ghosts," she notes, "immigration secrets whose telling could get us sent back to China" (183). Indeed, Maxine feels silenced by both the ghostlike immigration authorities and her parents, who admonish her not to tell. "Sometimes I hated the ghosts for not letting us talk; sometimes I hated the secrecy of the Chinese. 'Don't tell,' said my parents, though we couldn't tell if we wanted to because we didn't know" (183).[32] She writes, "even the good things are unspeakable. . . . If we had to depend on being told, we'd have no religion, no babies, no menstruation (sex, of course, unspeakable), no death" (185).

Memory, and remembering, are key to subjectivity and speech in *The Woman Warrior*. Yet the subjectivities in question are culturally specific:

> Normal Chinese women's voices are strong and bossy. We American-Chinese girls had to whisper to make ourselves American-feminine. . . . Some of us gave up, shook our heads, and said nothing, not one word. Some of us could not even shake our heads. . . . We invented an American-feminine speaking personality, except for that one girl who could not even speak up in Chinese school. (172)

Whispering is the way to become "American-feminine," and failing that performance, silence becomes a last resort. Interestingly, while silence is marked as a trait peculiar to being a Chinese girl, it is also implicated in becoming "American-feminine." While Western theories of subjectivity might imply that American identity is structured around acts of speech, for Maxine, part of attaining status as an American girl is learning how to whisper, how to be silent. Doing so, and making her life "American-normal," must involve pushing "the deformed into [her] dreams, which are in Chinese, the language of impossible stories" (87). The achievement of a specifically gendered American subjectivity, then, revolves around a process of disavowal of all things Chinese, including Chinese manners of speaking. Thus, Kingston disrupts the binaries often established between speech and silence, between American and Chinese. Also, for Maxine, the constraints of femininity and gender performance are marked by race and culture. Performing femininity is not enough—in the public space of school, she must perform a specifically white American femininity.[33]

Discussing the speech of her family members and others in the immigrant community, Kingston writes:

> The immigrants I know have loud voices, unmodulated to American tones even after years away from the village where they called their friendships out across the fields. I have not been able to stop my mother's screams in public libraries or over telephones. Walking erect (knees straight, toes pointed forward, not pigeon-toed, which is Chinese-feminine) and speaking in an inaudible voice, I have tried to turn myself American-feminine. Chinese communication was loud, public. (11)

Becoming American means learning to walk and talk differently. Kingston suggests that the loud, public modes of communication commonly employed by Chinese in China—the "strong and bossy" tones of Chinese women—are no longer appropriate in American contexts and that finding her American voice has meant learning to speak inaudibly or not at all. And it is not just the loudness of the Chinese language, she writes, but "the way Chinese sounds, chingchong ugly, to American ears. . . . We make guttural peasant noises and have Ton Duc Thang names you can't remember" (171–172). Because femininity is associated with (white) American-ness for the girls in school, feminine subjectivity provokes cultural and familial crises. Adopting "American-feminine" traits means further distancing themselves from what is perceived as authentically Chinese. It also throws into crisis the notion of an authentic way of being Chinese. However, Kingston's words also suggest contradictory impulses. The Chinese American girls in The Woman Warrior are configured as always already silent, silence being an inherent—and negative—cultural trait. At the same time, they are loud and in need of domestication —silencing—in order to be perceived as properly American. If silence, for her, signifies a loss of full subjectivity, it also implies her resistance to the process of mainstream acculturation and Americanization that is so difficult for her and her family members. To what extent, in these examples, might silence also be a means of resistance to the seemingly impossible task of becoming "American-feminine"? What of that "one girl who could not [would not?] even speak up in Chinese school"?

While this girl's silence may indeed represent her refusal to participate in the process of assimilation into American culture, Maxine cannot accept her actions. Her own silences cause her great suffering, at school and elsewhere. When she must speak, even in Chinese school, she writes, "the same voice came out, a crippled animal running on broken legs" (169). Hers, she writes, is a "bad, small-person's voice that makes no impact" (48). Further, "our voices," she notes, "were too soft or nonexistent" (167). Her voice is something that she cannot offer to Americans, whom she has been taught not to trust. But, as she states, "You can't trust your voice to the Chinese, either; they want to capture your voice for their own use. They want to fix up your tongue to speak for them" (169). In her narrative, she depicts with excruciating detail her painful interaction with the silent girl—her other self, according to some critics' interpretations[34]—in the bathroom after school one day.

Deciding that she will force this little girl to speak, she taunts her and physically torments her, pleading with her to make it stop by simply saying something. While the girl silently cries, the narrator admonishes her: "You're disgusting. . . . You're such a nothing. . . . Come on. Get tough. Come on. Throw fists. . . . O.K. O.K. Don't talk. Just scream, and I'll let you go. . . . Please. . . . There's nobody here but you and me. This isn't a classroom or a playground or a crowd. I'm just one person. You can talk in front of one person. . . . Why won't you talk? . . . If you don't talk, you can't have a personality" (178–180). Speaking, then, is a means to demonstrate subjectivity, a personality, and "toughness." Not speaking becomes equated, for Kingston's child narrator, with being disgusting and a "nothing."[35]

Yet examples from her narrative suggest otherwise. For the warrior woman of "White Tigers," writing becomes the means of reporting that saves family and community. Fa Mu Lan marches into battle with her grievances carved onto her back. She remains silent, however, so that others will not realize that she is a woman. While her words are powerful, her silence maintains self-preservation. Kingston, herself a woman warrior, suggests that it is the reporting—the writing—that signifies her vengeance and subsequent liberation, not necessarily her speech. She writes:

> The swordswoman and I are not so dissimilar. May my people understand the resemblance soon so that I can return to them. What we have in common are the words at our backs. The idioms for revenge are "report a crime" and "report to five families." The reporting is the vengeance—not the beheading, not the gutting, but the words. And I have so many words—"chink" words and "gook" words too—that they do not fit on my skin. (53)

Thus, Kingston recognizes that speech is not the only method of resistance. In the United States, where she is socialized into silence, she finds some sense of freedom through her writing, carefully distinguished in the text from speech, which she maintains is still difficult for her, even as an adult: "A dumbness—a shame—still cracks my voice in two" (165). As Cheung suggests, "it is clear that a quiet pupil can nevertheless be(come) an articulate writer" (1993, 89). Also, Kingston becomes aware that all acts of speech are neither guaranteed nor liberating.

The narrator's "no name" aunt, Kingston's father's sister who allegedly brought shame on the family name, is virtually erased from the familial history. For her, silence purportedly functions as a means of forgetting. Yet this aunt is not forgotten; her history is narrated to Maxine as a warning and a "story to grow up on," to test her "strength to establish realities" (5). To put her story into words, Kingston risks not only the censure of her family but also that of the deceased aunt's ghost. She writes, "My aunt haunts me. . . . I do not think she always means me well. I am telling on her, and she was a spite suicide, drowning herself in the drinking water" (16). This telling, while illustrative of the multiple silences and secrets circulating within Kingston's family, frees neither the aunt nor Kingston, necessarily. The retribution is symbolic, as the old villagers are by now dead, their identities buried within family secrets and immigration lies. To tell her aunt's story fails to counter the namelessness of this "No Name Woman," a quality suggestive of the repercussions of being unnamed, misnamed, or distorted through stereotypical representations in the United States, a condition Maxine herself experiences in the narrative.

Finally, Maxine, who seeks intimacy with her mother through mutual speaking, is forced to question notions ascribing power and "truth" to speech. At one point she writes, "I thought talking and not talking made the difference between sanity and insanity. Insane people were the ones who couldn't explain themselves. There were many crazy girls and women. Perhaps the sane people stayed in China to build the new, sane society. Or perhaps our little village had become odd in its isolation" (186). Incidentally, it is the girls and women for whom speech appears most difficult who are subsequently labeled "crazy." Again, speech and silence are conceptualized as gendered means of communication, shaped by subject position, immigration status, and sanity. While Maxine believes that her mother cut her tongue in order to silence her, Brave Orchid argues that she did it so that her daughter would never be "tongue-tied." She tells Maxine, "Your tongue would be able to move in any language. You'll be able to speak languages that are completely different from one another. You'll be able to pronounce anything. Your frenum looked too tight to do those things, so I cut it" (164). When Maxine counters, "But isn't 'a ready tongue an evil'?", her mother responds, "Things are different in this ghost country" (164). While Kingston believes Chinese in China speak freely and that to be "American-feminine," she must be silent, her mother argues that speech is also necessary for them in the United States. By cutting her daughter's tongue, she attempts to free her daughter from linguistic limits and constraints. However, for Maxine, speaking is always painful and not speaking is generally accompanied by throat pain and teeth gnashing (101, 197, 200, 205).

Kingston narrates the details of her attempt to become closer to her mother through speech, writing: "Maybe because I was the one with the tongue cut loose, I had grown inside me a list of over two hundred things that I had to tell my mother so that she would know the true things about me and to stop the pain in my throat" (197). By sharing with her mother all the "true things" about herself, her mother finally will be able to know and understand her. However, when Maxine attempts to tell these two hundred things, nothing happens. According to Maxine, "I had talked, and she acted as if she hadn't heard" (199). When they fight over their consistent miscommunication, Brave Orchid admits, finally, that speech is not always necessarily accurate and that language does not always convey the truth:

> "I didn't say you were ugly."
>
> "You say that all the time."
>
> "That's what we're supposed to say. That's what Chinese say. We like to say the opposite."
>
> It seemed to hurt her to tell me that—another guilt for my list to tell my mother, I thought. And suddenly I got very confused and lonely because I was at that moment telling her my list, and in the telling, it grew. No higher listener. No listener but myself. (203–204)

That there is no "higher listener," indeed no listener at all but herself, suggests to Maxine the limits of language and that fact that speech is always shaped by the laws and conditions around her. After repeatedly struggling against silence, Kingston also writes, "Be careful what you say. It comes true. It comes true. I had to leave home in order to see the world logically, logic the new way of seeing" (204).

Interestingly, many critics have commented on the so-called authenticity (or lack thereof) of this text, presumably missing the fact that Kingston herself introduces these themes as compelling questions.[36] For Kingston, Chinese identity is neither static nor essential. Rather, she is forced to constantly wonder what makes her Chinese American. Is there, or can there be, such a thing? She writes:

Chinese-Americans, when you try to understand what things in you are Chinese, how do you separate what is peculiar to childhood, to poverty, to insanities, one family, your mother who marked your growing with stories, from what is Chinese? What is Chinese tradition and what is the movies? (5–6)

Is silence inherently Chinese? Is speech? She suggests that such attributions are indeterminate, writing, "I continue to sort out what's just my childhood, just my imagination, just my family, just the village, just movies, just living. Soon I want to go to China and find out who's lying" (205).

Paralleling Maxine's quest for something truly "Chinese," critics and readers of The Woman Warrior have sought the authentic "Chinese" memoir. For instance, Cheung writes:

> Asian American intellectuals have endlessly debated the "authenticity" of The Woman Warrior. Those who attack Kingston for blurring the line between reality and fantasy seem unmindful of the narrator's insistent admissions of her own penchant for fabrication and her inability to discern fact from fiction. Even those on the author's side tend to defend her autobiography on the ethnographic ground that the narrator's experience accords well with their own. (1993, 78–79)[37]

Kingston herself comments, "After all, I am not writing history or sociology but a 'memoir' like Proust" (1982, 64). She makes it clear within the framework of her narrative that her memoirs involve truth, fiction, and fantasy. Describing the outlawed knot-makers of ancient China who "tied strings into buttons and frogs, and rope into bell pulls" and one knot "so complicated that it blinded the knot-maker," she notes, "If I had lived in China, I would have been an outlaw knot-maker" (163). While her child narrator continues to search for "truth," Kingston recognizes the complicated relationships between fact and fiction, especially in terms of autobiographical writing or an "authentic" Chinese experience. And while The Woman Warrior, as Kang points out, is often read as a sociological or ethnological document; in fact, it was marketed as a "memoir" primarily because Alfred Knoft, publishers of the first edition, "felt it would sell better as autobiography" (Iwata, cited in Kang, 2002, 31). She continues: "This marketing strategy proved successful, both commercially and critically, by inviting the text to be read as a transparent window onto Maxine Hong Kingston and her family" (2002, 31).

Even within the text, the narrator of *The Woman Warrior* constantly questions the possibility of any authentic Chinese or Chinese American culture, identity, or experience. Recounting her parents' lies, she writes, "I don't see how they kept up a continuous culture for five thousand years. Maybe they didn't; maybe everyone makes it up as they go along" (185). Maybe Kingston, too, makes it up as she goes along, inventing the past and her memories as part of a strategic renaming/remembering, the outlaw knots that reflect her own ambivalent relationship to remembering.

The act of renaming (and, in some cases, inventing), however, relates directly to historical "silences" and distortions in the United States of the histories of people of color and other marginalized groups. Mohanty, in her essay "Cartographies of Struggle," writes that "not only must narratives of resistance undo hegemonic recorded history, but they must also invent new forms of encoding resistance, of remembering" (35). Following this line of thought, inventing the past enables new possibilities, new ways of conceptualizing lived realities: "Resistance is encoded in the practices of remembering, and of writing. . . . The very practice of remembering against the grain of 'public' or hegemonic history, of locating the silences and the struggle to assert knowledge which is outside the parameters of the dominant, suggests a rethinking of sociality itself" (38–39). In other words, remembering our histories is part of resisting hegemonic discourses and master narratives. When our own histories are not available or accessible to us, when our pasts comprise a history of silence, we must rely on speaking and writing practices such as "remembering against the grain" and "invention." As Mohanty suggests, these new ways of thinking are directly related to "our daily practices of survival and resistance" (39). Yet, in what ways may silence also represent a strategy for remembering and for reinventing history?

Maclear provides an illuminating example. In her personal critical essay, she recalls an incident at a workshop on oral history and pedagogy. While screening a video oral history made by an Asian Canadian man about the experiences of Japanese Canadians in internment camps during World War II, Maclear was struck by the testimony of an old man whose silences were more telling than his words. The pauses and unedited silences in the film represented to Maclear "the lapses and disjunctures attendant in processes of remembering" (9). She writes, "They guided me to what he was not telling and reminded me that some things will always remain unspoken—and unknowable" (9). Other viewers discounted the film as "too slow" and difficult to understand, as they took the silences for absence, for "a lacking of sentiment and depth of reflection" (9). However, Maclear understood the silences as meaningful and as signification of the problems involved in reconstructing history. Implicit in the assumptions of the other viewers, who wanted more words and more explanations of the "experiences" in the camps, was a notion that somehow there can be a way to know the "truth" about the past—that history is more authentic when it is seen and spoken clearly. Maclear herself concludes with questions such as "Can silence ever be a self-evolved form of expression for people from oppressed groups? Given the material realities of racism, sexism, and other forms of institutionalized oppression, can we ever separate silence from mechanisms of domination that force us to 'be quiet' or that 'silence us'? Can we ever freely choose silence?" (11). I argue in this book that in some instances silence can and has been chosen as an expression and strategy of resistance by the writers to be discussed in subsequent chapters.[38] While I argue for an understanding of the multiple forms of resistance implied by specific gestures of silence, I do not mean to suggest an uncritical celebration of silence. Rather, a close examination of the complex and varied meanings of silence can highlight the ways in which Asian Pacific American women employ and contextualize various methods of resistance, including silence.

Thus, with speech comes silence—not simply the forgotten, the denied, or the disavowed but also the refusal, the protest, or the resistance that silence might also signify. Historicizing silence(s) forces us to recognize its "many faces" and to validate the *differences* between varied contexts of time and place, as well as the differences among those discourses deployed by various social and political groups. Also, historicizing silence may allow us to examine the consequences for simply mapping one set of theoretical assumptions that may apply to, for example, gender, onto contemporary racial discourses. While I argue for the interrelatedness of these social categories and attempt to refrain from compartmentalizing and/or overemphasizing their separateness, I also would like to move away from simple race-sex analogies and from arguments for universalizing theories of "difference." For example, "silences" in gay and lesbian history and "silences" in Asian American women's history, while certainly connected, are not necessarily similar ways of unsaying.

Silence, then, is particular to lived realities and histories. It performs different functions and produces distinct interpretations in various contexts. It is not simply loss, lack, absence, or repression. As a will to unsay, it is also that which makes speaking, or saying, possible, as it constructs and shapes meaning. As Trinh suggests, it is "a language of its own [that] has barely been explored" (1990, 373). And we have not listened enough to this language of silence, to its ever-changing meanings, to its resonances of possibility.

Having entered this world as an immigrant I felt I was living in a place where I had no history. Who was I? Where was I? When was I? . . . [T]o travel in the mind, through places one
has known, is also to scrape back history, reveal the knots, the accidental markings of
sense and circumstance that make up our lives. To disclose ordinary lives as they cut
against the grand narratives of history, the rubric of desire gritty against the supposed
truths we have learnt. —Meena Alexander, *The Shock of Arrival*

That's what all of America was like to me. When you see it for the first time, it glitters, beautiful, like a dream. But then, the longer you walk through it, the more you realize that
the dream is empty, false, sterile. You realize that you have no face and no place in this
country.—Nora Okja Keller, *Comfort Woman*

two

What Makes an American?
Histories of Immigration and Exclusion
of Asians in the United States in Maxine
Hong Kingston's *China Men*

Le Thi Diem Thuy, in her poem "Shrapnel Shards on Blue Water," recounts family memories, tracing her parents' daily lives in both their native land of Vietnam and their current home, the United States. She writes:
"Know this about us / we have lived our lives / on the edge of oceans /
in anticipation of / sailing into the sunrise / i tell you all this / to tear apart
the silence / of our days and nights here / i tell you all this / to fill the
void of absence / in our history here" (3). Vietnam, she writes, "is not /
a word / a world / a love / a family / a fear / to bury" (4). Vietnam "is
NOT A WAR. . . ." (4). Writing against History, the official historical
"facts" that render invisible her experiences as a Vietnamese American
woman, she asserts that Vietnam is much more than its simple colonialist conflation with the war. To tell "all this," in Le's case, is to "tear
apart the silence" and to "fill the void of absence in our history here."

Likewise, as noted in my preface, Maxine Hong Kingston asserts the necessity of documenting Asian American lives and experiences, sometimes against the dominant histories that have excluded them. In an interview with Timothy Pfaff about her fictionalized autobiographical account, China Men, Kingston describes the lack of awareness about Chinese American history within the United States, stating, "That ignorance makes a tension for me, and in [China Men] I just couldn't take it anymore. So all of a sudden, right in the middle of the stories, plunk—there is an eight-page section of pure history. It starts with the Gold Rush and then goes right through the various exclusion acts, year by year. There are no characters in it. It really affects the shape of my book, and it might look quite clumsy. But on the other hand, maybe it will affect the shape of the novel in the future. Now maybe another Chinese American writer won't have to write that history" (15). Describing China Men itself as a "history book," Kingston explains in an interview with Paul Skenazy that her manipulation of genre was a direct result of her need to compensate for her readers' lack of knowledge about Chinese American history (108). Fully aware that most readers would be unable to adequately contextualize her writing, and knowing that that would affect their understanding of the text, Kingston created an alternative form with China Men—part fiction, part autobiography, part history.

Both Kingston's The Woman Warrior and China Men participate in this narrativizing of history. Yet, these family memoirs construct, as Patricia Chu suggests, a "repressed history that haunts the American-born narrator" (2). She continues: "Although [The Woman Warrior] seems to suggest that the narrator's primary quarrels are with her parents and community, whose methods of socializing her seem too Chinese and out of step with the family's life in America, the grimness of that life is gradually revealed to be rooted in the Asian American past in America, the invisibility of that past to mainstream Americans, and its consequent resistance to narration" (2). In this context, speech and authorship, according to Chu, are "symbolic of and instrumental to survival and the search for fullness of being" (2). History and narration thus become intertwined in Kingston's works, and the controversies over Kingston's writings foreground such questions of identity, authenticity, history, and belonging.[1]

In actuality, relatively little is known of Asian American history. Such a lack of knowledge about Asian American history exists within a context of racism, stereotyping, anti-immigrant sentiments, and the rendering insignificant or irrelevant of most actions or events involving Asian Americans.[2] This lack of visibility has been perpetuated not only during historical periods of time under consideration but also during processes of historicization, through exclusions in the writing of history. Asians in America have been excluded from history for a number of reasons, not the least of which, as Ronald Takaki suggests, has been the tendency to equate "American" with "white" or "European" in origin. Also, because "American" has implied maleness, middle-class status, and heterosexuality as well as whiteness, "other" Americans—people of color, women of all races, poor and working-class people, lesbian, gay, bisexual, and transgender people—have often fallen outside such a narrow definition of what it means to be considered "American." As Takaki states, "We need to 're-vision' history to include Asians in the history of America, and to do so in a broad and comparative way" (1989, 7). In other words, including Asian Americans in U.S. history in meaningful and transformative ways must mean changing how we conceptualize history and the act of historicization.[3]

Thus, one logical starting point for any discussion of Asian Americans, especially one focused on historical silences within Asian America and critical rewritings of American historical narratives, is the history of Asian immigration to the United States. In the first part of this chapter, I provide a general overview of this history, relying on Kingston's China Men to illustrate the ways Asian American women's writings are shaped by and shape such history. Also, this chapter offers historical contextualization of texts discussed in subsequent chapters. Then, to extend my analysis of Asian American immigration history, I explore issues surrounding race and racial structure in the United States. As mentioned in my introduction, I seek a framework capable of moving beyond the oppositional thinking that characterizes much contemporary discussion of race within the popular and scholarly imagination of American culture. To simply insert "Asian American" as a term, concept, history, or group of "citizens" into an already defined structure performs a disservice to all racial and ethnic groups in the United States. It renders invisible all of those marginalized racial groups deemed "other" and reinforces the seemingly clear-cut (and unequal) polarity between "black" and "white" racial identities. In other words, race is conceptualized most often as a binary system in which white and black are oppositional and hierarchical. Also, "race" in the United States is mapped onto the bodies of black people so that race itself is defined as "black" race (thereby removing white people—and whiteness—from discussions of race altogether).[4] In such a framework, Asian American people and other people of color are not even categorized as "other"; they simply do not exist.

As mentioned in the introductory chapter, I do not attempt a comprehensive literary review or analysis of Kingston's texts. *China Men*, like *The Woman Warrior*, has inspired a great deal of literary criticism; thus, such a project is clearly beyond the scope of this study.[5] Rather, I introduce significant passages from *China Men* to illustrate key historical events and patterns in Asian—specifically Chinese—immigration to the United States.[6] Kingston's writings represent perhaps the most well-known and most heavily studied texts by an Asian American woman writer. However, my objective in including discussion of such texts is not to fully incorporate them into my study but simply to suggest that both *China Men* and *The Woman Warrior*—two canonized texts within Asian American literary studies—engage and foreground issues of Asian American immigration history and silence.

The History of Asian American Immigration

According to Sucheng Chan, nearly one million Asian immigrants entered the United States during the late nineteenth and the early twentieth centuries, emigrating predominantly from China, Japan, Korea, the Philippines, and India. Chan reports different reasons for emigration, including searching for work, influenced by a growing global capitalism, being recruited for work as coolie or indentured labor or as sugar plantation contract laborers, as well as fleeing native lands for safety and/or survival. "Asian international migration," Chan writes, "was part of a larger, global phenomenon: the movement of workers, capital, and technology across national boundaries to enable entrepreneurs to exploit natural resources in more and more parts of the world" (1991, 4). Thus, the early immigration of Asians to the United States operated within a global framework that set the terms for that immigration and for the experiences of the immigrants.[7]

Asian immigrants came to the United States in search of "Gold Mountain," a mythic land of wealth and opportunity; members of some ethnic groups were recruited as contract laborers on Hawaiian sugar plantations. Or, they found themselves being "pushed out" of their homelands due to famines and increasing political tensions, often the results of West-ern imperialist forces having "opened up" their countries to trade, the proselytizing of Christian missionaries, diplomatic relations, navigation, and Western militaristic occupation. Also, though rarely noted, accord-ing to Gary Okihiro, some early Chinese and Asian Indian coolies were sold to American ship captains, restrained in crowded pens (called "pigpens"), and brought to the United States against their will (41–42).[8] In Hawaii and all along the Pacific coast of the United States, Asian immigrants provided most of the strenuous labor as plantation workers, miners, com-mercial agriculture and farm laborers, domestic servants, factory oper-atives, cannery workers, and public works laborers (Chan, 1991, 5; Ta-kaki, 1989, 13). Also, racism and "ethnic antagonism" led to a dual-wage system in which Asians were paid less than their white counterparts for the same jobs.[9] Such a practice later led to white laborers demanding that further restrictions be placed on Asian workers, as well as the exclu-sion of future Asian immigrants (Takaki, 1989, 13).

Takaki (1989) discusses in detail the ways in which early white Amer-ican businessmen sought to "conquer" the U.S. western frontier (thought of as a physical and moral wilderness) by bringing "civilization" to it—through industry, capitalism, and big business such as railroads and sugar plantations. Such conquests depended on the labor of people of color. In Hawaii in the late 1800s, plantation owners from the mainland first at-tempted to use native Hawaiians as their source of labor. When Hawai-ians refused to work for low wages, they decided to import labor from China, believing that Chinese workers would be less troublesome and more obedient. Similarly, in the American West, capitalists set out to build transcontinental railroads by importing Chinese coolie labor as an inexpensive strategy (Takaki, 1989, 21–27).[10] Thus, to "tame" the wilder-ness, white men required the labor of people of color and immigrants, whom they continued to view as less than human. In fact, in business and shipment orders, this fact was often bluntly suggested by lists for supplies, as documented by Takaki (1989): In 1890, the Davies Com-pany, a Honolulu Mercantile company, submitted requisitions for "bone-meal, canvas, Japanese laborers, macaroni, a Chinaman." In 1898, planters of the Davies Company ordered "Laborers. . . . 75 Japanese" along with "Mules and Horses." In 1908, a letter sent from a sugar plantation listed in alphabetical order on its "shopping list"—"Fertilizer, Filipinos. . . ." (25). Not only were Asian immigrant laborers commodified as objects to be ordered along with food supplies and fertilizers, but they were also ordered according to "quotas" designed to keep them in their place through a complex divide-and-conquer system. Chinese immigrant laborers on Hawaiian sugar plantations were further dehumanized on the plantations, where they were often forcibly held to a certain plantation for a set number of years under the Master and Servant Act of 1850. In addition, the minimal wages that laborers were paid were often in the form of "payment in kind" and "script," good only at the plantation store (Amott and Matthaei 198–199).

In 1898, the United States colonized Hawaii and then, because of U.S. restrictions on Chinese immigration, could no longer "import" Chinese laborers. Thus, business and plantation owners turned to Japanese laborers. Worried that the "Japs," as they were called, were becoming too numerous (and therefore capable of organizing strikes), plantation owners then turned to Korea for new labor (Takaki, 1989, 26). When the Gentlemen's Agreement of 1907 between the United States and Japan brought the immigration of Korean laborers to a halt, U.S. sugar plantation growers turned to the Philippines, also annexed by the United States in 1898, for labor.[11] Filipinos/as, because of their legal status as members of a U.S. territory, could travel with American passports, so the Gentlemen's Agreement and immigration laws barring other groups of Asians did not apply to them. However, as members of a U.S. colony, Filipinos/as were not entitled to U.S. citizenship and were thus excluded from the rights of citizens.

Meanwhile, men and women in the Punjab region of Northwest India, having been colonized by the British, suffered increasing poverty and dispossession of their land because of the introduction of heavy taxation systems. They, too, came to the United States in search of work. Along the way, plantation owners also "ordered" Portuguese workers, African Americans from the South, and Puerto Ricans to come to labor on plantations. However, the preference of planters seemed to be to divide the workforce "about equally between Oriental nationalities" (quoted in Takaki, 1989, 26), in order to better control workers, and to pit the two groups against one another, thereby precluding workers' organizing (Takaki, 1989, 26; Amott and Matthaei 199). Such strategies were explicitly stated as mechanisms of control in various writings by planters at the time. During the 1850s, for example, Chinese laborers were used to "set an example" for Hawaiian workers, thereby creating antagonism between the two groups by setting them in competition against one another (Takaki, 1989, 25). With the aid of stereotypes about both Hawaiians and Chinese, plantation owners were able to demonstrate control over their laborers. Planters in the 1880s explained: "We lay great stress on the necessity of having our labor mixed. By employing different nationalities, there is less danger of collusion among laborers, and employers [are able to] secure better discipline" (as quoted in Takaki, 1989, 25). In 1896, a company representative wrote in a letter to a planter: "Regarding the proportion of Chinese and Japanese laborers we beg to advise, that the Hawaiian Sugar Planters' Association and the Bureau of Immigration have agreed upon 2/3 of the former and 1/3 of the latter. For your *private* information we mention, that the reason for this increasing [sic] the percentage of the Chinese laborers is due to the desire of breaking up the preponderance of the Japanese element" (Takaki, 1989, 26). Thus, as Takaki argues, one group of laborers—deemed most easily exploited at a particular time—was used by the plantation owners to better control and discipline the workers, and "diversity was deliberately designed to break strikes and repress unions" (1989, 25–26).

At the same time in California, powerful forces in business recognized Chinese immigrants as a steady labor force willing to work below the wages paid to white laborers. Again, those in power employed calculated methods, using Chinese workers (and other people of color) to control the possible outbreak of strikes and keep wages down. As Takaki suggests, "The resulting racial antagonism generated between the two groups helped to ensure a divided working class and a dominant employer class" (1989, 29). Here as well, after the Chinese Exclusion Act of 1882, employers sought labor from Japan. For a period of time, Japanese immigrants picked fruit at wages almost no other workers would accept. When Japanese farmworkers began to demand higher wages and better living conditions, the popular journal *California Fruit Grower* recommended looking for "Asian-Indian" laborers. The following year, farmers began employing Indian immigrants as "'a check on the Japanese,' paying them twenty-five cents less per day" (Takaki, 1989, 29–30). In the 1920s, the majority of farm laborers were Mexican; however, under the threat of a quota basis determined by the Immigration Act of 1924, farmers feared that Mexicans would not be permitted into the United States, and they began to "import" Filipino laborers (Takaki, 1989, 30). As in Hawaii, heterogeneous groups of laborers were favored, as farmers believed that "'laborers speaking different languages [were] not as likely to arrive at a mutual understanding which would lead to strikes'" (quoted in Takaki, 1989, 30).

Thus, under the economic regime of capitalism in the United States, Asian immigrant workers in the early part of the twentieth century were exploited in numerous ways. Having struggled to enter the United States, Asians found themselves able to find work only in segregated labor markets where they earned the lowest wages and were often pitted against one another (as well as other groups of working-class people and people of color) in order to prevent strikes and other forms of resistance.[12] For many immigrants, however, self-employment offered one method of economic advancement. In his historical record, Takaki mentions the numerous Asian immigrants who sought to become owners of small businesses; he explores the propensity toward self-employment—becoming shopkeepers, merchants, small-business owners, etc.—not as an "Asian trait" or innate cultural trait but as a means and strategy of survival, a way to control one's own labor, and "a response to racial discrimination and exclusion in the labor market" (1989, 13). Also, Amott and Matthaei discuss the ways in which Asian immigrants opened family businesses— "for the Chinese, laundries and restaurants; for the Japanese, truck farming; and for the Koreans, grocery stores" (195). Going into business for oneself, then, became one small way of circumventing racism by attempting to keep out of such a system of exploitation, although the historical oppression of and violence against immigrant owners of small businesses is a whole story in and of itself. Because white people frequently tried to stop the development of Asian-owned businesses, many Chinese shops were established in Chinatowns, ghettoized in poor neighborhoods, and/or established in the South to serve African Americans, who often could not get served in white-owned businesses (Amott and Matthaei 206).

Both Takaki and Chan contextualize the history of Asian immigration within a shifting and dichotomous global paradigm in which the West (Europe, the United States) relied on the non-West (Asia, Africa, Latin America, the Pacific Islands) to define itself as a site of power and capital. Takaki argues that under the global system of capitalism, "core" nations like the United States, England, France, Spain, and Portugal penetrated politically and economically the less-developed, "semi-peripheral" areas of Asia, Africa, and Latin America in their search for new markets, raw materials, and sources of labor. European and American colonialism disrupted economies there and also increased problems of poverty. The "necessities" of the "modern world-system" powered international labor migration, "pushing" workers from Africa and Asia and "pulling" them to Latin America, the West Indies, and the United States. . . . Asian immigrants constituted a unique laboring army of "strangers" . . . of alien origin, they were brought here to serve as an "internal colony"—nonwhites allowed to enter as "cheap" migratory laborers and members of a racially subordinated group, not future citizens of American society. (1989, 31)

Similarly, Chan sums up the early immigration experience for Asians and its relationship to Western domination in the following way:

Asian immigration into Hawaii and the United States was but one aspect of a larger historical process that has sometimes been called the "expansion of Europe." For several centuries, colonists, capitalists, soldiers, and missionaries from Europe roamed the earth in search of lands, profits, power, and souls. When Americans joined this venture, they justified it as part of their manifest destiny. But in many places, white men could not accomplish their goals without the sinews of nonwhite men. Where the local population did not supply the needed labor, the Europeans or Americans brought workers from other countries.

British actions in China and India indirectly started the emigrant stream from those countries to California and British Columbia, while American schemes facilitated the outflow of people from Japan, Korea, and the Philippines to Hawaii and the Pacific Coast. Because what Euro-Americans desired was muscle power, the vast majority of the Asians they enticed to the other side of the Pacific were young men in their prime working years, most of whom came without wives, parents, or children. Abused and maligned, their deeds unsung, these men were an indispensable work force that helped to build the American West. (1991, 23)

Indeed, the early immigration experiences of Asian Americans were characterized by 1) extreme control, culminating in numerous exclusionary laws and practices and often erupting into violence and threats of vio-

lence; 2) a peculiar gender dynamic, in particular extreme gender dis-
parities among immigrants; and 3) distinct and shifting understandings
of citizenship and "race," with Asian immigrants often classified as "permanent aliens," outsiders, and "guests" of this nation.[13]

Institutionalized Exclusionary Practices[14]

Immigration exclusion laws against Asians were numerous and complex.
Some of their consequences included the institutionalization of racism
and racial discrimination, the further exploitation of Asian immigrants,
and the destruction of Asian family systems and traditional gender and
familial roles. Also, violence against Asian immigrants, while rampant,
was rarely prosecuted. Chan notes the hostile reception of Asian Indians
in the United States: "In September, 1907, 600 Euro-American workers
drove some 200 'Hindus' out of Bellingham, Washington, where they
had found employment in the lumbermills" (1991, 23). Indians were
forced southward into California, and eventually—in 1917—exclusionary laws were formally imposed to keep them out altogether. Other groups
suffered violent attacks from white workers, sometimes culminating in
mob lynchings or the burning of homes. Chan categorizes the violence
against Asians into three patterns: "the maiming and wanton murder of
individuals, spontaneous attacks against and the destruction (usually by
fire) of Chinatowns, and organized efforts to drive Asians out of certain
towns and cities," documenting the widespread occurrence of all three
types of violent acts (1991, 48).

   According to Amott and Matthaei, white mobs attacked Chinese in
San Francisco, Los Angeles, Seattle, Tacoma, Denver, and Rock Springs,
Wyoming. In 1871, a mob lynched nineteen Chinese immigrants after
attacking Los Angeles' Chinatown and stealing $40,000. The "Great Driv-
ing Out" of Asians included the expulsion of Chinese from towns and
cities all over the American West, and white workers of California initiated the slogan "The Chinese Must Go" as part of its assault against
Chinese laborers (Amott and Matthaei 203). In 1885, according to Chan,
"an Anti-Chinese Congress convened in Seattle, [and] issued a manifesto
demanding that all Chinese leave Tacoma and Seattle by 1 November"
(1991, 50). On the third of November, five hundred residents of Tacoma forcibly removed at least six hundred Chinese from the city, leaving them without shelter during a heavy rainstorm. Subsequently, Ta-

coma's Chinatown was burned down. In Seattle, anti-Chinese mobs gathered in attempts to expel Chinese from the city (Chan, 1991, 50–51). Other Asian immigrant groups suffered violence and threats, as well as being physically removed from their residences. A number of Japanese men were stoned by groups of white boys; Korean farmworkers were surrounded by white mobs threatening violence; Filipinos were attacked and beaten by white mobs during a taxi dance. In many of these incidences, fatalities also occurred (Chan, 1991, 51–53).

Chan argues that it would be a mistake to interpret such acts of violence as isolated and/or spontaneous. Rather, she states that they were "an integral part of what historian Alexander Saxton has called the 'growth sequence' of the anti-Chinese movement—and, by extension, movements against other Asian groups" (1991, 53). After anti-Asian acts of violence, politically motivated groups developed in order to rid the country of the specific Asian groups targeted. Even nonviolent citizens often sympathized with the ideologies and assumptions of the perpetrators, as the violence itself was sustained by certain ideas about race. Chan argues that

> elaborate "scientific" explanations of nonwhite "inferiority" and the belief that minorities should be kept in their place were widely accepted by the late nineteenth century and provided an ideological justification for treating not only Asians, but other people of color, in a discriminatory and exploitative manner. To preserve Anglo-Saxon purity, it was argued, no interracial mixing should be allowed. The outbreaks of violence, therefore, served two functions: they were at once intimidation tactics to drive out Asians and expressions of frustration over the fact that, even after exclusionary laws had been passed, sizable numbers of the "undesirable" aliens remained. (1991, 54)[15]

Kingston, in China Men, recounts tales of a lonely grandfather, separated from his wife and family, who helped build the railroads of the American West. Describing what his experiences must have been like, she explains that it was his participation in such an endeavor that made him an American: "'Only Americans could have done it,' they said, which is true. . . . [Ah Goong] was an American for having built the railroad" (145). Indeed, he even purchases and proudly carries American citizenship papers, though he has been tricked and the papers are false. Nevertheless, he claims America as his own. However, when the dangerous work of the railroad is completed, and many Chinese men have died, the "driving out" begins. Kingston writes, "It was dangerous to stay. . . . Ah Goong does not appear in railroad photographs" (145). As symbolized by the lack of visual (photographic) evidence, any historical record of his participation is virtually erased. Documenting the history of violent expulsion, Kingston speculates about Ah Goong's journey, writing,

> Good at hiding, disappearing—decades unaccounted for—he was not working in a mine when forty thousand chinamen were Driven Out of mining. He was not killed or kidnapped in the Los Angeles Massacre, though he gave money toward ransoming those whose toes and fingers, a digit per week, and ears grotesquely rotting or pickled, and scalped queues, were displayed in Chinatowns. . . . If he got kidnapped, Ah Goong planned, he would whip out his Citizenship Paper and show that he was an American. He was lucky not to be in Colorado when the Denver demons burned all chinamen homes and businesses, nor in Rock Springs, Wyoming, when the miner demons killed twenty-eight or fifty chinamen. . . . The count of the dead was inexact because bodies were mutilated and pieces scattered all over the Wyoming Territory. No white miners were indicted, but the government paid $150,000 in reparations to victims' families. There were many family men, then. There were settlers—abiding China Men. And China Women. Ah Goong was running elsewhere during the Drivings Out of Tacoma, Seattle, Oregon City, Albania, and Marysville. (148)

By explaining where he was *not*, Kingston documents several incidents of violence against Chinese Americans during the late 1800s. The same lack of historical evidence that renders Ah Goong invisible, however, emerges as fortuitous when the San Francisco Hall of Records is destroyed during the earthquake and fire of 1906. "An authentic citizen, then, had no more papers than an alien. Any paper a China Man could not produce had been 'burned up in the Fire of 1906.' Every China Man was reborn out of that fire a citizen" (150). Hence, for Chinese immigrants, silence emerged both as absence and erasure *and* as a tactical device of survival, protection, even U.S. citizenship.

The racial discrimination against Asians underlying U.S. public policies generated nearly fifty laws passed between 1850 and 1950, created specifically to restrict and subordinate Asian immigrants. In her section of *China Men* called "The Laws," Kingston documents America's exclusionary laws against Chinese immigrants (152–159). Such laws prohibited Asians from testifying in courts against white people, prevented them from owning land, excluded them from public schools, levied special taxes on them, and prohibited their employment in corporations (although this final restriction was later struck down when the corporations required the cheap labor of Asian immigrants) (Amott and Matthaei 195–204). In some areas, the racism underlying such laws was subtle yet designed to discriminate against Asian immigrants, such as the fourteen separate ordinances concerning laundries, as documented by Chan, which were created to curtail and control Chinese laundries in San Francisco.[16] According to Amott and Matthaei, such laws culminated in legislation that excluded the immigration of Asians altogether. For example, the Chinese Exclusion Act of 1882, the first law to single out a particular group solely on a racial basis, cut off any further immigration from China; Japanese immigration was curtailed 1907–1908 and again in 1924 with the National Origins Act, which prohibited Japanese immigration while permitting thousands of European immigrants to enter the country; Indian immigration was cut off in 1917; and Filipino/a immigration was curtailed in 1934 with the Tydings-McDuffie Act, which provided for the independence of the Philippines and limited Filipino immigration to fifty persons a year (Takaki, 1989, 14).

As Donald Goellnicht suggests, Kingston's section "The Laws" is ironic. This irony is evident in some of the historical facts she states,[17] but most pronounced in her tone. He explains:

> By imitating the monological voice of authorizing History—the history imposed by the dominant culture that made the laws—this section uncovers both the dullness of this voice and its deafness to other, competing voices, those of the minorities suffering legalized discrimination. This undertone of irony becomes most resonant when Hong Kingston quotes from the exclusionary laws enacted by federal, state, and municipal legislatures against Chinese workers and immigrants, especially when we measure these "laws" against the "invented" biographies of China Men that make up the rest of the text. Paradoxically, the imagined/fictional history proves more truthful than the official version. (1992, 196)

Kingston's China Men offers a richly imagined, unofficial history as counternarrative to the dominant histories that have excluded and marginalized Asians in America. By centering her own history, "The Laws," within her text, she provides a necessary context and offers a challenge to the widely known American history that, through its legislation and subsequent narratization, erased her family's experiences.[18]

Gendered Patterns of Asian Immigration
to the United States

Wives of male European immigrants were allowed to enter the United States freely, while women married to Asian (male) immigrants were excluded on the basis of their classification as "aliens ineligible to citizenship" (Takaki, 1989, 14). As Takaki suggests, the National Origins Act of 1924 encouraged the formation of families among European immigrant communities as European immigrants were legally permitted to return to their homelands and re-enter the United States with their spouses and families. Asian immigrants, on the other hand, were prevented from forming families. Women from China, Japan, Korea, and India were barred from entering the country, and even U.S. citizens could not bring Asian wives into the country (Takaki, 1989, 14). Thus, there were very few early Asian immigrant women present in the United States, contributing to the "bachelor societies" of Asian immigrant men at that time. Between 1850 and 1852, according to Teresa Amott and Julie Matthaei, a period in which more than 100,000 Chinese men emigrated to the United States, only 8,848 Chinese women entered the country (199). In 1860, the ratio of men to women among Chinese immigrants was 19 to 1; in 1900, among the Japanese, it was 25 to 1; and in 1930, among Filipino/a immigrants, the ratio was 14 to 1 (Amott and Matthaei 195). As Chan points out, recent scholars have documented the relatively small number of Asian women and attributed it to "the patriarchal, patrilineal, and patrilocal nature of Chinese, Japanese, and Korean societies" (1991, 103–104). Chan states, "In societies where girls are reared to serve men and to procreate, respectable women did not travel far from home" (1991, 104).

The rationale behind the exclusion of Asian women from the United States had to do with patterns of racism against Asians in general, traditional attitudes toward women in their homelands, stereotypes in the United States about Asian women in particular, and from an economic standpoint, employers' desires to cut costs. From the beginning of Asian labor recruitment for sugar plantations in the late 1800s, managers specified that "no batch of workers could contain more than twenty-five percent women" (Chan, 1991, 12). Employing unmarried male workers was more cost-efficient for plantation owners, and the workers were more likely to survive under rough conditions and more likely to continue working despite discrimination and even violence without their wives and children present. Also, reports of sexual abuse and violence by sailors further deterred Asian women from traveling abroad (Amott and Matthaei 199). As Amott and Matthaei state,

> Chinese labor was favored by U.S. and Hawaiian employers who were able to contract able-bodied young men for work and to prevent the married workers' wives and children from joining them. By 1852, 11,787 Cantonese Chinese had come to the United States, only seven of whom were women. Although workers did send some wages home to their families, most of the costs of producing another generation of workers and caring for the infirm and aged were borne in China. This allowed employers to keep wages very low, especially by U.S. standards. As single men, Chinese workers were ideal for migrant farm work, mining, and railroad construction: employers could move them around easily and house them in cheap dormitory-style structures rather than family homes. (196)

And, as Chan points out, from the workers' point of view, "it was less costly to sustain their families in their homelands than to feed them in the United States" (1991, 104).

Meanwhile, in China, families commonly believed that keeping the wives of emigrants at home was one way to ensure that money would be sent home for the support of the extended family (Chan, 1991, 104). According to Chinese custom, a married woman lived with her husband's family, where she was subservient to her mother-in-law (Amott and Matthaei 200–201). Thus, thousands of Chinese women remained in China, married to men who lived in the United States, many of whom never returned. Such women were referred to as Gum-Shan-Poo ("Gold Mountain ladies"), and the distinct familial arrangements within which they lived have been referred to by Evelyn Nakano Glenn as the "split-household family system."[19] Chinese men were encouraged to marry before departing the country, and other emigrants came home from the United States in order to marry only to leave their wives behind. In fact, because of anti-miscegenation laws, in effect in the United States until 1948, male Asian immigrants who wished to marry and have families had few options but to return to their homelands. Sons of such families often joined their fathers, brothers, uncles, and grandfathers in the United States when they were old enough to do so, while daughters were expected to remain at home in China (Chan, 1991, 104; Amott and Matthaei 200).

Slightly different patterns emerged for immigrants of other Asian ethnic groups. For example, Japanese family arrangements differed because of cultural differences and distinctions between immigration exclusions placed upon Chinese and Japanese immigrants. Whereas Chinese exclusion was imposed abruptly with the Chinese Exclusion Act, restrictions on Japanese immigrants occurred more slowly, over stages (Chan, 1991, 107). With the Gentlemen's Agreement of 1907, unskilled Japanese men were barred from entering the United States, contributing to the decline of Japanese immigration. However, unlike the Chinese, Japanese men were permitted to bring their wives and relatives into the country. Because of the high cost of passage between Japan and the United States and the fact that Japanese men risked losing their deferred military status if they remained in Japan for more than one month, many Japanese men had few options for marriage. Thus, common to marriage patterns among Japanese immigrants was the phenomenon of "picture brides," a practice that accounted for more than half of the Japanese women who arrived in the United States between 1909 and 1923. Picture brides were, for the most part, young Japanese women who never met their husbands prior to marriage; they were matched with husbands through photographs and letters, often through family and friends. These women, who were typically at least ten years younger than their prospective husbands, went through marriage ceremonies alone in Japan, applied for passports and the necessary papers, and then traveled to the United States, where their husbands were required to meet them in person at the docks. Upon their arrival, the picture brides were subject to intimidating inspections and humiliating medical examinations before they could join their husbands. As Amott and Matthaei point out, they were immediately refitted into Western-style clothes and encouraged to assimilate into American cultural practices as soon as possible (Chan, 1991, 107; Amott and Matthaei 221–223).

Other Asian immigrant women arrived in the United States in much smaller numbers. Some Korean, Filipina, and Indian women accompanied their husbands to the United States. More than one thousand Korean women arrived as picture brides before 1924. Other women arrived on their own to find work or were brought to the United States as concubines or prostitutes (Chan, 1991, 109–110; Amott and Matthaei 201, 239–240).[20] During these time periods, as Kang suggests, Asian women were "designated as alternately worthy of and ineligible for immigration, naturalization, and citizenship" (2002, 114).

The issue of Asian women working as prostitutes in the United States involves a complicated history. Whereas prostitution was a reality for many Asian immigrant women, as a practice it was also heavily influenced by immigration legislation, by a limited range of options for survival for Asian women, and by cultural myths and stereotypes. The fact that Asian American women continue to battle controlling images of deviant and/or hypersexuality, both within and outside of the sex industry, testifies to the significant impact of this history.

A significant number of Asian immigrant women worked as prostitutes in the late 1800s and early 1900s. My discussion here takes the example of Chinese women who worked as prostitutes during this time period, as historians have documented their experiences more so than any other Asian ethnic group. Because immigration laws constricted the entrance of Chinese women into the United States and even kept Chinese men from bringing their wives into the country, reinforcing the split-household system, many communities of Chinese immigrants were characterized, as mentioned above, by uneven sex ratios. As Amott and Matthaei state, "the unbalanced sex ratio among whites further fueled the demand for Chinese prostitutes—in the total California population in 1850, there were over 12 men for every woman" (201). Men living in these so-called bachelor communities were forbidden by law to intermarry with white women.[21] While some Asian men formed relationships with non-Asian women of color, others depended on prostitutes for sexual liaisons and companionship (Yung 30). As Amott and Matthaei suggest, citing the work of Lucie Cheng, "prostitution was also supported by white capitalists, who wanted to keep wives and children from immigrating and increasing labor costs, and by racists who wanted to keep the Chinese from reproducing in the United States" (201). Thus, prostitution among Chinese women flourished as Chinese prostitutes made up a high percentage of the Chinese female population. In San Francisco's Chinatown, there were 159 brothels in 1870 (Amott and Matthaei 202). In 1860, between 85 and 97 percent of Chinese immigrant women in San Francisco worked as prostitutes; in 1870, the figure was 71 to 72 percent; and in 1880, it dropped to 21 to 50 percent (Yung 29).

According to Yung, while a relatively small number of women came to the United States to work as prostitutes of their own will, many others who entered the country and subsequently worked as prostitutes were sold or tricked into doing so. Historians Amott and Matthaei and Yung document the lives of such notorious women as Ah Toy, who, in 1849 arrived in San Francisco to "better her condition," worked independently as a prostitute, and later became the madam of a Chinese brothel.[22] Yet, the large number of young Chinese girls and women who were forced to work as prostitutes lived lives of degradation, illness, and poverty, and many were parts of organized tongs. Tongs, or secret societies of Chinese patriarchal clan associations, organized prostitution, controlling and even "importing" the women. According to Amott and Matthaei, the major tong, Hip Yee Tong, "earned an estimated $200,000 between 1852 and 1873 by importing an estimated 6,000 women, 87 percent of all Chinese women arrivals" (201). Tongs sent agents overseas to recruit, purchase, or kidnap young girls into prostitution.

According to Yung, while most white women working as prostitutes were independent professionals working for wages in brothels, "Chinese prostitutes were almost always imported as unfree labor, indentured or enslaved" (27). Most, she argues, were purchased, kidnapped, or lured by procurers in China and then resold in the United States to a barracoon or to the highest bidder (27).[23] Often these women were forced to sign contracts of service, establishing that they would work a set number of years and then achieve freedom. However, many soon realized that the allowable ten days of absence in their contracts were not sufficient to cover such things as illness, pregnancy, or even menstrual periods, and, thus, such contracts could be extended indefinitely, the years of service extended again and again (Yung 28). While a small number were sold to wealthy Chinese men in San Francisco as concubines or mistresses, most of these women were forced to live in miserable conditions, where they were subjected to physical and emotional abuse and offered no legal protection. As Yung points out, few actually outlived their contract terms of four to six years (28). They were harshly treated, many of them were kept locked up and closely guarded, and most of them eventually succumbed to sexually transmitted diseases, as they were often forced to service any man who could pay their owners' fees. Yung argues that they enjoyed no political rights, no protection from discrimination, and no legal recourse. In the United States, they lacked family ties, faced a language barrier, and were forced to endure racism, earning less money for their services than white women. Finally, along with prostitutes from Latin American countries, they were ghettoized and "consistently singled out for moral condemnation and legal suppression, even though white prostitution was more prevalent" (Yung 31).

White Americans' response to Chinese prostitution was extremely negative. According to Yung, Chinese women were accused of "disseminating vile diseases capable of destroying 'the very morals, the manhood and the health of our people . . . ultimately destroying whole nations'" (32). In this way, national leaders and media representatives characterized Chinese women as constituting a national threat, thereby sanctioning the widespread public sentiment that Chinese women and men should not be allowed to enter the United States. White Americans attempted to either confine Chinese women working as prostitutes to isolated areas or to drive them out completely. Often, chiefs of police and/or local boards of health relocated Chinese prostitutes outside city limits. According to Chan, "Chinese prostitutes in San Francisco were the first Asians whom the host society tried to remove to a confined geographic locality outside of municipal limits" (56). As she points out, "the efforts to isolate Chinese prostitutes soon became generalized to a desire to segregate all Chinese persons," culminating in an 1879 law passed by the California State Legislature obligating all incorporated cities and towns to remove Chinese persons from their territories, which was later overturned based on its unconstitutionality (56).

When Americans were unable to drive Chinese prostitutes out of their cities, they often relied on an array of stereotypes suggesting that Chinese women were sexually deviant, exotic, and innately promiscuous. Thus, the same stereotypes that drew many white male patrons to Chinese prostitutes were also the representations used to legitimate the mistreatment and exclusion of Chinese women in general.[24] All Chinese women were believed to be potential prostitutes. According to Yung, the passing of the Chinese Exclusion Act had severe consequences for Chinese women and families, as it limited the number of Chinese women who could enter the United States to only a privileged few. In fact, she argues, "rigorous enforcement of the act, along with the implementation of anti-Chinese measures regulating prostitution such as the Page Law of 1875, kept even those Chinese immigrant women with legitimate claims out of the country and made immigration to America an ordeal for any woman who tried to enter. Immigration officials apparently operated on the premise that every Chinese woman was seeking admission on false pretenses and that each was a potential prostitute until proven otherwise" (23–24).[25] Amott and Matthaei cite an 1856 *New York Tribune* editorial: "The Chinese are lustful and sensual in their dispositions; every female is a prostitute of the basest order," arguing that the perceived immorality of the Chinese was a determining factor in the Chinese Exclusion Act (202). Such stereotypes remain in place today, evidenced by immigration requirements that necessitate Asian women testifying that they have never worked as prostitutes.

While the conditions for Chinese prostitution were indeed miserable, as documented by a number of historians, there were possibilities for escape. As Yung suggests, women sometimes escaped through marriage, mostly to Chinese laborers who saved enough money to "purchase" their wives from the owners. Some women ran away, and others escaped by going to the police, or, as Yung states, "through insanity or suicide" (33). Finally, a number of women were "rescued" by white Christian missionaries such as Margaret Culbertson and Donaldina Cameron, who, with police assistance, organized raids on Chinese brothels in order to free the Chinese women, whom they viewed as "the ultimate symbol of female powerlessness" (Yung 35). In this way, approximately fifteen hundred Chinese girls and women were rescued by the Presbyterian Mission Home between 1877 and 1907. At the Mission Home, Chinese women were subjected to intense Christian proselytization and cultural values based on white, middle-class Victorian standards. While some of the Chinese women chose to return to China or to return to their former conditions, many married Chinese Christian men and started new lives in America (Yung 35–36).

This history suggests both the complicated relationship Chinese women had with their "saviors," who were often racist and/or condescending in their treatment of Chinese women, and the agency imparted by Chinese women, who often strategically shaped new cultural values and gender systems in order to survive. While it is true that American missionaries sometimes did provide much needed services and assistance to Chinese women in exploitative and often dangerous circumstances, it is also important to note the damaging effects of such work on Chinese communities. As Yung suggests, the missionaries

> not only infringed on the civil rights of an already disenfranchised population, but also helped to perpetuate negative stereotypes of the Chinese, thus adding fuel to anti-Chinese sentiment and legislation. . . . [Also], [r]escued women were often pressured into adopting gender roles that emphasized female purity, piety, and Christian home life. Because missionary women strongly believed that the Chinese home should center on the moral authority of the wife and not the patriarchal control of the husband, they worked hard to turn Chinese women against traditional Chinese marriages and family life, alienating the Chinese community and subjecting the women to cultural conflict and social ostracism as a result. (36)

Peggy Pascoe argues that missionaries' acceptance of racial stereotypes "helped maintain white American dominance over minority groups" (140). Yet, Chinese women who entered missionary homes were, as Yung suggests, "neither powerless victims nor entirely free agents, but women who lived in a world with many constraints and few opportunities" (36–37). As such, they often took what they needed from the missionary homes and doctrines, accepting values that they could use in order to improve their lives and conditions and rejecting those cultural traits that conflicted with their needs. As Pascoe argues, Chinese women, through their acceptance and rejection of various aspects of the missionaries' Christian and Victorian indoctrination, were able to shape new gender relations that fit their new circumstances in America.

Thus, Asian women affected and were often affected by U.S. immigration practices whether they found themselves in the United States or not. They were forced to deal with multiple conflicts in terms of their traditional gender roles, from split-household families to encounters with Western attitudes to stereotypes about their sexuality. Likewise, Asian men in the United States found themselves subjected to different forms of attack on their traditional gender roles and identities. Conventional gender roles were disrupted for Asian men through processes of feminization in the eyes of mainstream America. Located at the bottom of the labor tier, in a geographical location where very few women of any race were present, Asian men were forced to occupy traditionally "feminine" domains in their work as houseboys, doing domestic work, laundry, and food service (Amott and Matthaei 197).[26]

In *China Men*, Kingston invokes the historical feminization of Chinese men in the United States in her first chapter, "On Discovery," which subsequently frames the entire narrative. Written as a myth (and based on a legend from the eighteenth-century Chinese classic *Flowers in the Mirror* by Li Ju-Chen),[27] the chapter details the life of Tang Ao, a man who went searching for Gold Mountain and ended up in the Land of Women. There, women captured him, chained him up, and bound his feet. Joking that they were "sewing [his] lips together"—and thereby suggesting, as Goellnicht writes, that silence is "part of the female condition" (1992, 192)—they dressed him in women's clothing, fed him only "women's food," painted his face, and forced him to serve their queen, during which "his hips swayed and his shoulders swiveled because of his shaped feet" (5). Kingston writes, "In the Women's Land there are no taxes and no wars. Some scholars say that that country was discovered during the reign of Empress Wu (A.D. 694–705), and some say earlier than that, A.D. 441, and it was in North America" (5). As Goellnicht suggests, Kingston employs "characteristic interrogation of all her sources" and "gives us two possible dates for this mythic event, but the narrator seems certain that the location of the Land of Women 'was in North America'" (191). Presented as history and "fact," this feminization presumably occurred in the United States—the Gold Mountain. Such emasculation of Chinese immigrant men enacts, for Kingston, as much of a silencing—sewing (his) lips together—as does the subsequent historical erasure of Chinese American men's presence and actions in the United States.[28]

Resistance to Oppression

While I have documented many of the hardships faced by early Asian immigrants, it is important to note also the many ways in which these immigrant men and women consistently challenged and resisted the oppressive forces working against them, as well as negative mainstream American ideologies circulating about them. From the beginning of Asian immigrants' experiences in the United States, they were cognizant of the discriminatory ways in which they were treated economically, politically, and socially. Both Chan and Takaki note that Asian immigrant workers of every ethnicity have risen up in revolt against injustice. Documenting the history of strikes among Chinese, Japanese, and Filipino workers from the latter part of the nineteenth century into the twentieth century, Chan maps a history of organized resistance. Members of these groups struck for living wages, equitable to the wages paid other racial/ethnic groups; for reasonable working hours and days, including at least one day or half-day off each week; for better working conditions; and for an end to the abuses they suffered from overseers that sometimes culminated in deaths and maimings of their fellow workers.

As Takaki argues, it was the organization of strikes among Asian immigrants that solidified and structured their resistance. While individualistic forms of violence and sabotage were significant, they rarely resulted in changes in the daily conditions and experiences of the workers. Strikes, however, demonstrated group solidarity and organized resistance to economic discrimination and exploitation. Takaki, documenting the emergence of the strike among Hawaiian sugar plantation laborers in the early part of the twentieth century, suggests that "striking constituted a particularly effective expression of labor resistance, for it could lead to a positive transformation of the plantation structure. Moreover, striking could enable men and women of various nationalities to gain a deeper understanding of themselves as laborers, to develop a working-class identity and consciousness" (1989, 150). In 1867, Chinese transcontinental railroad workers organized a strike involving two thousand men that lasted one week (until their food rations were depleted). In 1891, another group of Chinese laborers, this time in Hawaii, struck to protest unfair deductions from their wages until they were ruthlessly whipped by policemen, who destroyed their campsites. In 1900, Japanese plantation workers in Hawaii organized a strike after the death, due to careless management, of three mill hands. In 1909, seven thousand Japanese plantation workers went on strike at Oahu for four months for higher wages (Takaki, 1989, 150–151).

While most early strikes were organized within particular ethnic groups, workers of different ethnic groups also joined together at times to organize strikes, as in the cases of Chinese and Japanese laborers working together to strike a Hawaiian sugar plantation in 1900 (Takaki, 1989, 149); Japanese and Mexican farmworkers collaborating to demand higher wages in California in 1903 (Chan, 1991); and Filipinos, Japanese, Spanish, Portuguese, and Chinese laborers joining together in Hawaii in 1920. Also, both men and women participated in strikes in Hawaii during the early twentieth century (Takaki, 1989, 149). Although plantation owners often attempted to diffuse strikes by reliance on a divide-and-conquer strategy of employing workers of other ethnicities as "strike breakers," they could not completely curtail the emergence of interethnic organizing and solidarity. The Hawaiian strike of 1919–1920, for example, involved Japanese and Filipino laborers joining together to protest low wages, urged by newspaper statements such as the following, printed in the Japanese *Hawaii Shimpo*: "Our sincere and desperate voices are also their voices. Their righteous indignation is our righteous indignation. . . . Fellow Japanese laborers! Don't be a race of unreliable dishonest people! Their problem is your problem!" (Takaki, 1989, 152–153). As a result, workers of various ethnicities joined together, realizing that they shared common concerns as workers in a capitalist regime.

Also, members of unions began to realize the need for interethnic labor organizations, leading to the creation of, for example, the Hawaii Laborers' Association, a multiethnic labor union that brought together members of several nationalities with a common vision of struggle (Takaki, 1989, 154–155). However, the Asian immigrant labor organizations that formed were not supported or accepted by white-dominated American groups such as the American Federation of Labor, whose president, Samuel Gompers, once stated, "Every incoming coolie means the displacement of an American, and the lowering of the American standard of living" (as quoted in Chan, 1991, 87).

Asian immigrant workers continued to strike, to organize unions and resistance efforts, and to develop a group consciousness and solidarity. While very few strikes were completely successful, employers often conceded in small ways, and the stereotypes that Asian workers were docile and obedient were successfully challenged (Chan, 1991; Takaki, 1989). Also, as Takaki has argued, striking involved the development of a new consciousness among Asian immigrants and, specifically, a transformation in their identities from "sojourners" to "settlers," in the case of Japanese immigrants, "from Japanese to Japanese Americans" (1989, 151). By striking, they signaled their desire to change their current living conditions in the United States and hopefully improve the situation for their children, thereby implying their decision to remain in this country. Also, their use of methods such as strikes and litigation signified their acceptance of U.S. channels for social change and transformation, implicitly suggesting their claim to American status and full cultural participation.

Another important method of resistance often employed by Asians in the United States, according to Chan, was litigation, generally undertaken not by the working classes but by the more educated and economically privileged Asian immigrants. By Chan's count, more than one thousand litigation cases involving Chinese plaintiffs or defendants were undertaken between 1882 and 1943. Since, as she argues, only about one-tenth of actual cases were reported, we can speculate that there were tens of thousands of cases involving Asian immigrants seeking justice through the courts (1991, 90). According to Chan, the three most significant issues to Asian immigrant litigants were economic discrimination, naturalization rights, and immigration exclusion. She writes, "Chinese tried hardest to fight exclusion: more than 90 percent of their reported cases arose from efforts to gain entry into the United States. Japanese, Asian Indians, and Koreans were most concerned about acquiring citizenship through naturalization, while Chinese and Japanese were determined to remove impediments to their right to earn a living" (1991, 90).[29] While most of the cases brought by Asian immigrants were unsuccessful, a few did win, and the sheer numbers of litigations had an effect on perceptions of Asian immigrants and on the ways in which Asians in the United States perceived themselves and understood their rights and claims to citizenship.

Asian immigrants also organized around issues of nationalism, recognizing the global contexts of the abuses and discriminations they faced in the United States. Chan writes, "As Asian immigrants went on strike and went to court, some of them increasingly realized that the host society found it easy to discriminate against them because their countries of origin were weak" (1991, 96). Immigrants from colonized countries, in particular, faced mistreatment in the United States, including what Chan refers to as "legally sanctioned subordination" (1990, 39). Understanding the connections between the subjugation of their homelands (often to the United States or other Western forces) and their own subjugation within the United States, some individuals worked to organize liberation efforts for their homelands from foreign domination and occupation. For example, Korean immigrants formed nationalist organizations and collected money from members of immigrant communities in their desire to liberate their country. Likewise, Asian Indians worked within the United States to end the British colonization of India (Chan, 1990,

50–55). In such efforts, the immigrants themselves realized that their movements away from their home nations were often the direct results of such colonialist aggressions. They also were cognizant of the fact that "as despised subjects of a colonized country, they had no protection of any sort against racial discrimination" in the United States (Chan, 1990, 55). Chinese women in San Francisco, from the beginning of the twentieth century, tied their feminist activism to nationalist efforts, arguing that women's oppression was inextricably tied to the foreign domination of China, and therefore women's rights must be linked to Chinese nationalist movements (Yung 52). Such efforts resulted in the development of a new political consciousness among many Asian immigrants.

Sometimes, Asian plantation workers countered the violence and abuses they suffered with their own violence directed against overseers and plantation holders. According to Takaki, workers often developed subtle, ingenious means of resistance, designed to sabotage the smooth operation of the plantation. In various instances they destroyed property; they started fires; they counterfeited script (or payment in kind, to be used only in plantation stores) to distribute among workers; they feigned illness and/ or injury; and in the words of Takaki, they "became skilled practitioners in the art of pretending to be working" (1989, 144). Other avenues of escape from the drudgery of plantation labor included the use of alcohol and opium, as well as actually running away from the plantations and from their "contracts" (often at the risk of being caught and returned to the plantations).[30]

One ingenious method of resistance is detailed in *China Men*. In describing her great-grandfather's experiences in Hawaii as a coolie, Kingston explores his resistance to authority. Having signed a contract to come to the Gold Mountain, Bak Goong becomes a laborer on a sugar plantation. There, it is not the backbreaking work that makes him suffer but the rule that laborers are not allowed to talk at work. "I wasn't born to be silent like a monk," he thinks, claiming that he needs to cast out his voice to catch ideas (100). Also, he links this silence of the monk to the lack of sexual possibilities available to Chinese men at the time: "Apparently we've taken a vow of chastity too. Nothing but roosters in this flock" (100). He breaks the rule against talking and is whipped. He sings during work and is fined. Finally, because the work has made his breathing difficult, he solves the problem of not being able to speak by coughing his thoughts and ideas. "The deep, long, loud coughs, barking and wheezing, were almost as satisfying as shouting" (104). When the overseer beats his horse, he coughs his angry response, and, as Kingston notes, "he felt better after having his say. He did not even mind the despair, which dispelled upon his speaking it" (104). When he becomes ill along with other Chinese men on the plantation, he diagnoses their illness as "congestion from not talking" and proposes that they "talk and talk" (115). He tells the other men a story about a king who shouted his secrets into the ground, relieving himself of the pain of keeping it all in. Whenever the wind blew after that, the king's secrets could be heard throughout the land. The next day in the fields, the other men dig a hole into the ground and fill it with their words. "They had dug an ear into the world, and were telling the earth their secrets. 'I want home,' Bak Goong yelled, pressed against the soil, and smelling the earth. 'I want my home,' the men yelled together. 'I want home. Home. Home. Home. Home. . . .' 'That wasn't a custom,' said Bak Goong. 'We made it up. We can make up customs because we're the founding ancestors of this place'" (117–118).

Of this history, Kingston writes, "What stories the wind would tell" (118). Just as they claim America for their own by making up tradition, they make the land and wind theirs by speaking into it. Kingston remembers her trip to Hawaii where she was shocked to learn of a stretch of the island of Oahu called Chinaman's Hat. The name is offensive to her, a racist slur. Yet in the wind she hears the island singing and wonders about the lives of her ancestors. "I have heard the land sing," she writes. "I have seen the bright blue streaks of spirits whisking through the air. I again search for my American ancestors by listening in the cane" (90). The offensive name is also a tribute, honoring those ancestors: "It's a tribute to the pioneers to have a living island named after their work hat" (90). As Patricia Linton argues, this name that at first estranged Kingston also makes her proud. "Retelling provides a way to change the meaning, to force the slippage of the signifier" (44). By appropriating speech and land, the Chinese immigrants make both their own. Bak Goong's history, Linton suggests, is a complex, powerful metaphor "that demonstrates how people appropriate the land, making it so completely their own that the land itself tells their story" (45). Similarly, Kingston makes the history her own, resisting her exclusion from the United States and the official historical narrative, shifting the terrain of Chinese immigration to the United States.

Other historians and writers also urge Asian Americans to tell their stories, arguing that it is the telling that makes the difference. In his historical work about Asian Americans, Takaki (1989) urges Asian Americans to break their silence and to speak out. He documents the silencing of Asian immigrants in the United States as one of the most oppressive actions used against them by the dominant culture and suggests that in order to be viewed as subjects and agents of their own history, Asian Americans must claim their own voices, "their own words and stories as told in their oral histories, conversations, speeches, soliloquies, and songs, as well as in their own writings—diaries, letters, newspapers, magazines, pamphlets, placards, posters, flyers, court petitions, autobiographies, short stories, novels, and poems" (7–8). He writes, "In the telling and retelling of their stories, the elderly immigrants reclaim the authorship of their own history. They want the younger generations to know about their experiences" (9). Kingston, in The Woman Warrior, relies on a similar argument regarding speech and silence when, after describing the heroic acts of the woman warrior, Fa Mu Lan, she names her narrator a woman warrior also, noting that her words symbolize her "vengeance." In this context, it is the telling itself that renders Kingston a warrior woman, as the reporting of crimes represents an act of vengeance and a means of resistance and empowerment.

Yet, to what degree have the experiences of Asian American men and women been similar, and at what point do they diverge? Many of the forms of resistance I have documented in early Asian immigration history refer explicitly to Asian American men. While women participated in strikes, they made up a smaller percentage of the workforce and therefore were less visible in such demonstrations. Women were also far less likely to employ litigation as a method of resistance, a context that was both racist and sexist. Speaking out has offered one significant form of challenge to the dominant order, but in the United States, where speech has been a protected right only for some members of society, Asian American women and men have most often been silenced, both literally and figuratively. As I have demonstrated, this silence, which may be appropriated as a strategy for multiple relocations, also causes problems.

Similarly, in China Men, Kingston suggests that silence, a powerful means of protection, also causes great pain. What she desires most of all is to know the truth of her father's history. But her father, who was a poet and scholar in China, is silent in the United States and therefore unknown and unknowable to her. Goellnicht suggests that this silence relates to the enforced feminization suffered by Kingston's father, who breaks his silence "only to utter curses against the women as a means of releasing his sense of frustration and powerlessness in racist America" (1992, 201). To her father, Kingston writes, "Worse than the swearing and the nightly screams were your silences when you punished us by not talking. You rendered us invisible, gone. . . . We invented the terrible things you were thinking: That your mother had done you some unspeakable wrong, and so you left China forever. That you hate daughters. That you hate China. . . . You say with the few words and the silences: No stories. No past. No China" (14). His silence is interpreted by his daughter to mean that he hates girls, women, and China. Incidentally, Kingston's paralleling of China and daughters also suggests that China itself is gendered female. Her only conclusion is to internalize such hatred, despising herself for being born female and Chinese. She writes, "What I want from you is for you to tell me that those curses are only common Chinese sayings. That you did not mean to make me sicken at being female" (14).

Because China and the United States are so often posited as binarily opposed, and Chinese and American identities appear to be mutually exclusive, she wonders if, to be truly American, her father has had to cast off all vestiges of his former (Chinese) self. There are no photographs of him in China or in Chinese clothing. "Have you always been American?" she wonders. "Do you mean to give us a chance at being real Americans by forgetting the Chinese past?" (14). (And, does becoming American, for a Chinese person, entail giving up speech?) Of course, as she is fully aware, there is reason to be silent in America. Even his name must be shielded, she notes, or he may be traced and deported (29). The "immigration lies" she recounts in The Woman Warrior coexist uneasily with silence. She even remembers a time when her father changed his name regularly, using aliases to escape the police—new names for each situation—"'because the white demons can't tell one Chinese name from another or one face from another.' He had the power of naming" (242). Aware that her father refuses to speak of the past, she states,

> You fix yourself in the present, but I want to hear the stories about the rest of your life, the Chinese stories. I want to know what makes you scream and

curse, and what you're thinking when you say nothing, and why when you do talk, you talk differently from Mother.

I take after MaMa. We have peasant minds. We see a stranger's tic and ascribe motives. I'll tell you what I suppose from your silences and few words, and you can tell me that I'm mistaken. You'll just have to speak up with the real stories if I've got you wrong. (15)

For Kingston, silence has multiple meanings. Her father's silence, however, is oppressive and painful to her. And, as Goellnicht argues, it is not a "positive" silence but "the silence of resignation that signals withdrawal and humiliation, the inability to articulate his own subject position so that he is doomed to the one—that of inscrutable, passive 'chinaman'—created for him by the dominant society" (1992, 201–202). She begs him to correct her, to tell her the "real" story, his story.[31] Instead, she must create her own story of what his life could have been like, inventing a history for him and for herself in opposition to the erasure and historical silencing of their lives in America. "I think this is the journey you don't tell me" (49), she writes, as she begins her narrative of him. Such self-creation is necessary because, as Linton suggests, "so much of the actual family history is undocumented or fraught with contradiction" (38). Kingston's imagined accounts are juxtaposed uneasily against the "factual accounts" she challenges. In creating her own history, she reinscribes dominant conventional historical narratives that exclude her and tells a different kind of American history, one in which her ancestors, too, are Americans.

Race, Racial Formation, and Racism

At this point, I turn to common conceptualizations of "race," "racism," and racial formation in the United States in order to provide a brief and general overview of such concepts. By doing so, I hope to provide a basic context and framework against which to examine the roles Asian Americans have played in the racial history of this country and to begin to envision new ways to make sense of race in order to develop paradigms capable of invoking the complexity and contradictions of race and racism in the United States. Such background will also provide an important context for my subsequent discussion of the uses of language and silence in texts by Asian American women writers. As Michael Omi and Howard Winant point out, theories of race in the United States are ever shifting, influenced by existing racial relations at any given historical moment. In their work *Racial Formation in the United States*, they provide an examination of three common approaches to understanding race and racial relations, based on ethnicity, class, and nation, offering critiques of each model and proposing their own theory of "racial formation." I will briefly discuss each of the three theories as well as the model they rely on to make meaning of race, and then I will discuss how other theorists attempt to make sense of race and racism.[32]

The first of the approaches discussed by Omi and Winant, the ethnicity paradigm, has been the most commonly used approach to understandings of race in the United States. The model, based on the integration of Europeans into U.S. culture, relies on certain assumptions about both assimilation and cultural pluralism. In short, this theoretical framework is based on the assumption that all immigrants, from all national origins, can and should assimilate into American culture, thereby becoming "American," as European Americans have done. Predicated, as the authors argue, on the European immigrant model of assimilation, proponents of this model argue that assimilation is the "most logical, and 'natural,' response to the dilemma imposed by racism" and that if immigrants of European descent can successfully assimilate, then members of all cultural groups should be able to do so (17). At the same time, following the reasoning suggested by a model of cultural pluralism, all ethnic (and national, cultural) groups are viewed as existing equally, with histories, customs, and traditions holding equal value in the United States.

However, as Omi and Winant argue, not all cultural groups are perceived as equal in this country, and people of color have generally not been able to fully assimilate into American culture. Because of structural barriers, including racism, members of racial minority groups have not followed the same trajectory of integration into mainstream U.S. culture, and in fact many people of color have rejected the aspirations of such a model. As the authors state,

> Substantial criticism has been directed at the ethnicity school for its treatment of racially defined minorities as ethnically defined minorities, and for its consequent neglect of race *per se*. These arguments point to the limits of the immigrant analogy in addressing what was in many cases a qualitatively dif-

ferent historical experience—one which included slavery, colonization, racially based exclusion, and in the case of Native Americans, virtual extirpation. In addition, it has been argued, the paradigm tends to "blame the victims" for their plight and thus to deflect attention away from the ubiquity of racial meanings and dynamics. (20)

Finally, Omi and Winant question the use of terms such as "black" and "Asian" as they are often used, juxtaposed against categories such as "Irish" or "Jewish." What becomes, they wonder, of ethnicity *among* blacks or *among* Asians? And what about national origin, religion, language, and other cultural differences among ethnic black, Asian, Native American, and/or Latino groups, rarely considered as they are among European ethnic groups? There is, in fact, they argue, "a subtly racist element in this substitution—in which whites are seen as variegated in terms of group identities, but blacks 'all look alike'" (22), the effects of the misapplication of a paradigm based in white ethnic history inappropriately mapped onto racially defined groups.

Next, Omi and Winant discuss and critique the class paradigm of race, which relies on the notion that "social divisions which assume a distinctively racial or ethnic character can be attributed or explained principally by reference to economic structures and processes" (Stuart Hall, as cited in Omi and Winant 24). Thus, by this approach, race is understood as being rooted in exchange relationships and in the unequal exchange that characterizes a "class system." Omi and Winant discuss three class-based approaches, the market relations approach, stratification theory, and class conflict theory, representing three different, related ways to conceptualize economic inequality. While granting value to each of these approaches, Omi and Winant ultimately argue that it is impossible to understand race solely in terms of a class relationship because "race cuts across class lines as well as dividing classes internally" (32). They argue that it would be more accurate to state that "race and class are competing modalities by which social actors may be organized" (32). In short, while cognizant of the need to address issues of class in any discussion of race and racism, and the relationships among race, class, and other social categories, the authors critique this approach as narrow and shortsighted in that it fails to adequately address the complexities of race in the United States.

Finally, Omi and Winant discuss a nation-based theory of race, one that had precursors in the writings of Martin Delaney, Paul Cuffe, and W. E. B. DuBois and gained currency in the United States in the mid-1960s with the rise of black nationalism. Rooted primarily in a critique of colonialism, a nation-based theory of race attempts to explain racism in the United States by understanding people of color as members of an internal colony, oppressed within the United States as the nations of origin are dominated and/or occupied by the United States and other Western forces. Of particular importance are this model's emphases on inequality, political disenfranchisement, territorial and institutional segregation, and cultural domination (37). Cultural nationalism, in which members of racial minorities attempt to understand themselves within diasporic contexts, also represents a significant aspect of this racial theory. Yet, Omi and Winant ask, "How effectively does the nation-based paradigm account for racial dynamics?" (47) and ascertain that the connection is, at best, tenuous. Conditions of colonization, they argue, do not always automatically carry over into postcolonial contexts, and it is, at times, difficult to specify what, exactly, is "national" about racial oppression in the United States (47).

In their own model of race, Omi and Winant begin by dissolving any presumptions that race can be understood as being about mere skin color or human physiognomy or through an "either-or logic" that posits a black-and-white dualistic framework (54). They argue that we must challenge both the idea that race is an essence, fixed, concrete, and stable and the notion that race is an illusion, "a pure ideological construct which some ideal non-racist social order would eliminate" (54). To make sense of race, they propose to understand it as "an unstable and 'decentered' complex of social meanings constantly being transformed by political struggle" and a "concept which signifies and symbolizes social conflicts and interests by referring to different types of human bodies" (55). Also, according to these authors, race must be understood as "always and necessarily a social and historical process . . . [with] no biological basis for distinguishing among human groups along the lines of race" (55). Thus, race cannot be understood through the concept of essentialism.

Omi and Winant define their project, then, as an attempt to make sense of the fact that and ways in which race continues to both structure and represent social reality. To do so, they rely on the theoretical approach of "racial formation," defined as "the sociohistorical process by which racial categories are created, inhabited, transformed, and destroyed" (55). Directly related to racial formation is the concept of "racial project"—"simultaneously an interpretation, representation, or explanation of racial dynamics, and an effort to reorganize and redistribute resources along particular racial lines" (56). They make their argument by suggesting that specifically situated racial projects shape racial formation and are linked to the practice of hegemony.

In order to make sense of race, we must understand the ways in which racial formation occurs at both structural and representational levels. In other words, race is shaped and transformed by both institutional, systematic forces and cultural, ideological tools. Indeed, racial formation occurs at multiple levels, including the macro level, at which race may be understood in terms of social structure along a broad spectrum of political realities, and the micro level of everyday experience, during which, the authors argue, racial formation is shaped by a "common sense" approach in which everyday reality is shaped by stereotypes, cultural images, and persistent beliefs about what race is and should be. Meanwhile, the authors state, "it is not possible to represent race discursively without simultaneously locating it, explicitly or implicitly, in a social structural (and historical) context. Nor is it possible to organize, maintain, or transform social structures without simultaneously engaging, once more either explicitly or implicitly, in racial signification" (60). Racial formation, then, depends upon the interactions of multiple racial projects, institutional and cultural.

Omi and Winant trace a trajectory of the modern conception of race in order to explain contemporary understandings of race, suggesting that the emergence of such a conception occurred only with the rise of Europe and the arrival of Europeans to the Americas. Europeans' "discovery" of the "natives" prompted them to develop a worldview in order to distinguish themselves (Christian, civilized, human) from the animal-like "others." According to the authors, the origins of modern racial awareness were precipitated by the "Conquest of America," which signaled the "advent of a consolidated social structure of exploitation, appropriation, domination" (62). Such historical processes began the ideological work of centering Europe and Europeans while marginalizing nonwhite people as peripheral, inferior, and subordinate. Religious justifications, however, soon gave way to scientific ones, conceived to justify the exploitation, enslavement, and genocide of African American, Native American, Latin American, and Asian American people. Within the domain of science, race was newly interpreted as biological, suggesting that racial difference was a matter of difference among species and thereby rationalizing the inequitable allocation of resources and social and political rights (63–64).[33] Finally, in more recent years, and often due to intellectual and political struggles on the part of people of color, race has been conceptualized as political, with emphases on civil rights and anticolonialism (65).

To understand the historical underpinnings of race in America is to understand also the work of hegemony in a racial dictatorship. Omi and Winant argue that for nearly three hundred years, this nation has constituted such a dictatorship, characterized by the exclusion of nonwhite people from politics, the conflation of "American" identity with whiteness, the establishment of a "color line" as the fundamental division in our society, and the consolidation of an oppositional racial consciousness among people of color (65–66). Organized by both coercion and consent, the hegemonic racial structure of the United States intersects with other "regions" of hegemony, including gender, class, and sexual identity.

Similarly, Evelyn Brooks Higginbotham argues that an explication of race must involve analysis of its relationships to other social categories, including gender, class, and sexuality. In her essay "African-American Women's History and the Metalanguage of Race," Higginbotham engages three simultaneous and interrelated strategies to make meaning of race: defining the various "technologies" or workings of race; exposing the role of race as a "metalanguage" by exploring "its powerful, all-encompassing effect on the construction and representation of other social and power relations" (252); and recognizing both the oppressive and liberatory functions of race.

Relying on definitions of race by scholars such as Henry Louis Gates and Barbara Fields, Higginbotham defines race as "a social construction predicated upon the recognition of difference and signifying the simultaneous distinguishing and positioning of groups vis-à-vis one another. More than this, race is a highly contested representation of relations of power between social categories by which individuals are identified and identify themselves" (253). Thus, while race is often believed to be "natural" and essential, Omi and Winant and Higginbotham describe it as socially constructed and constituted through relations of power in our society. Furthermore, race structures and is structured by other social categories, including gender, class, and sexuality, in that race determines how one's gender may be perceived. Take, for example, African American women's relationship to the "cult of true womanhood" of the nineteenth century, in which women were defined as pure, pious, submissive, and domestic, and in which whiteness defined womanhood as much as gender did. Black women, on the other hand, who were forced to work "like men" in the public sphere, and who were often denied access to their own bodies, their sexuality, and their children, were often forced to prove that they were indeed women, as in the case of Sojourner Truth. To Truth's question, "Ar'n't I a woman?" Higginbotham suggests, America's legal system replied no, ruling that black women existed "outside the statutory rubric 'woman'" (257). Similarly, while black women were never considered "ladies," white women of the working class (and white women who transgressed sexual boundaries of propriety) were also denied such status. For Asian American women, gender and notions of femininity are also racialized, exemplified by the fact that young Maxine of The Woman Warrior must learn to perform "American (white) femininity" in order to assimilate into U.S. culture.

Race, according to Higginbotham, then serves as "global sign" and a "metalanguage." It "speaks about and lends meaning to a host of terms and expressions, to myriad aspects of life that would otherwise fall outside the referential domain of race" (255). As such, it operates, as Gates puts it, as the "ultimate trope of difference" (cited in Higginbotham 253), thereby shaping identity, culture, and social relations. And yet, the ways in which race affects society have included both negative, oppressive consequences and liberatory transformations of consciousness. Higginbotham suggests that race is a "double-voiced discourse" for African Americans, serving both the oppression and the liberation of black communities. Thus, as Fields points out, while race was often taken as a sign of biological inferiority, African Americans reinvented the concept to include cultural identity, heritage, and even nationalist pride (cited in Higginbotham 268–269). By appropriating language and ideology as tools of resistance, African Americans have challenged both representational and structural, institutional forms of oppression. However, as Higginbotham suggests, claiming cultural unity in the face of oppression often results in the masking of differences among members of the cultural group. Thus, race remains a site of contestation, power, and conflict, as well as one of possible resistance to oppression.

In order to further their theory of race and racial formation, Omi and Winant attempt also to make sense of *racism*. Explaining that racism has commonly been understood, since the 1960s, as prejudice and discrimination, these authors attempt to broaden this definition, arguing that racism, like race, has shifted in its meanings over time. They define racism as that which "creates or reproduces structures of domination based on essentialist categories of race" (71). As a historical construct and "product of centuries of systemic exclusion, exploitation, and disregard of racially defined minorities" (69), racism also encompasses institutional inequality and must be differentiated from race. Acknowledgment and discussion of race does not equal racism, and all racisms themselves are not the same in value or meaning. Even the "strategic essentialisms" often deployed by members of racially oppressed groups must be seen as distinct from racism, which essentializes as a process of domination.[34]

Other theorists, too, have attempted to develop theories of race by offering interpretations of racism. In her essay "Something About the Subject Makes It Hard to Name," Gloria Yamato defines racism as "the systematic, institutionalized mistreatment of one group of people by another based on racial heritage" (22). To Yamato, racism is constantly transformed by social and political forces. "Like a virus, it's hard to beat racism, because by the time you come up with a cure it's mutated to a 'new cure-resistant' form" (20). Racism, then, must be analyzed and challenged on multiple levels. Yamato identifies four prevalent forms of racism in circulation today: 1) aware/blatant racism, in which the racism is clear and unapologetically expressed and easily identified by both its victims and onlookers; 2) aware/covert racism, a subtle form of racism in which racist acts are carefully veiled, usually in order to protect the perpetrators; 3) unaware/unintentional racism, often manifested in the behavior of white liberals who appropriate, exoticize, and stereotype the histories, cultures, and identities of people of color; and 4) unaware/self-righteous racism, another subtle and insidious form of racism. Yamato explains it in the following way: "The 'good white' racist attempts to shame Blacks into being blacker, scorns Japanese Americans who don't speak Japanese, and knows more about the Chicano/a community than the folks who make up the community" (21). In her development of a four-pronged theory of racism that includes analyses of several racial projects, Yamato formulates also an understanding of the complexities of race in the United States, cognizant of the workings of hegemonic power in racial oppression that sometimes manifests itself through internalized racism.

Like Yamato, Rita Chaudhry Sethi also attempts to expand on existing conceptualizations of racism, focusing specifically on racism against Asians in the United States in her essay "Smells Like Racism: A Plan for Mobilizing against Anti-Asian Bias."[35] Critiquing the ways in which race is so often framed in simplistic binarisms in the United States, resulting in a black/white polarity, Sethi interrogates the role Asian Americans play in U.S. racial relations and conflicts. She finds that racist acts directed against Asian Americans are, at best, trivialized, and at worst, ignored and dismissed, not only by white mainstream America but also by other groups of people of color. She suggests that Asians in the United States remain a safe target for racism because of "the perspective that excludes the experiences of Asians (and other people of color) from the rubric of racism" (236). And, she states,

> Whites would deny us our right to speak out against majority prejudice, partially because it tarnishes their image of Asians as "model" minorities; other people of color would deny us the same because of monopolistic sentiments that they alone endure real racism. . . . The perspective of some people of color that there is a monopoly on oppression is debilitating to an effort at cross-ethnic coalition building. (236–237)

Thus, until our society can broaden its definitions of race and racism to acknowledge the complexities of these concepts, anti-Asian sentiments and practices will continue to escalate. To challenge such attitudes, Sethi proposes a new model of interpretation for racism, one that takes into account the "intraracism" occurring among various racial groups, the internalized racism experienced by people of color, and a wide array of culturally discriminatory practices rarely recognized as racist.[36] Such acts include prejudice and discrimination on the basis of accent and English-language abilities, cultural practices, food, attire, and religion, as well as appropriative and exoticizing tendencies and the proliferation of media stereotypes. Citing vandalism, violent acts, and murders committed against Asian Indians in New Jersey in the late 1980s by self-proclaimed "Dotbusters," Sethi analyzes the police and prosecutor's reluctance to recognize any of the events as racially motivated, stating "[The Asian Indians'] experiences were unrecognizable as the caricature of racism, and there was a collective refusal to be expansive and open-minded in interpreting what was happening. . . . [T]he main reason why justice was not served was because the racism that Indians were enduring did not fit the neat, American paradigm for racial violence" (245, 247).[37]

Of course, the fact that Asians do not fit neatly into the racial framework of the United States has a historical basis. As Takaki and Chan demonstrate, the racial history of this nation depended on assumptions of whiteness as the norm, with racial difference being defined most often as a black/white difference. As mentioned earlier, within the oppositional racial framework of the United States, Asian Americans (and other nonblack people of color) are generally perceived as positioned outside of racial discourse altogether. When they are marked as people of color —and subsequently "raced"—they are often described as if being on a continuum between black and white (not quite black but not white either).[38] Such assumptions lead people to imagine that Asian Americans' experiences of racism are not really as damaging as the racism enacted against African Americans and that Asian Americans as a group aspire to whiteness (hence, the myth of the "model minority"). Even today, most racial theories fail to take the experiences of Asian Americans into account. Chan suggests that existing frameworks of "race" oversimplify the conditions of Asian Americans. For instance, historians and other scholars have generally not agreed over whether Asians in the United States have been oppressed as a class, a race, or a "nationality." While Omi and Winant might dismiss the categories of class and nationality (as well as ethnicity) for a discussion of race that subsumes the other categories, Chan argues that in fact Asian immigrants, like other immigrants of color, have suffered from all three forms of inequality and oppression. She writes, "It is clear that the immigrants themselves realized their suffering had multiple causes. As workers, they struck for higher wages and better working conditions; as nonwhite minorities 'ineligible to citizenship' they challenged laws that denied them civil rights on account of their race; and as proud sons and daughters of their countries of origin, they supported political movements to free those lands from foreign encroachment" (1991, 81). Thus, Asian immigrants themselves recognized the multiple sites they occupied and resisted oppression at all levels.

However, due to the 1790 naturalization law that restricted American citizenship to "free white persons," Asians in America found themselves directly confronting what it meant to be American. When the law was amended after the Civil War to include African Americans, Asians were still excluded from the rights of citizenship (as were Native Americans). As Amott and Matthaei suggest, because Asians were unable to attain the status of citizenship, they remained "permanent 'aliens' (non-citizens), and whites were able to pass numerous laws which restricted their rights simply by referring to their alien status" (194). Asians, because they were denied citizenship, were unable to vote, own land or property, marry white women or men, and/or access many public resources, including schools and government programs. Also, the 1922 Cable Act stated that any American women who married "aliens ineligible to citizenship" themselves forfeited U.S. citizenship (Takaki, 1989, 14–15). The naturalization law that equated American identity with whiteness was not rescinded until 1952.[39] Its effects remain evident today.

In *China Men*, Kingston explores constructions of race and racialization for Asian Americans in her section "The Brother in Vietnam." This brother, a high school teacher and pacifist, dreads the war and fears the destruction of his beliefs and values. When he is drafted, he hears that Vietnam is especially dangerous for Asian American soldiers, who are not seen as really American. "The rumor also went that the brother's draft board was channeling hippies and blacks into the infantry. And 'Orientals' belonged over there in Asia fighting among their own kind" (277). Even as a teacher in the United States, his ideas are often not taken seriously by his students. "Any criticism he had of America they dismissed as his being gookish" (279). Because he is seen as a guest—and an ungrateful one at that—he is not entitled to the same privileges enjoyed by those who belong, including the privilege to critique the system. When he is recruited to teach the young men aboard his Navy ship how to read and write, they tell him, "You speak English pretty good" (290), suggesting his status as an outsider. And when he is promoted and subjected to a security check, he holds his breath for fear of his family being deported. Kingston writes, "The government was certifying that the family was really American, not precariously American but super-American, extraordinarily secure—Q Clearance Americans. The Navy or the FBI had checked his mother and father and not deported them. . . . The government had not found him un-American with divided loyalties and treasonous inclinations" (299). He is cleared but remains aware that his status, and that of his family, could change at any moment.

However, "while his services were needed for the undeclared American-Vietnam war, the family was safe" (299).

Takaki suggests that we examine the very language used in representing Asian immigrants. He writes, "the view of Asian immigrants as 'sojourners' and European immigrants as 'settlers' is both a mistaken notion and a widely held myth" (1989, 10). The effects of such a notion and myth can be seen in the fact that Asians in America have always been perceived as outsiders, as strangers, and as guests. Again, Takaki suggests that many Asian immigrants "found they were not allowed to feel at home in the United States, and even their grandchildren and great-grandchildren still find they are not viewed and accepted as Americans" (11). Because Asians, as a group, have not been able to "pass" and/or easily assimilate into American culture, other Americans have often viewed them with suspicion and prejudice, a fact that becomes especially evident in the history of the internment of people of Japanese descent during World War II, the subject of the next chapter.

The exclusion of Asians from the United States, exclusions experienced by Asians in the United States from citizenship and its rights (leading to exploitation, oppression, racial discrimination, and even violence), and the relative absence of documentation and historical research about Asians in the United States all represent silences in Asian American history. The effects of such silences have included continuing anti-Asian legislation and sentiments in the United States, widely held stereotypes and/or perceptions regarding the insignificance and nonexistence of Asian Americans and their contributions to American culture, and the rendering invisible of Asian American women's writings about their lives and experiences in this culture. In short, the effects have been, at best, demoralizing, and at worst, dehumanizing.

In her book *Compositional Subjects* Kang suggests more attention to the processes of exclusion of Asian American women at the level of historiography. Rather than attempting to recover a "lost" history or merely adding on to what is already known about Asian American women in order to render a more "complete" history, an engagement that "affirms the disciplinary purchase of history to produce a faithful yet objective account of the past" (2002, 147), Kang emphasizes what she refers to as a "genealogy of unbelonging" (2002, 146). Similar to Jennifer Terry's "effective history" (discussed in the previous chapter), Kang's genealogy would alert us to not only the exclusions and elisions within conventional historical narratives but also the processes underlying such omissions. What are the suppressed, irretrievable, even "unthinkable" aspects of history? What has been rendered unintelligible? Such questions provoke crises of historical narration and evidence. She writes:

> [H]ow can a writing of Asian American women's history stress—in the sense of both emphasis and pressure—the archives not as preserving the residues of the past but as displaying an ongoing crisis of what counts as reliable historical data in different presents, and how they then induce, enable, and preclude certain narrations of the past? (2002, 150)

Because "a remarkable detail of the originary moment of Asian/American women in U.S. history is scored not by their presence but their striking absence" (2002, 150), Kang asserts that a critical historiography of Asian American women would highlight the limits of conventional historizing processes, as well as the archival documents commonly read as historical "evidence" (2002, 159). Yet, where does a geneaology of unbelonging belong? What are its methods, and how should they be applied? To address such questions, we must distinguish between various forms of history and history making, challenging dominant History with unofficial histories that imagine different accounts of the past.

Asian American writers have challenged their own historical omissions through multiple strategies, including the use of silence. While silence, as discussed in the previous chapter, has had multiple meanings for Asian Americans in U.S. history, it may also represent a significant site for resistance. Priscilla Wald, in her text *Constituting Americans*, discusses the conflicts faced by members of marginalized groups in the United States when confronting the dominant narratives of "We, the People," official stories that constitute Americans. In her discussion of the relationship between cultural identity and literary production in the United States, Wald argues that members of oppressed groups, when attempting to tell their own stories and histories, face a choice between conforming to cultural prescriptions or being rendered incomprehensible and unintelligible (3). Yet, she suggests, "[their] untold stories press for a hearing" (1). Discussing her analysis of works written in the margins of American cultures, she states,

> My readings attend to disruptions in literary narratives caused by unexpected words, awkward grammatical constructions, rhetorical or thematic disso-

nances that mark the pressure of untold stories. The authors I consider arrived at their understandings of untold stories in response to the imperatives each experienced—in his or her way—to tell the story of the nation. (1)

Thus, the forms the writers employ to tell their previously untold stories include varied ways of saying, closely tied to their relationships to the dominant culture. As such, adequate historical contextualization, as well as close analysis of their language use, is imperative.

In my analysis of texts by Asian American women writers, I attempt to link the authors' writings to their specific cultural and sometimes familial histories in the United States in order to make sense of the varied motivations behind each of their uses of silence. I argue that because of their continuing status as outsiders in a nation that perceives them as "foreigners" even while they, themselves, may claim American identity, the writers of this project engage unique relationships with the subject position of the writing "I." Each of them, in their attempts to tell a new story, risks being rendered unintelligible and therefore silenced again. And yet each of them deploys some form of silence in their writings, an attempt to unsay or a strategic reclamation and resistance.

There is a silence that cannot speak.

There is a silence that will not speak.

Beneath the grass the speaking dreams and beneath the dreams is a sensate sea. The speech that frees comes forth from that amniotic deep. To attend its voice, I can hear it say, is to embrace its absence. But I fail the task. The word is stone.

I admit it.

I hate the stillness. I hate the stone. . . .

Unless the stone bursts with telling, unless the seed flowers with speech, there is in my life no living word. The sound I hear is only sound. White sound. Words, when they fall, are pockmarks on the earth. They are hailstones seeking an underground stream.

—Joy Kogawa, *Obasan*

three

White Sound and Silences from Stone: Discursive Silences in the Internment Writings of Mitsuye Yamada and Joy Kogawa

In Janice Mirikitani's collection of poems entitled *We, the Dangerous* (1995), she takes as one of her central themes the involuntary internment of persons of Japanese descent in the United States during World War II.[1] Along with exploring the feelings of helplessness and anger associated with the internment, Mirikitani also examines what it means to be an American in a context in which Asian Americans are still perceived as foreigners and visitors to the United States, even when they are American citizens who consider this country their home. Her first series of poems in the collection, "Looking For America," includes works that critique the white-centered beauty standards of U.S. culture, the internalization of racism and self-hatred by people of color, and the invisibility of Asian Americans in media representations and national discourse.

In Mirikitani's poem "We, the Dangerous" (1978), she explores the misconception that Japanese Americans during World War II constituted a threat to national security—the "yellow peril"—a remnant of earlier anti-Japanese and anti-Asian hostility and scapegoating. Because of widespread hysteria and racist panic, Japanese Americans during World War II were considered dangerous and/or in danger of violence, and therefore they were incarcerated both for the protection of the American public and "for their own good." Relating the imprisonment of more than 120,000 Japanese Americans to the pervasive stereotypes about Asians at the time, Mirikitani writes: "We, closer to the earth, / squat, short thighed, / knowing the dust better. . . . / We, akin to the jungle, / plotting with the snake, / tails shedding in civilized America. . . . / We, who awake in the river / Ocean's child / Whale eater. . . . / We, the dangerous, / Dwelling in the ocean. / Akin to the jungle. / Closer to the earth" (26–27). Explicitly commenting on the association between stereotypes of Asian Americans (animal-like, uncivilized, savage, closer to nature) and the forced incarceration of Japanese Americans during World War II, Mirikitani attempts to explode any notion that such an incarceration was necessary or justified. Rather, as she suggests, the widescale removal of an entire group of Americans based solely on ethnic heritage represented an attempt by the U.S. government—and public—to "devour," "humble," and "break" the Japanese in America. Drawing on the strength of their history as Asian Americans and relating the crisis of internment to other atrocities committed against Asian people, Mirikitani writes, "Hiroshima / Vietnam / Tule Lake / And yet we were not devoured. / And yet we were not humbled. / And yet we are not broken" (27). Her words reflect perseverance in the face of racist hostility and adversity and a reclamation of her own identity as a Japanese American.

In two subsequent pieces contained in the second section of her book, entitled "Bowl of Rage," Mirikitani explores the silences surrounding internment. Both "Breaking Silence" and "Prisons of Silence" attempt to account for the multiple silences surrounding Japanese Americans' experiences in the concentration camps. In her dedication to "Breaking Silence" (1982), which was written for her mother, Mirikitani writes, "After forty years of silence about the experience of Japanese Americans in World War II concentration camps, my mother testified before the Commission on Wartime Relocation and Internment of Japanese American Civilians in 1981" (56).[2] In the body of the poem, Mirikitani includes her mother's testimony and her own modifications to that testimony, writing, "We were made to believe our faces / betrayed us. / Our bodies were loud / with yellow screaming flesh / needing to be silenced / behind barbed wire" (57). And later, "Mr. Commissioner . . . when you tell me I must limit / testimony, / when you tell me my time is up, / I tell you this: / Pride has kept my lips / pinned by nails / my rage coffined. / But I exhume my past / to claim this time. . . . / Words are better than tears, / so I spill them. / I kill this, / the silence . . . / There are miracles that happen / she said, / and everything is made visible. . . . / Our language is beautiful" (58–59).

To kill the silence, in the poem, is to reclaim one's language and oneself. To replace tears with words implies that the pain of internment can be confronted and alleviated by engaging in discourse about it. Breaking silence is likened to making the history of Mirikitani's mother's experience in internment *visible*, both to herself and to outsiders, the members of the Commission on Wartime Relocation and Internment before whom she testifies. Also, as Traise Yamamoto suggests, the silence described in this poem is likened to the repression of racial identity; subsequently, "the mother's testimony bears witness to and reverses the internment's erasure and silencing of the 'yellow screaming flesh'" (233). Thus, it is the process of making the past visible, of speaking out, that is the "miracle." And it is the act of speaking that renders the language "beautiful," hence powerful and empowering to both Mirikitani and her mother, as well as others who share their racial identity and/or their experience of internment, in the double narration of the poem.

In the following poem, "Prisons of Silence" (1983), Mirikitani is concerned again with breaking silences. She writes, "The strongest prisons are built / with walls of silence" (60). The imprisonment Japanese Americans were forced to endure during World War II is linked to a cultural silencing of Japanese Americans. Constrained behind barbed wire for the duration of the war, they were unable to speak for themselves while their presence in the United States was virtually erased from national discourse. In the poem, silences are related to abandonment and betrayal by one's own government: "Jap! / Filthy Jap! / Who lives within me? / Abandoned homes, confiscated land, / loyalty oaths, barbed wire prisons / in a strange wasteland. / Go home, Jap! / Where is home? / A country of betrayal. / No one speaks to us. / We would not speak to each other. / We were accused" (61). Silence becomes the prevailing condition not only because others refuse to acknowledge—to see or hear—Japanese

Americans but also because they are unable to speak to one another. The accusations, the shame, and the confusion of internment render the imprisoned speechless while fragmenting their communities and families, dividing them from one another through silence. Thus, the silences are enforced, but they are also adapted as a means of protection and survival.

In this way, silence may represent containment and a measure of safety until the rage buried beneath the surface threatens to destroy the narrator and the life she has rebuilt. "I have kept myself contained / within these walls shaped to my body / and buried my rage. / I rebuilt my life / like a wall, unquestioning. / Obeyed their laws . . . their laws" (63). What threatens to destroy the illusion of safety is the narrator's revelation that the silences in which she must live are imposed by others —the dominant group of the United States—who enforce "their" laws upon her subjectivity and racial community. Also, the silences Mirikitani critiques represent the unspoken assumptions undertaken by the U.S. government in its illegal imprisonment of Japanese Americans: "All persons of Japanese ancestry / filthy jap. / Both alien and non-alien / japs are enemy aliens. / To be incarcerated / for their own good / A military necessity / The army to handle only the japs. / Where is home? / A country of betrayal" (63). She fears the threat of silence and raises the questions, What is unsaid? What is coded in the dominant language? What is masked by euphemisms and the language of racist hysteria?

Lastly, as mentioned above, silence is the prison itself; the internment embodies and enacts the greatest silence of all. It is through the breaking of such silence that one becomes free: "We give testimony. / Our noise is dangerous. . . . / We soar / from these walls of silence" (65). Breaking free of silence is likened to breaking free from the imprisonment Japanese Americans were subjected to during World War II. To free oneself, according to Mirikitani, one must break silence. It is through language and discourse, she seems to suggest, that we can know the truth of what happened and move toward a new life. While Mirikitani is attentive to the nuances of silences in the poems mentioned above, she remains steadfast in her assertion that silence exists opposite speech and that it must be through speech that we locate freedom and subjectivity. While speech is certainly an avenue toward social change, I argue that silence may also represent a significant method of resistance, especially in the case of Japanese American women's writings about internment. Also, I question the contradistinction so often posited between speech and silence and suggest that we explore instead the ways in which silence may enact a method of discourse in its own right, often in relation to speech. Finally, as mentioned in the first chapter, I must question the logic implying that speech ensures freedom and social liberation, particularly in a context in which the notion of free speech has historically applied only to a chosen few—the dominant groups of this nation. While marginalized people have sometimes successfully deployed the master's tools, including the dominant language, on their own behalf, we must continue to acknowledge the limitations and interrogate the social and political consequences of doing so.

In this chapter, I focus on two narratives of internment/dispersal, Mitsuye Yamada's *Camp Notes and Other Poems* and Joy Kogawa's *Obasan*. Contextualized against the history of World War II and the North American decision to incarcerate or exile individuals of Japanese ancestry, these writings engage the themes of silence, speech, and language in complex ways, suggesting that silence cannot necessarily be equated with lack of subjectivity or resistance and that it may in fact embody multiple meanings, including a denial and disavowal of the national narratives that have heretofore neglected to include the histories of Asian Americans. To question official national histories, both writers address family histories—especially the fragmentation of Japanese American and Japanese Canadian families during and after World War II—in relation to themes and strategies of silence.

Mitsuye Yamada's *Camp Notes* and the World War II Internment of Japanese Americans

At the onset of World War II, there were approximately 127,000 people of Japanese ancestry living in the United States, predominantly in California, Washington, and Oregon. At least two-thirds of them had been born in the United States and were American citizens. Immediately following the bombing of Pearl Harbor by the Japanese military in 1941, a new wave of anti-Asian—specifically, anti-Japanese—sentiment swept the United States. Because of rumors of "fifth column" activity among Japanese Americans, the FBI began to imprison community leaders considered to be "pro-Japanese," and the financial resources of the Issei— first-generation Japanese immigrants—were frozen (Matsumoto 438).[3] In the midst of public outcry and media sensationalism that vilified all

Japanese people during World War II, President Franklin Delano Roosevelt signed Executive Order 9066, which "evacuated" all persons of Japanese ancestry to a number of designated concentration camps in which many of them were forced to remain for the duration of the war.[4]

Second-generation Japanese in the United States—the Nisei—attempted to divert such animosity by proudly claiming their American citizenship and status. They displayed American flags in their windows, they helped with the war effort, and some of them even attempted to enlist in the armed services. Yet the anti-Japanese sentiment continued to grow. Community leaders continued to be arrested and taken into custody by the FBI; their illegal actions included religious and cultural leadership. Japanese homes and businesses were raided for so-called contraband weapons, radios, and cameras; curfews were imposed on Japanese women and men; and those of Japanese ancestry were required to withdraw from the Western Defense Command (Hatamiya 11; Brimner 28–29; Matsumoto 438). Lieutenant General John DeWitt, director of the command, argued that ancestry was probable cause enough and ordered the removal of ethnic Japanese from the West Coast. In the face of arguments that there had been no acts of sabotage, he stated that "such lack of action . . . was proof that there eventually would be" (Brimner 30; Nagata 3). Thus, ethnicity alone was enough to determine one's loyalty to the United States.

While Japanese Americans of the Nisei generation believed their constitutional rights would be protected, more and more politicians and columnists were calling for the removal of all Japanese people. Without justification for such removal, these spokespeople grew more and more blatantly racist, proclaiming their hatred and fear of Japanese people. Brimner states that "it was in this climate of hostility, racism, paranoia, and greed, that Franklin Delano Roosevelt issued Executive Order 9066. . . . In spite of the fact that no Japanese American was *ever* charged with, brought to trial for, or convicted of any act of espionage or sabotage, the way was cleared for individuals and groups to be excluded from specific areas based, at least officially, on military necessity" (32). Another misguided justification for the incarceration of Japanese Americans included the notion that it would be for their own protection. Because Japanese Americans were the victims of crimes caused by wartime hysteria, including shootings and killings, and local police and sheriff departments did not offer them protection or come to their defense, some leaders argued that internment would be for the Japanese Americans' own good—offering a measure of protection for them against racist violence (Hatamiya 13; Nagata 4).[5] Thus, Executive Order 9066, which did not distinguish between citizens and noncitizens, or between Japanese and Japanese Americans, was signed, forcing more than 120,000 individuals into the camps.[6]

Complex emotional reactions to internment are demonstrated in the writings of Mitsuye Yamada. In her book of poems entitled *Camp Notes and Other Poems,* Yamada chronicles her life before, during, and after her experiences in internment.[7] As Nagata and Hatamiya both suggest, it is not uncommon for Japanese Americans to organize and interpret their lives in contemporary American culture in terms of the camps, often organizing memories around pre–World War II (or, pre-camp) and post–World War II (post-camp). Such reference points have come to define Japanese American history, indeed Japanese American experience and identity, according to Hatamiya (preface, x). In the first section of Yamada's collection, "My Issei Parents, Twice Pioneers, Now I Hear Them," she includes seven poems that weave the voices of her parents and grandparents with her own as an introduction to their lives in America. Section 2, entitled "Camp Notes," the largest section of the text, deals explicitly with her experiences in the internment camp in Minidoka, Idaho. And section 3, "Other Poems," includes pieces that explore the aftermath of her internment experiences, especially her treatment by others immediately after leaving the camp and her subsequent thoughts on issues of racism and American identity.

Yamada, by tracing her lived experiences through her grandmother's stories, memories of her Issei parents, and the Nisei community to which she belongs, roots this collection of poems firmly in the analysis and deconstruction of terms such as "family" and "community." Also, repeatedly, *Camp Notes* represents tensions between personal and national histories. As Traise Yamamoto suggests, "the recovery of history [in *Camp Notes*] is inextricably tied to the recovery of the voice that recovers history" (203). Beginning with the poem "What Your Mother Tells You," in which she writes "What your mother tells you now / in time / you will come to know" (1), Yamada establishes her mother's voice, and her memory of her mother, in this collection. In this way, she frames the text within her genealogy, closing with a poem dedicated to her son, "Mirror, Mirror." The book itself is contained within the generations of her family, in direct contrast to the internment camp experiences that disrupted and threatened to destroy that family. In fact, Yamada includes an ideograph on the cover of *Camp Notes*, used in constructions such as *wa(keru)*, *wa(kareru)*, *wa(karu)*, which in the context of the first poem of the collection, used with other characters to write *wakatte kuru*, translates to "in time you will come to know" or "in time you will understand." However, on the cover, alone, this Kanji character translates as "divide," "to be divided," "to part," "to separate from." The significance of division and separation, in *Camp Notes* and for thousands of Japanese and Japanese American families during World War II, has been documented. The juxtaposition of "to be divided" and "in time you will understand" is critical to Yamada's use of strategic silences.

Translation operates as a significant feature of the text in other ways, too. In these first seven poems, Yamada appropriates the voices of her family members, translating their words to readers in various forms. From "Great Grandma," a poem about her grandmother's philosophy of life, to "A Bedtime Story," in which she narrates her father's telling of a bedtime story, Yamada is concerned with how to tell the stories of her parents and grandparents. There is, however, a significant difference between Yamada's retellings of her mother's words and her father's words. The two poems that embody Yamada's attempts to understand Japanese culture through her father's words, "A Bedtime Story" and "Enryo," according to Susan Schweik, are both "narratives of failed translations, characterized by impasses between the storytelling father and the listening child" (235). Contrasting these failures of translation to the poems in which Yamada translates her mother's voice, a voice that "speaks without interruption, without mediation" and represents "an almost seamless identification of mother and daughter" (235), a general pattern emerges among these poems: "in the 'mother' poems, narrative works, stories are recovered and found to be worth the telling; in the 'father' poems, narrative warps, stories fall on deaf ears, fall short" (Schweik 235).

In "Marriage Was a Foreign Country," presumably the narrative of Yamada's mother's journey to the United States, the narrator of the poem speaks what is commonly referred to as "broken" or "fragmented" English. "Your father I see him on the dock / he come to Japan to marry / and leave me / I was not a picture bride / I only was afraid" (3). The brokenness of the language suggests her accented English, while Yamada's transliteration of it alludes to a quality of fragmentation within the content of her words, suggesting the fear the narrator speaks of, the abandonment, and the threat of danger. The mother's voice in "Home-coming" is presented similarly, in "broken" English, and in "What Your Mother Tells You," her words are in Japanese, followed by the daughter's (Yamada's) English translation. Meanwhile, the father speaks in "perfect" English in Yamada's poems "Enryo" and "A Bedtime Story." In each of the poems, "Papa's" words are flawless and complete by the prevailing standards of middle-class American English.

While the "translation" of her mother's voice may appear intact, as Schweik would argue, Yamada's verbatim retelling of her mother's immigration story, rather than a polished, cleaned-up version in grammatically correct English, also suggests a quality of brokenness, a fragmentation in and of itself. As Amy Tan suggests in her personal essay "Mother Tongue," many Asian Americans speak multiple languages, including multiple versions of English, depending on with whom they are communicating. For instance, they may speak a different language, even a different version of English with first-generation immigrant parents than with American-educated peers and colleagues. Tan also observes that "the language spoken in the family, especially in immigrant families that are more insular, plays a large role in shaping the language of the child" (318). For Tan, to speak and to listen to her mother in what has become their own personal language—an alternative language, a "broken" English, a language of intimacy, and a "different sort of English that relates to family talk" (315)—is to show respect for her mother, while also representing a promise to listen carefully for what is not spoken, for what may be signaled by body language, pauses, and/or the absence of words. She is critical of those who claim to not understand her mother's English, suggesting that they are not listening carefully, and she is just as critical of the American sentiment that the quality of one's English, again by the standards of the dominant group in the United States, reflects the quality of what he or she has to say (317). For Yamada, then, to narrate her mother's voice in such a language suggests, simultaneously, an urge to reproduce her mother's words as she heard them—to translate in such a manner as to be "faithful to the original" (Lowe, 1994)—and an urge to suggest the rupturing of the dominant American narrative of marriage and family. For Yamada's mother, marriage is driven by necessity and centers on immigration to the United States and the justified fears that accompanied immigration for Asians at the time—racism, exclusionary laws, detainment at Angel Island—not the dominant paradigm of heterosexual courtship, love, and romance. As such, the retelling itself suggests a fracturing.

It is just such an urge to complicate the retellings that impels Yamada's quality of "translation" when it comes to the narratives of her mother and father. Schweik writes,

> The histories Yamada's text admits intact are those that exhibit the qualities Foucault has attributed to "general" histories, which provide alternative models of approach to the past. General histories, unlike "total" histories, as Foucault defines them, narrate and incorporate "segmentation, limits, difference of level, timelags, anachronistic survivals, possible types of relation." *Camp Notes* constructs Yamada's history itself as part of a "general history": a story not of center but of circumference; a retelling of the story that never allows either teller or listener to forget its limits, its lags, the differences that threaten to circumscribe or silence it; a transcription of the story that never pretends to be the *whole* story. Permanently marginal, perpetually in opposition to the dominant versions of its events, energized by its interruptions, *Camp Notes* reaches toward the construction of a discourse of discontinuity. (237)

Thus, what Yamada interrupts and interrogates are the "total" histories of her father, represented especially in the poems "Enryo" and "A Bedtime Story." In "A Bedtime Story," a poem in which her father tells the narrator a traditional Japanese story that emphasizes traits such as self-sacrifice and the acceptance of wrongs committed against an individual, the father's smooth narrative within the poem is rudely interrupted by Yamada's insertion of her narrator's voice: "Papa paused, I waited. / In the comfort of our / hilltop home in Seattle / overlooking the valley, / I shouted / 'That's the *end?*'" (7). Rather than accept the unhappy fate of the old woman in Papa's story, Yamada's child narrator questions the narrative and challenges the ending. Implied is a refusal to accept such an ending and a critique of the attitudes of *shikata ga nai* ("it cannot be helped"), a lesson of acculturation Yamada refuses to learn. Yamada's child narrator seems to argue that "it"—the bad situation for the old woman in the story, the oppression and exploitation of Japanese in the United States, the internment of Japanese Americans—*can* in fact be helped, and that the ending of the story can and must be changed.[8]

Similarly, in "Enryo," a child narrator asks "Papa" what the Japanese word *enryo* means. In the role of acculturator, "using his stories in an attempt to shape and dominate his daughter's behavior" (Schweik 237), Papa explains that enryo is "pride in disguise" (9): "Even so / it is holding back / saying no / thank you / saying no / trouble at all" (9). Here again, the child narrator questions Papa's wisdom: "Enryo is a Japanese word / which sounds like / in leo. / What does being in a lion / have to do with humility / I asked Papa" (9). The questions signify Yamada's narrator's unwillingness to accept the father's easy, whole narratives. Rather, she refutes traditional values associated with proper behavior and modesty.[9] However subtly, Yamada's words suggest a profound critique of the social and cultural context in which she finds herself, a context in which the internment of Japanese Americans was not only able to occur but then to be smoothly evaded and virtually erased from this nation's official history for a number of years.

Later, in the middle section of the text, the section about the internment-camp experience, Yamada leaves two of her father's poems intact. Under the heading "P.O.W.," Yamada translates her father's poems, attaching his pen name, "Jakki," and including a note about her father's internment by the FBI during the years 1941 to 1944. Yamada does not question the narratives of these two poems. In fact, doing so is unnecessary; neither of these poems locate themselves within the "total"—and totalizing—histories of the United States. As such, "the two sad, short poems question themselves from inside. Their quality of self-questioning, the sense they give of severe, radical discontinuity and of contradictions between and within cultures, is precisely what allows the 'P.O.W.' poems to be translated by the daughter" (Schweik 237). Such an interpretation suggests that the experience of the camps is one of such severe dislocation and unnaming that even the all-knowing Papa is transformed. Or rather, it is the daughter's—Yamada's—vision of her father that is destabilized.

The final poem of section 1, entitled "Dialogue," offers a dialogue supposedly between Yamada's parents that is not actually a dialogue at all. Rather, her father is unable to listen to the silence her mother projects: "I said / Don't / after twenty years / you know she's leaving / you / must listen to / her / stop / and listen. / He said / But I did / I called her in here / I asked / her / I hear / you have something / on your mind / WHAT / but she stood right / there / dumb / looking out / the window" (10). The poem is framed by Yamada's voice as narrator, who begins, "I said . . ." in an attempt to insert her own voice and to demand an act of accountability from her father. Yet he fails to hear the silent communication of her mother, presumably signaling her discontent, dissatisfaction with the situation, and/or disagreement. The mother's silence, which seems to go unquestioned by Yamada herself (or the narrator of the poem)—who seems to understand the meanings of that silence—is unheard and therefore rendered meaningless by the father.

As in "Marriage Was a Foreign Country," the two actors of "Dialogue" represent both woman and man and Japan and the United States. In terms of the colonialist policies enacted by the United States against Japan, as well as the context of World War II internment, it is possible to interpret these figures within current conceptualizations of gender, patriarchy, and colonization, in which either/or dichotomous thinking obscures reality and links one form of oppression with another. Either/or dichotomous thinking, according to bell hooks, is the "central ideological component of all systems of domination in Western society" (1989, 29) and involves the categorizations of objects, ideas, and even human beings in terms of their differences from one another. And as Patricia Hill Collins suggests, dichotomies are framed around gender (male/female), race (white/nonwhite), sexuality (heterosexual/homosexual), and a host of other relations of difference and domination (e.g., mind/body, reason/emotion, culture/nature, and subject/object). Collins asserts that such entities then gain meaning only in relation to their counterparts. While one part of the polarity dominates and objectifies the other—which, quite literally, comes to be seen and known as "other"—those who are dominated lose access to establishing their own identities, naming their own histories, and defining their realities (69).

In the case of these two poems, the husband/father is linked to the United States; indeed, in "Marriage Was a Foreign Country," this connection is quite explicit. For the Nisei who were interned, the United States was indeed their "fatherland," as Japanese could be said to represent their "mother tongue." In such a neocolonialist context, it is the "husband" who refuses to hear what is not made explicitly clear (in his—the ruler's—language) and the "wife" who is unable to speak what there is no language to convey. At the same time, it is the "father's" voice that generates "total" histories and is subsequently challenged by Yamada, while her "mother's" voice, while fragmented (silent?), resonates more closely with the narrator's own reality. Japanese American writers and activists continue to document forms of resistance during the internment that were unacknowledged or masked behind euphemisms and the objectification of people of color. Thus, Yamada comments on the ways in which familial disunity and fragmentation, for Japanese Americans, is directly influenced by the social, political, and economic conflicts of World War II, at the same time that she locates the large-scale and global political issues of the war within familial contexts.[10] Moreover, she also wonders what meaning or power silence can possess without acknowledgment? In the words of Trinh, while silence "as a refusal to partake in the story does sometimes provide us with a means to gain a hearing" and is a "voice, a mode of uttering, and a response in its own right," what happens to such silence when it exists in isolation—when it is not heard? "Without other silences . . . my silence goes unheard, unnoticed; it is simply one voice less, or more point given to the silencers" (83).

In "Evacuation," any power of silence is circumvented by those who dominate and silence Japanese Americans:

As we boarded the bus
bags on both sides
(I had never packed
two bags before
on a vacation
lasting forever)
the Seattle Times
photographer said
Smile!
so obediently I smiled
and the caption the next day
read:
Note smiling faces
a lesson to Tokyo. (13)

Not only are the actions of the narrator misconstrued to her disadvantage and subsequent erasure, but the very language used to describe the process of what is happening to her further masks the reality of the situation, enacting a denial of "even the representation of resistance" (Yamamoto 209). Similarly, in "Desert Storm," Yamada writes: "this was

not / im / prison / ment. / This was / re / location" (19). Her splinter-
ing of each word suggests the evocative power of language, including
government euphemisms that distort reality. As researchers have indi-
cated, certain terms are problematic in the discussion of internment, including "relocation," "evacuation," and "assembly centers." While the
government has used and continues to reinforce such language usage
where the experiences of Japanese Americans during World War II are
concerned, organizations such as the Civil Liberties Public Education
Fund (CLPEF) and the National Japanese American Historical Society
(NJAHS) recommend the use of more accurate terms for what happened,
including "imprisonment," "incarceration," "internment," "detention,"
"confinement," or "lockup." For the camps, they advise that we use "internment camps," "detention camps," "prison camps," or "concentration
camps"; to describe those who were confined, they suggest "detainee,"
"internee," "inmate," or "prisoner." The report of NJAHS posits that
"continued use of these misnomers would distort history. . . . The choice
of term must reflect the fact that the inmates were not free to walk out without getting shot."[11] Thus, while silence may be misunderstood, speech,
too, is dangerous. Language, controlled by those with power, may distort, stereotype, and control while concurrently shaping and defining reality for those who are dominated and/or marginalized. As Yamamoto
argues, "the internment illustrates with terrible clarity that the power
of language to define and name is not equally applicable to all who use
it. Racist rhetoric capitalizes on the unequal power relations between the
'us' who uses speech and the 'them' to whom speech is applied" (208).

Locating political strife within a familial context—and commenting
on the disintegration of her family and other Japanese American families
during World War II—Yamada includes several poems that continue to
explicitly emphasize the crises posed for Japanese American families, including her own. In the middle section of the text, "Camp Notes," one
recurring theme is the physicality of the camps in terms of daily survival
and material hardship: "Lines formed for food / lines for showers /
lines for johns / lines for shots" ("Harmony at the Fairgrounds," 15);
"Turn off your lights / it's curfew time! . . . Off with your lights / there
must be no light" ("Curfew," 16); "Our collective wastebin / where the
air sticks / in my craw / burns my eyes / I have this place to hide /
the excreta and / the blood which / do not flush down / nor seep
away" ("In the Outhouse," 20); "I'll bet you a home-made apple pie /

you'll never get out of here in / a hundred years. / That's impossible. / Where in the world would you / get apples?" ("Some People Walked Through," 28); "The Mother drew my eyes / to her smiling mouth / but still I saw her / pinch her daughter who let drop / the handful of mushy beans / shrieked a soundless cry / and abundant tears" ("Mess Hall Discipline," 29). Other recurring images include dust and dust storms, cages, and snakes.

According to numerous historians, families reported having to sleep on floors in crowded conditions in stalls formerly used to house animals, while in the "assembly centers" in which they were housed before being taken to the camps (Matsumoto, Hatamiya, Nagata, Brimner). When they were finally removed to the actual camps, their situation changed little. They shared crude bathroom accommodations or outhouses and were fed in mess halls with meager foods many of them were unaccustomed to eating. They were provided inadequate medical facilities, which, along with harsh weather conditions and poor nutrition, contributed to numerous health problems and deaths.[12] The ten permanent camps were located in Topaz, Utah; Amache, Colorado; Minidoka, Idaho; Manzanar and Tule Lake, California; Heart Mountain, Wyoming; Denson (Jerome) and Rohwer, Arkansas; and Poston and Gila River, Arizona. Each of the ten camps was located on a deliberately isolated site in order to keep the Japanese away from other Americans. All of the camps were in the desert or in swamps, and former internees recall the dust storms and intense heat in the summers and harsh cold and snowstorms in the winters (Brimner 50–54).

Former internees report the large number of armed men with guns pointed toward them upon their arrival, the barbed wire fences surrounding the camps, the watchtowers in which armed guards stood, and the limited and supervised visits from outsiders (Brimner 36–44). Many Japanese Americans resorted to cooking their own meals and building their own furniture from scrap lumber in an attempt to make their situations bearable (Brimner 50; Matsumoto 440; Hatamiya 20). Any opportunities to leave the camps, even temporarily, involved the separation of family members and therefore a significant shift for traditional Japanese family structures.[13] Also, families were disrupted in other ways. Valerie Matsumoto writes: "Family unity deteriorated in the crude communal facilities and cramped barracks" (439). She describes the camp living arrangements in the following way:

The standard housing in the camps was a spartan barracks, about twenty feet by one hundred feet, divided into four to six rooms furnished with steel army cots. Initially each single room or "apartment" housed an average of eight persons; individuals without kin nearby were often moved in with smaller families. Because the partitions between apartments did not reach the ceiling, even the smallest noises traveled freely from one end of the building to the other. There were usually fourteen barracks in each block, and each block had its own mess hall, laundry, latrine, shower facilities, and recreation room. (439)

Because of a lack of privacy in the camps, family members began to spend as little time as possible in their barracks. In the mess halls, family members often ate separately, sitting with peer groups instead of with one another: fathers sat with other men, mothers with small children, and adolescents with their friends. Finally, because family members were expected to work at assigned jobs within the camps, varying work schedules also interfered with family unity and time together (Matsumoto 440). Understandably, conflicts emerged among Issei and their American-born children, the Nisei, and among those who were angered about their internment versus those who wanted to maintain and demonstrate their loyalty to the United States. The camp experience, as Donna Nagata suggests, "directly opposed" Japanese cultural values of filial piety and deference to one's elders" (11) by placing relatively more power in the hands of the Nisei while at the same time severely disenfranchising their parents, the Issei, who were unable to hold office within the camp governance system and who also faced language barriers within the United States in general.

In *Camp Notes*, Yamada layers the theme of family disintegration over that of physical hardship. Not only are the family members forced to wait in lines for meals, for showers, and to use the bathroom, but they must sleep on the ground, endure dust storms, and have access only to inadequate food and medical supplies. Family members began to eat and work separately. Men lost the customary power they had enjoyed as heads of household in a patriarchal cultural tradition. And in the culture of the internment camp, parents and children exchanged roles. In her poem "Inside News," Yamada writes: "Mess hall gossips / have it that / the parents / with samurai morals / are now the children" (21). While such permutations may have provided relatively more power and opportunities for women and for Nisei children in the camps, they came with a high cost to the traditional family structure. While Matsumoto suggests that one positive outcome of the camps was the fact that women workers in the camps received wages equal to those of their male counterparts, all received extremely low wages—wages that would have barely been livable outside of the camps at that time.[14] Matsumoto also points out that while women in the camps experienced severe trauma and racism, they also experienced new opportunities. Older women experienced more leisure time. Younger women escaped traditional expectations for arranged marriages and instead received new opportunities for work, education, and travel (436).

However, the relative equality achieved by women in the camps must be acknowledged in its proper context. To make pay equal to men of their race should be a sign of progress, but it is not necessarily, especially when all members of the race make wages on which they would be unable to survive outside of the camps. Rather than focusing solely on the situation of women as improving due to the camps, as some authors focus their study, I argue that we should pay more attention to the ways in which Japanese American men, too, were exploited and oppressed during World War II. First-generation Japanese immigrants also suffered particular difficulties in the camps, contributing to negative family relations. Because Issei were unable to attain U.S. citizenship, they faced more severe consequences for any perceived challenges to authority in the camps. The confusion provoked by such changes is illustrated by Yamada's words: "A small group / huddles around a contraband / radio / What? / We / are losing the war? / Who is we? / We are we the enemy / the enemy is the enemy" ("Inside News," 21).

In other poems, Yamada's poetry subverts traditional understandings of family and family life. Two poems in particular reflect on the changes in the narrator's family and on her place in the world. In "Night Before Goodbye," Yamada writes:

Mama is mending
my underwear
while my brothers sleep.
Her husband taken away by the FBI
one son lured away by the Army
now another son and daughter

lusting for the free world outside.
She must let go.
The war goes on.
She will take one still small son
and join Papa in internment
to make a family.
Still sewing
squinting in the dim light
in room C barrack 4 block 4
she whispers
Remember
keep your underwear
in good repair
in case of accident
don't bring shame
on us. (31)

In this poem, Mama's domestic sphere and practice of mending is sub-
verted not only by her context ("room C barrack 4 block 4) but also by
the fact that her work of mending on behalf of the family (and therefore
nurturance of her family) occurs in opposition to the damage of the war
and internment upon that same family (Schweik 229). Presumably, the
mother has chosen to leave the camp at Minidoka for the higher-security
Tule Lake prison camp, in which Yamada's father was interned, in order
to "make a family."[15] As Schweik points out, the threats to this mother's
family are both "outward and alien"—the conflict of the war, the U.S.
government's policing and imprisonment of Japanese Americans, external pressure to enlist in the U.S. military, and the actual physical separation of her family—and internal, as demonstrated by the "lure" and
"lust" that pull her children away from her and the camps and "toward
the ironically designated 'free world' (which in this 'before' poem still
retains the illusion of freedom)" (229). Locating Mama's gift of mending
within a literary tradition of mothers and daughters, Schweik wonders
about the "disturbing obsession with the daughter's decorum at the expense of concern for her actual well-being" (230). The mother of this
poem, she argues, "anxiously socializes her daughter on Papa's behalf"
(230) becoming a complicit participant in the policing of her daughter's

body, symbolized—and enacted by—internment. As for the daughter, "to be a good daughter, she must render herself doubly invisible, as impervious to notice or comment as possible, even at the moments of greatest vulnerability and display of her body" (230). Significantly, any such moments are sure to be "accidents" and not caused by the intentions of the narrator or those around her (230). Thus, not only is her agency obscured but what the daughter may suffer in terms of shame or humiliation is reduced to mere "accident," not the result of purposeful harm or endangerment. Yamamoto also comments on the irony of the mother's words, reliant as they are on scripts of white femininity, and suggests that while Japanese American women were degendered during the internment (with race enacting the primary operating term during World War II), it is in this poem that Yamada re-enters a realm of femininity, emerging as a subject shaped by both gender and race (Yamamoto 210–211).

The following poem, "Cincinnati," narrates the young woman's departure from the camps and "freedom at last." Yet this "freedom" is quickly circumscribed by a racist act of violence. "Freedom at last / in this town / aimless / I walked against the rush / hour traffic / My first day / in a real city / where / no one knew me. / No one except one / hissing voice that said / dirty jap / warm spittle on my right cheek. / I turned and faced / the shop window / and my spittled face / spilled onto a hill / of books. / Words on display . . . Everyone knew me" (33).[16] Not only is the "freedom" she expected only illusory, but the narrator also faces the "national fictions" embodied by the window of books, "words on display." Schweik writes:

> The books here represent the full weight of "national fictions"; they embody the dominant popular culture to whose angers, desires, and fears the identity of the Japanese-American is subjected and by whose words she is defined. In opposition to the hill of books stands the single image of the speaker's "spittled face." That face, spat-upon and, as the poem will reveal, crying, signifies both the brutalities "words on display" evade and the subjectivity of a woman for whom "words on display" do not speak. (231)

The narrator's experiences conflict with the national fictions evidenced by the words on display. Such official, total histories are consistently interrogated and challenged by Yamada, often by her insertion of oppositional histories—narratives framed by particularity, quite aware of their own partiality and liminality. *Camp Notes* itself privileges the power of voice, a particular kind of voice: "its own authority derives from its claim to vocal veracity and authenticity, its representation of itself as a particular woman's voice speaking up, telling her own story, a true story" (Schweik 234). Thus, in opposition to the general and official histories of the United States, *Camp Notes* is fully aware of its limits and of the factors that threaten to silence it. It embodies the "transcription of the story that never pretends to be the *whole* story" (237). As such, the text forces a questioning of the seamless and totalizing histories provided by national fictions. Yamada's critique of dominant discourses seeks not to replace the dominant narrative with her own story but to challenge any notion of a singular, definitive history, especially one that precludes examination of the histories of Japanese Americans during World War II.

Readers, therefore, must be cognizant of both the silences surrounding the text (the silences surrounding internment that threaten this telling at all), as well as the silences *within* the text, some of which are strategically deployed by Yamada in order to "tell" her story. In the central section of the text, Yamada explicitly details memories of experiences in the camps. The poems that constitute this section were actually written during or immediately following World War II but subsequently kept from publication until 1976. Schweik contextualizes such self-censorship against the more widespread censorship of any writings by Japanese Americans during the war years and for many years afterward. She discusses Toshio Mori's book *Yokohama, California*, already scheduled for publication in 1941, that was then suppressed by its publishers for nine years. Other writings, she argues, were most likely "suppressed or repressed at earlier stages" (226):

> From 1941 until well after 1945, any narrative or for that matter any act of public speech by a Japanese-American posed an unacceptable threat to the national fictions embodied and organized in established U.S. literary institutions. Dominant constructions of national identity, permissible representations of the "American people" as they faced their Enemies, depended, first of all, on an almost complete elision of the existence of a Japanese-American population. . . . [T]he disturbing fact of the concentration camps, and the realities of the Japanese-American population the camps contained, threatened dominant representations of a nation "all in it together." Books like Mori's,

which explored Japanese-American culture in detail, constituted double threats, both in their subject matter and in their very existence. (226–227)

Thus, writings such as Yamada's threatened the seamless version of national identity and history embodied by official narratives of U.S. participation in World War II, narratives that posited specific conceptualizations not only of American identity but also of war and wartime experience. Such conceptualizations precluded wartime experiences of American people of color and all women, except in highly formulaic paradigms, as the mothers or wives or American "heroes" whose experiences of the war were distant and removed from the "front lines." Yet, Japanese Americans also survived war, and Japanese American women experienced their own version of the war: "either denied citizenship or stripped of their rights as citizens, forcibly exiled from their homes, exposed to humiliation and violence, imprisoned in desert camps in the interior of an ostensibly sheltered and sheltering nation, [they] experienced the war very much 'at firsthand'" (Schweik 225).

Yamada's *Camp Notes*, then, which details her firsthand experience of World War II from her location within an American concentration camp, explodes the existing narratives of America's experience—and Japanese American women's experiences—of World War II. The fact that it took such a long time for her collection to reach publication is a question she herself seeks to examine, especially in the context of the agonizingly slow emergence of Asian American women's writings in general. In her essay "Invisibility Is an Unnatural Disaster," Yamada writes about Asian Americans finally attempting to claim their own history in this country and suggests that Asian American women are only recently emerging as a powerful and vocal force in U.S. culture. Of this, she writes: "It took forever. Perhaps it is important to ask ourselves why it took so long" (36).

Of course, that the poems would be delayed makes sense in the context of the extreme social and political repression Japanese Americans were forced to endure, as it also makes sense that many Japanese Americans attempted to erase the experiences of internment from their memories and to shield their children from the truth of what happened. As Matsumoto suggests, "Given the tenor of the times and the situation of their families, the pioneers in resettlement had little choice but to repress their anger and minimize the amount of racist hostility they encountered" (444). Yamamoto discusses the "masks" worn by Japanese

American women as a form of nondisclosure and self-protection, in this case a sign of Yamada's awareness of the limits of language and her subsequent distancing. Yamada comments explicitly on such a process in her poem "Thirty Years Under":

> I had packed up
> my wounds in a cast
> iron box
> sealed it
> labeled it
> do not open . . .
> ever . . .
>
> and traveled blind
> for thirty years
>
> until one day I heard
> a black man with huge bulbous eyes
> say
> there is nothing more
> humiliating
> more than beatings
> more than curses
> than being spat on
>
> like a dog. (32)

Like Mirikitani's mother and the narrator of Joy Kogawa's historical novel *Obasan*, Yamada has kept her silence for thirty years. The poem and collection in which it is published represent her coming to voice about her experiences in the camps as much as they also represent her silences about the event. Significantly, it is not until she hears the black man's words that she is able to identify her own cause of suffering and humiliation. By relating to his oppression, she is able to acknowledge her own.[17] In contrast to the dehumanization of "being spat on like a dog," Yamada consistently reasserts her own humanity and that of other Japanese Americans who were interned. In her poem "The Watchtower," she writes: "This is what we did with our days / We loved and we lived / just like people" (22).

As artist Mine Okubo suggests, thirty years after her experience in a relocation camp, "The impact of the evacuation is not on the material and the physical. It is something far deeper. It is the effect on the spirit" (as cited in Matsumoto 436). Similarly, Nagata discusses the emotional and psychological impact of the internment on both the Issei and Nisei generations. Many Issei, in their fifties and sixties by the end of the war, never fully recovered from the experiences of the camps. She writes, "They lost the ambition to restart their lives, and many remained dependent on their Nisei children for the rest of their lives" (30). The Nisei, on the other hand, were pressed to work as hard as possible in an attempt to prove their loyalty and their worth. However, as Nagata suggests, they suffered a direct assault on their self-esteem and identity as Americans. Having experienced abandonment and betrayal by their own country, many Nisei internalized feelings of self-blame and unworthiness similar to the feelings experienced by other trauma survivors, and many used strategies such as denial and silence to help combat their feelings of helplessness and anger (30–35). Furthermore, Japanese cultural expectations such as those demonstrated by concepts like *shikata ga nai* and *gaman*, or the "internalization or suppression of emotions" (Nagata 101), contributed to feelings of compliance.[18] Such attitudes and values also made many Japanese Americans all the more reluctant to discuss what had been done to them. As Nagata suggests, other cultural values contributed to their silences, including "an emphasis on indirect, nonverbal communication of emotional topics, an avoidance of disruptive confrontations, and an avoidance of family conflict and embarrassment" (101). Thus, any discourse concerning Japanese Americans' experiences of internment during World War II was made problematic by multitudinous circumstances. Furthermore, as stated earlier, it is clear that the internment was enabled and bolstered by a context of extreme racism and stereotypes such as those discussed in the previous chapters, which normalized the exclusion and silencing of Asian North Americans in general.

In her review of *Camp Notes*, Marian Yee attributes Yamada's change in perspective, because of her identification with the black man of "Thirty Years Under," to a relocation of vision that is necessary for the claiming of one's own identity. She writes, "Expressing that experience so that someone else can identify with it is a way of unlocking in order to re-see" (246). Such revision is necessary for a parallel revisioning of the history that continues to erase, distort, and misname the experiences of

Japanese Americans. Yamada goes on to guide her son, in "Mirror, Mirror," to view himself differently. To his words, "Trouble is I'm american on the inside / and oriental on the outside," she replies, "Turn that outside in / THIS is what American looks like" (56), offering him, according to Yee, "another vision of himself" (246). In doing so, Yamada also questions what it means to look—and be—American. Yee suggests that it is Yamada's capacity to "re-see" that allows her to make a place between the "Here" and "There" of her two poems of the same names, juxtaposing "I was always / a starting person / like sprouts and shoots / or a part person / like slices and slivers / which is why / neighbor boys called out / MIT SUEY CHOP SUEY" (42) and "Once I went back / to where I came from / I was sent to school / in clothes 'Made in Japan' / and small children along the riverbank stopped jumping / rope and sing-sang: / American no ojo-o san / doko ni iku-u . . . Girl from America / where are you going?" (43). Rather than suggesting that because she has conflicted relationships with both Japan and the United States she belongs nowhere, Yamada asserts both her sense of displacement *and* her place in both locales, claiming each as her own.

Of course Yamada's silences, which are varied and nuanced, continue to exist in opposition to another, more powerful silencing, that of the dominant culture and its "official" narratives, which seek to preclude the telling her words enact as well as the bicultural identity she asserts. She remains vigilant where such silencing occurs, juxtaposing the power of silence (as a language of its own) against the perils of silence, the dangers of being unheard or misheard, of being misunderstood or erased. Silence, then, emerges as both a condition that contextualizes the text's (delayed) production and a prominent theme within the text. In "The Speech," Yamada addresses such a tenuous position: "Zambia stood before the Council of Churches / a prepared text held upright / under one corner of the dashiki / covering his black naked body. / The delegates in silent hundreds / stood openly / ready and willing for the roar / to tear their flesh. / 'We . . . ' / Then for five full minutes, / Zambia, 50, wept" (44). While the hundreds of delegates remain silent awaiting the "roar," Zambia is unable to speak. The "prepared text" he holds upright is inadequate to fully communicate what it is he needs to say. Yet his "speech," of the title of the poem, is just that—a silence that speaks and an attempt to unsay. While his silence—and weeping—may speak volumes, there is a danger that the delegates of the Council of Churches (who, presumably, hold power in the situation) will not listen carefully enough to what he is telling them. Also, there is the presumption addressed in the poem that with age and maturity, with full subjectivity, should come speech. By juxtaposing "Zambia" with "50" in the last line of the poem, Yamada seems to be suggesting that it is all the more surprising that he is unable to speak, as he is a mature representative. Silence, on the other hand, is generally understood in terms of children and the powerless.

In her poem "To the Lady," Yamada emphasizes the power of voice, expressing anger at those who refuse to listen and "read between the lines." The poem begins with the following lines: "The one in San Francisco who asked / Why did the Japanese Americans let / the government put them in / those camps without protest?" Yamada, wondering what it would have taken to make this woman comprehend what actually happened, replies:

Come to think of it I
      should've run off to Canada
      should've hijacked a plane to Algeria
      should've pulled myself up from my
      bra straps
      and kicked'm in the groin
      should've bombed a bank
      should've tried self-immolation
      should've holed myself up in a
      woodframe house
      and let you watch me
      burn up on the six o'clock news
      should've run howling down the street
      naked and assaulted you at breakfast
      by AP wirephoto
      should've screamed bloody murder
      like Kitty Genovese

Then

YOU would've

      come to my aid in shining armor
      laid yourself across the railroad track

marched on Washington

tattooed a Star of David on your arm

written six million enraged

letters to Congress

But we didn't draw the line

anywhere

law and order Executive Order 9066

social order moral order internal order

YOU let'm

I let'm

All are punished. (40–41)

The "lady's" assumption that Japanese Americans "let" the U.S. government put them in camps without protest overlooks the ways in which Japanese Americans did in fact resist their internment. Yamada's reply and her anger signify a claiming of her own voice as well as an evasive and ironic strategy. By listing all the actions she should have taken (and the reactions such actions would have provoked on the part of the woman in question), she highlights what little recourse Japanese Americans actually possessed during the time of World War II. The power to "run off to Canada" is ineffectual when Canada also imprisoned people of Japanese descent. The ability to "hijack a plane," "bomb a bank," or practice "self-immolation" were also circumscribed by such governmental restrictions as the imposed curfew, the seizure of property, and the immediacy of the "removal" and internment. At the time, who would have allowed Japanese Americans air time on the six o'clock news? Media representations, controlled by white Americans, consisted of distorted and stereotypical depictions of Japanese and Japanese Americans as the enemy, as threats to national security. The notion that Yamada could have successfully achieved any of the actions she describes in the poem is so implausible as to be laughable.[19]

In her essay "Asian Pacific American Women and Feminism," Yamada attempts to draw connections among the internment, her identity as an American, the feminist movement, and voice. Here, she describes another woman she encountered:

[The woman] said she was deeply moved by my "beautifully written but not bitter camp poems which were apparently written long ago," but she was distressed to hear my poem "To a Lady" [sic]. "Why are you, at this late date, so angry, and why are you taking it so personally?" she said. "We need to look to the future and stop wallowing in the past so much." I responded that this poem is not at all about the past. I am talking about what is happening to us right now. . . . As a child of immigrant parents, as a woman of color in a white society and as a woman in a patriarchal society, what is personal to me is political.

These are connections we expected our white sisters to see. It should not be too difficult, we feel, for them to see why being a feminist activist is more dangerous for women of color. They should be able to see that political views held by women of color are often misconstrued as being personal rather than ideological. Views critical of the system held by a person in an "out group" are often seen as expressions of personal angers against the dominant society. (If they hate it so much here, why don't they go back?) (1981, 74)

Noting how tenuous the position of women of color is in the United States, Yamada constantly raises tension between both speech and silence and visibility and invisibility. Both speech and silence, like visibility and invisibility, are potentially dangerous, especially for members of "out groups." Either action must be carefully negotiated, with attention to the appropriate social and political contexts. Meanings of silence are particularly significant in the case of Japanese American internment—an event in history so often silenced by the "official" histories and even silenced by Japanese Americans themselves. Some historical events are all the more difficult to discuss because there may be some things that simply cannot be said, made visible, or ever clearly known (Maclear 9). In some ways, Japanese Americans' experiences of internment have occupied such a position, existing outside the national imagination and vocabulary. Because it fails to neatly fit any paradigms of America's language or national narratives, any attempt to tell is to enact an unraveling of sorts, a gesture of doublespeak, stating one thing while at the same time saying another, or perhaps stating one thing while simultaneously unsaying it. Such a strategy has as its risk the rendering of experiences even more unknowable.

Yamada's silences exist for a multitude of reasons, and she herself wonders what happens when such silences go unnoticed. Silence may be powerful, but it must be noticed and recognized in order to have any impact. Silence and speech relate also to memory. Through both speech and silence, Yamada makes use of memory as a survival skill, "the constant reminder of a narrative which resists the forces that would silence it, but which must also acknowledge its own incompleteness, its own suppressions and suturings, its own internal silences" (Schweik 241). However, Yamada is not only aware of the internal silences and fracturing of her text, she deploys such strategies as a part of the telling. Thus, in not so many words, Yamada suggests the subtle evocative power of silence while at the same time alluding to the perils of having that silence go unnoticed.

Speaking the Silence: Joy Kogawa's *Obasan*

Japanese Canadians were also targeted during World War II and subjected to internment and dispersal in Canada, though their history has been even less documented than that of Japanese in the United States. Like the United States, Canada also has a history of anti-Asian legislation and public sentiment. For example, Ken Adachi comments on laws passed to exclude Asians from immigration to Canada, including the 1923 Chinese Exclusion Act, and laws passed to exclude Asians in Canada from rights like employment, naturalization, and suffrage.[20] Like Asians in the United States, Asians in Canada also faced racism, discrimination, exploitation, and even mob violence, culminating in the officially sanctioned "removal" of all persons of Japanese descent from the Pacific Coast during World War II (Adachi; Chua). Justified as military necessity, twenty-three thousand British Columbians were interned in Canada, 75 percent of whom were Canadian citizens. As both Cheng Lok Chua and Yamada suggest, the Canadian internment was even more drastic than that of the United States, as it "shunted able-bodied males to labor and 'concentration' camps . . . six weeks before moving all families to ghost towns and abandoned mining communities in the interior" (Chua 98; Yamada 1996). Not only were many families permanently fractured, but "[the] property of Japanese Canadians was confiscated and auctioned off to defray the costs of the removal" (Weglyn 56–57). Finally, "even after World War II ended in 1945, Canada refused to permit Japanese Canadians to return to Vancouver until four more years had elapsed; in fact, Canada attempted to deport as many of them as possible to war-ravaged Japan" (Weglyn 190–191). As Yamada states, Mackenzie King, the Royal Commissioner of Canada, established a "reconstruction policy" (often referred to as a policy of dispersal) that forced Japanese Canadians to choose between repatriation to Japan (a country to which many of them had never been) and dispersal "east of the Rockies to self-supporting jobs" (1996, 296). Such policy, she argues, should not be surprising given the fact that during World War II, Western nations espoused "evolutionary theories" of racism, and Canada, a commonwealth of Great Britain, "supported the policy of colonial aggression against 'inferior' peoples" (1996, 296).[21] Significantly, one of the primary texts to document the history of Japanese Canadian internment and dispersal is Joy Kogawa's historical novel, *Obasan*. A great deal has been written about *Obasan*. Often compared to Kingston's *The Woman Warrior* because it shares a wide readership and has been frequently chosen as a representative text of Asian North American literature, *Obasan* represents a remarkably complex range of issues for Japanese Canadians in particular and the field of Asian American literature in general.[22] As Scott McFarlane suggests, "no single text concerning the internment has had a greater impact on the Canadian imaginary than Joy Kogawa's *Obasan*. . . . [And it] has played, and continues to play, a significant role in the way the internment is understood" (402).

Obasan is a historical novel told from the point of view of Naomi, who survived the internment and dispersal of Japanese Canadians during her childhood, as Kogawa herself did. At the age of six, when World War II began, Naomi witnessed her family's devastation and fragmentation only to bury the memories of the experience for thirty years. In 1972, the "present" of the novel, Naomi's elderly paternal uncle, Isamu, dies. Returning to the home of her aunt, Aya (the Obasan—aunt—of the novel's title),[23] she finds a package sent to her from her maternal aunt, Emily, including documents, letters, and a detailed journal about the family's experiences during World War II. Prodded by Obasan's grief and Aunt Emily's words, Naomi begins to recount her own experiences during the war.

In this section, I present some of the influential criticism of *Obasan* in order to contextualize my discussion of the text. Then, I argue that *Obasan*, much like Yamada's *Camp Notes*, is a text that performs a gesture of doublespeak, enacting both speech and silence simultaneously in order to both tell and untell the history of internment. Juxtaposed with the dominant historical narrative of World War II, which elides the internment of Japanese Canadians and Americans in favor of a narrative of North

American struggle for democracy, freedom, and liberation, Kogawa's novel at once presents a counterhistory of Japanese Canadians' experiences during the war and suggests that readers examine the very concept of history as transparent and/or easily accessible through foundational understandings of "experience."

In her essay "The Evidence of Experience," Joan Scott discusses the use of "experience" in writings of histories of difference—histories detailing the lives of those subjects often left out of traditional histories. Scott challenges conventional notions of experience that lead to its privileged status in historical narration and, therefore, preclude analyses of the nature of experience. She argues that experience is not simply an essence that human subjects possess but rather that subjects are produced and constructed through experience. Thus, to historicize difference, and to historicize the experiences of marginalized groups of people— subjects often missing or misrepresented in the dominant narratives of official histories—we must first examine the "hidden from history" paradigm that suggests that our goal as historians of difference is simply to locate the always already existing histories of those "others" and then insert them (back) into history. Not only will doing so simply reinscribe the same paradigms and epistemologies of dominant history but, as Scott argues,

> [such] studies lose the possibility of examining those assumptions and practices that excluded considerations of difference in the first place. They take as self-evident the identities of those whose experience is being documented and thus naturalize their difference. They locate resistance outside its discursive construction, and reify agency as an inherent attribute of individuals, thus decontextualizing it. (399)

The idea that history, and historical experience, are transparent entities waiting to be known makes sense according to a certain logic that purports that seeing is knowing. Critiquing this metaphor of visibility as literal transparency, Scott writes:

> Knowledge is gained through vision; vision is a direct, unmediated apprehension of a world of transparent objects. In this conceptualization of it, the visible is privileged; writing is then put at its service. Seeing is the origin of knowing. Writing is reproduction, transmission—the communication of knowledge gained through (visual, visceral) experience. (398)

Yet, as Scott asks, what does vision offer? Why and how is visuality privileged over other "ways of knowing," and in what ways does such a privileging preclude questions of power, agency, and subject position?

Similarly, Maclear, in considering the video testimony of an internment survivor (as discussed in the introductory chapter), draws attention to the fact that history is mediated by subject positions and relations of power and suggests that silences, too, comprise historical narratives. Much like the idea that seeing is somehow knowing, there remains the Western belief that saying is knowing, that speech equals subjectivity and knowledge and even history. But silence, too, operates as a way of saying and a language in its own right, and silence forces us to reexamine notions of history. Not only can history never be transparent, but experience, too, is constructed and constructs each of us according to sociopolitical institutions, beliefs, and events. For example, the experiences of Asian Americans must be evaluated within the historical contexts that recognize their inscription as "Asian" as an effect of social, political, and economic movements. As Richard Fung suggests, "Asian" itself is a constructed social identity that "displaces specific national or regional identities and allegiances under the conditions of white racism, either expressed here in the diaspora, or through Western colonialism and imperialism in Asia" (1995, 125). Thus, "Asian" as a cultural process and a constructed identity is possible only because of the context of colonialism and white racism. As such, it becomes much more a move for political solidarity and counterdiscourse than an innate, essentialized identity. There is no such thing as an "Asian consciousness" for Asians in North America beyond the cultural context in which Asian Americans exist.

What makes an exploration of historical processes crucial to my analysis of Kogawa's novel is the fact that Kogawa attempts to problematize just this notion of transparent history, at the same time reinscribing a history based on her experience and the experiences of others who survived internment. As Manina Jones suggests, "*Obasan*'s discussion of the internment camps is both the documentary filling in of an untold story and a comment on the way the truth of that story has been excluded from the documents of history" (219). For instance, in her acknowledgments in the beginning of the novel, Kogawa thanks several individuals as well as the Public Archives of Canada for permission to use documents and letters from the files of Muriel Kitagawa, Grace Tucker,

T. Buck Suzuki, and Gordon Nakayama. Additionally, as McFarlane states, the character of Aunt Emily is based upon the historical figure Muriel Kitagawa, who published essays in the Japanese Canadian English newspaper *The New Canadian*, until 1952. About such documentation, David Palumbo-Liu writes:

> It is from these documents that Kogawa, like her protagonist Naomi, constructs her narration, a narration that juxtaposes the cold, orderly dictates of the Canadian government with the personal correspondence of the Japanese Canadians—the history of the dominant ideology versus the "unauthorised" [sic] minority representations of that historical moment. And they are unauthorized because those who wrote the texts are denied status as authors of history; they can only be subjects of it and subjected to it.
>
> Naomi's narration is engendered in the empty space left bare by these texts. (220)

Thus, Kogawa attempts to revise history while remaining attentive to the processes and risks concurrent to such revision. While Kogawa, too, relies on a notion of "experience" as history, she, like Yamada, offers only particular and partial histories articulated against Canada's official, totalizing historical narrative. In a sense, Kogawa's use of experience has more to do with memory and processes of remembering, functioning similarly to Kingston's strategies of remembering in *The Woman Warrior* and *China Men*. Additionally, the silences within *Obasan's* narration must be contextualized against the silencing of Japanese Canadians about the history of internment.

Palumbo-Liu goes on to document the tension between memory and history, arguing that one response of "minority" writers has been to challenge the historical "truths" presented by dominant narratives with counterhistories involving memory. History is a significant site of resistance for writers of color, not only because of the ways in which official historical narratives have so often been controlled by those in power and used to maintain control over the powerless but also, as Palumbo-Liu suggests, because "ethnicity is a product of material history—not a predetermined and static essence, but rather something always constructed and re-articulated with regard to a particular historical location of groups within a dominant culture" (211). He describes how, much like Scott's "experience," writers of color have privileged memory as an important discursive tool of counterhistory, used to challenge foundational histories of hegemonic power. Yet, much like the unqualified deployment of experience, memory, too, falls prey to simple reinscriptions of power and unequal relationships. Any counterhistory, according to Palumbo-Liu, "must legitimate itself by laying claim to a firmer epistemology than that claimed by the dominant history" (211). As he asks, "how can one deconstruct the dominant history on the basis of its ideologically suspect nature, and not admit that one's own revision is also overdetermined?" (211). However problematic, memory as history is also a significant site of resistance. Reliance on memory has always been part of the structure of dominant history, though often masked, and such memory has been institutionalized as history and "truth," surpassing the memory of those marginalized by the dominant narrative's ability to conceal power relations and smooth out inconsistencies and ruptures.

Palumbo-Liu relies on Heidegger's discussion of truth as both concealment and unconcealment, ultimately arguing that the writings of people of color, in their usages of memory, participate in a countermovement of "not forgetting." Thus, he "[uses] this notion of truth as problematized precisely by the work of ethnic memory to *un-forget* that which has been covered up in the historical accounts of ethnic peoples" (215, emphasis added). Problematizing history through memory, then, may involve the use of strategies such as "unconcealment," "unforgetting," and, as I argue, "unsaying." However, to deploy memory for the sake of counterhistory not only risks the reinscription of dominant historical paradigms but also the "instability in the margins" almost assuredly to be the fate of a contestive and contested narrative (Palumbo-Liu 218). In the case of *Obasan*, Palumbo-Liu argues that memory is engaged as a significant site of resistance in an attempt to supersede history. Cheung points out that Kogawa, through her presentation of Naomi's history, "counters historical manipulation of facts with novelistic record; in opposition to the social memory she offers Naomi's personal memorial" (1993, 154). This memory is made all the more important because history has attempted to elide the very existence of Japanese Canadians, and their memory of events has been rendered meaningless in the context of the dominant narrative of World War II. Memory, like experience, is related to speech. Western conceptualizations of history generally assume a close association between telling and remembering. Yet it is the narration, through speech and/or *silence*, that in fact shapes both the memory and the experience.

Clearly, then, reliance on experience and memory are problematic and risky ventures for writers of marginalized groups. While useful as strategies of revision, such tactics also risk reinscribing the same models of power and oppression their writers seek to challenge. Yet, what are we to do when the memories of the marginalized are devalued and all but erased from history—in effect, silenced—in relation to the omnipotent and powerful voices of the dominant culture? Perhaps this is one potential site in which silence itself can be enacted as an additional strategy of unsaying—critiquing the version of history that renders Japanese Canadians to liminality and critiquing the processes of historiography that make such elisions possible to begin with.

Scott McFarlane asks, "Why is it that so many Japanese Canadians feel silenced and subsequently the need to testify concerning their experiences of the internment? Why is it that so many *sansei* and *yonsei* feel shrouded in silence, detached from the experience of their parents and unable to articulate the impact of the internment on their lives?" (402). He argues that the idea that coming to language is easily understood as a healthy response to a negative event suggests that the history of internment exists as an objective, real, transparent history to be accessed simply through language. He adds, "Linguistic theorists since Sausaurre have given reasons to be wary of both the mimetic capabilities of language and a historiography based on hermeneutic assumptions" (402). Further, he writes,

> The intense accounting, recounting, and documentation suggests that the internment cannot be said to exist outside of language. That is to say, what "really happened" happens as an effect of language. This is why the redress movement was so concerned with control of the media and the language used to reconceive the events of the war. Furthermore, if the internment is an effect of language then it should be understood as a process to be continually negotiated. . . . [I]f the internment is a process of language then it is important to ask how it is being circulated in discourse. (402–403)

While assumptions continue to dominate public discourse, suggesting that silence equals passivity and acceptance (and speaking out about internment is the only route to healing from such a painful history), writers such as Yamada and Kogawa suggest multiple paths toward liberation.

Thus, Kogawa's double gesture involves both a rewriting of history—

or, more accurately, a counterhistory—and a critical examination of her own process of revision. While some might perceive such a double gesture as an undermining of her own liberatory possibilities, I argue that it is just such an ability to both say and unsay that makes *Obasan* as powerful a text as it continues to be. Kogawa, like her protagonist Naomi, is constantly negotiating the discursive potential of both speech and silence.

In *Obasan*, readers learn that during Naomi's childhood her family lived comfortably in Vancouver, British Columbia, and family members were close. Naomi narrates, "My parents, like two needles, knit the families carefully into one blanket. . . . We were the original 'togetherness' people" (24). When asked, Aunt Emily concurs, insisting that the families were not fragmented and that "the Nakanes and the Katos were intimate to the point of stickiness, like mochi" (24). However, things have changed since the war, as evidenced by Naomi's reflection: "If we were knit into a blanket once, it's become badly moth-eaten with time. We are now no more than a few tangled skeins—the remains of what might once have been a fisherman's net. The memories that are left seem barely real. Gray shapes in the water. Fish swimming through the gaps in the net. Passing shadows" (25). Thus, Naomi's memories are dislocated and inaccessible. Yet it is through her constant attempts to remember, prodded on by Aunt Emily, that she continues to "unconceal" her memories of the past.

At the onset of World War II, Naomi's mother and Grandmother Kato have just left for Japan to see Naomi's great-grandmother, who is very ill. At the sudden departure of her mother, with whom she shares an extremely close relationship, young Naomi wonders: "My great-grandmother has need of my mother. Does my mother have need of me? In what marketplace of the universe are the bargains made that have traded my need for my great-grandmother's?" (79–80). Missing her mother, Naomi lives with the fact that, even as an adult, she does not know what became of her mother after she departed for Japan. When she asks Obasan for a clue to the mystery of her mother's disappearance, her elderly aunt responds by giving her an old photograph of Naomi as a small child holding her mother's hand. "This is the best time. These are the best memories," she says (56). To Naomi, who can learn no more at this stage in the novel, memories themselves are too painful. "Some memories, too, might be better forgotten. . . . What is past recall is past pain" (54). Yet, still she tries to learn the truth about the past. Her attempts prove futile, as Obasan's silences grow thicker. Naomi narrates:

"The greater my urgency to know, the thicker her silences have always been. No prodding will elicit clues" (55). Yet, the memories remain, despite the confusion they bring. As Naomi herself states, there is no escape from remembering:

> All our ordinary stories are changed in time, altered as much by the present as the present is shaped by the past. . . .
>
> [W]e're trapped, Obasan and I, by our memories of the dead—all our dead—those who refuse to bury themselves. Like threads of old spiderwebs, still sticky and hovering, the past waits for us to submit, or depart. When I least expect it, a memory comes skittering out of the dark, spinning and netting the air, ready to snap me up and ensnare me in old and complex puzzles. . . . Why did my mother not return? . . .
>
> Obasan gives me no answers. (30–31)

Thus, Naomi is faced with not knowing and with an internal fragmentation that mirrors the dispersal of her family and community. About the photograph Obasan gives her, she narrates, "Only fragments relate me to them now, to this young woman, my mother, and me, her infant daughter. Fragments of fragments. Parts of a house. Segments of stories" (64).

Naomi's paternal grandparents, the Nakanes, are arrested and incarcerated at the beginning of the war. They are held under armed guard in "the Pool," in which they face crowded conditions in former livestock stalls and are separated into men's and women's areas. The men are forced to work on the roads, while the women, according to Aunt Emily, are "burdened with all the responsibility of keeping what's left of the family together" (120). Uncle Isamu (Obasan's husband) is then incarcerated, and Naomi's father, Mark Nakane, is arrested and imprisoned in the camps, where he develops tuberculosis. Aunt Emily and her father, Grandpa Kato, petition to move what is left of the family to Toronto, but because Uncle Isamu and Aunt Aya are Japanese nationals, they are not permitted to go. Thus, Naomi and her older brother, Stephen, go with Obasan to the ghost town of Slocan, where they inhabit a dilapidated two-room cabin in the woods. Years later, when Naomi returns to see once again where they had lived, there is no trace that they were ever there. "What remains of our time here?" she wonders (139). As Jones suggests, the family members "cannot find the location of their internment. They find instead the site of an erasure, a significant absence"

(219). As Naomi considers the absence of any imprint made by her family's presence, Kogawa simultaneously, throughout the novel, seems to consider the absence within Canadian history and discourse of what happened to Japanese Canadians during the war. As Jones suggests, Kogawa's attention to both physical location and citations of historical documents are instrumental in her narrative revision that seeks to expose the gaps in the (official) historical record (Jones 220).

During the three years that Naomi lives in Slocan, Grandma Nakane becomes ill and dies, and Uncle Isamu is released from prison and joins the family. Also, Naomi's father is released and arrives in Slocan, still very ill. However, in 1945, the family receives more orders for dispersal. Naomi and Stephen are forced to go to Alberta with Obasan and Isamu, who have received orders to move to Kaslo in order to await "Eastern placement," while their father, who is not considered "suitable" for Eastern placement, is ordered to remain in New Denver. Details are sketchy and chaotic, presented secondhand through Naomi's readings of Aunt Emily's papers. Upon learning why they left Slocan, Naomi narrates: "The orders, given to Uncle and Father in 1945, reach me via Aunt Emily's package in 1972, twenty-seven years later. The delivery service is slow these days. Understanding is even slower" (206). In the narrative, the letters "speak out of order" (Jones 222). Jones writes: "They never arrive in the sense that their meaning is fully determined. They become a 'broken record,' but not in the sense that they are involved in a process that merely repeats past events. Because repetition always involves difference, authoritative story order(s) is/are fragmented, 'his master's voice' re(pro)nounced" (222). In fact, Kogawa's text, like Camp Notes, resists a totalizing and authoritative history, suggesting instead a partial, fragmented record of events, cognizant of its own rupturing and the nature of that rupturing.

Aunt Emily's documents force Naomi to reevaluate her own memories of events as witnessed through the eyes of a child. Reading her aunt's journal entries from 1941, she thinks, "I feel like a burglar as I read, breaking into a private house only to discover it's my childhood house filled with corners and rooms I've never seen. Aunt Emily's Christmas 1941 is not the Christmas I remember" (95). Upon finding a newspaper clipping of "[facts] about evacuees in Alberta," she is jarred by the contrast between the "grinning and happy" depiction of "Jap Evacuee" beet farmers and her recovered memories. "Facts about evacuees in Alberta?

The fact is I never got used to it and I cannot, I cannot bear the memory. There are some nightmares from which there is no waking, only deeper and deeper sleep. There is a word for it. Hardship. . . . 'Grinning and happy' and all smiles standing around a pile of beets? That is one telling. It's not how it was" (232, 236). The chaos represented by Naomi's memories parallels the chaos experienced by the family members at the time of their multiple dispersals. Naomi resists both the chaos and the knowing:

> I want to get away from all this. From the past and all these papers, from the present, from the memories, from the deaths, from Aunt Emily and her heap of words. I want to break loose from the heavy identity, the evidence of rejection, the unexpressed passion, the misunderstood politeness. . . .
>
> Aunt Emily, are you a surgeon cutting at my scalp with your folders and your filing cards and your insistence on knowing all? The memory drains down the sides of my face, but it isn't enough, is it? (218, 232)

It is not enough, not for Aunt Emily, who lives by the canon: "Write the words and make it plain" (38). For Emily, there is truth; for her, "the vision is the truth as she lives it" (38). What is remembered must be written, documented painstakingly. "All her life," Naomi notes, "Aunt Emily toiled to tell of the lives of the Nisei in Canada in her effort to make familiar, to make knowable, the treacherous yellow peril that lived in the minds of the racially prejudiced" (49).

But for Naomi, for whom the truth is "more murky, shadowy and gray" (38), remembering is painful, and she cannot bear the pain. Also, she wonders what good all the words and memories do. "None of this bears remembering," she thinks. But Aunt Emily tells her, "You have to remember. . . . You are your history. If you cut it off you're an amputee. Don't deny the past" (60). To such an argument, Naomi can only wonder what they can hope to gain from such painful processes of remembering. She thinks,

> All of Aunt Emily's words, all her papers, the telegrams and petitions, are like scratchings in the barnyard, the evidence of much activity, scaly claws hard at work. But what good they do, I do not know—those little black typewritten words—rain words, cloud droppings. They do not touch us where we are planted here in Alberta, our roots clawing the sudden prairie air. The

words are not made flesh. Trains do not carry us home. Ships do not return again. All my prayers disappear into space. (226)

The fact that their lives do not change—no train carries Naomi home, Uncle's beautiful ship is never returned, her mother is lost forever—forces Naomi to challenge her Aunt Emily's position through much of the novel.

Not only is nothing changed, but Naomi is convinced that what happened to her family will only continue to happen. She continues to question her aunt: "What is done, Aunt Emily, is done, is it not? And no doubt it will happen again, over and over with different faces and names, variations on the same theme. . . . Greed, selfishness, and hatred remain constant as the human condition, do they not? Or are you thinking that through lobbying and legislating, speechmaking and storytelling, we can extricate ourselves from our foolish ways? Is there evidence for optimism?" (238). As Naomi's experiences indicate, there is not. During the years in Alberta, Naomi learns that her father has died and has been buried near his parents, Grandma and Grandpa Nakane. Still, she hears nothing from her mother or maternal grandmother. In the present of the novel, Naomi is still living in Alberta, working as a schoolteacher in the small town of Cecil, where she evades her students' questions about love and ignores their words for her—"spinster" and "old maid"—while also ignoring her own needs and desires.

If the memories do not "bear remembering," neither can they bear the telling. Naomi has difficulty with the verbalization of such a history of pain. She narrates, "People who talk a lot about their victimization make me uncomfortable. It's as if they use their suffering as weapons or badges of some kind. From my years of teaching I know it's the children who say nothing who are in trouble more than the ones who complain" (41). Such a narration demonstrates Naomi's understanding of the nuanced meanings of silence. As a language of distress, and as the quietly resistant language of her mother and Obasan, silence functions as telling in its own right. Finally, Naomi's suggestion that there is no evidence for optimism underscores her question, Can words change anything? Indeed, when free speech is only free for some, what is the power of language? What use value can Emily's "lobbying and legislating, speechmaking and storytelling" enact?

Language is a powerful medium, but as such it operates differently for those in power and for the powerless. In *Obasan*, "words spoken by the powerless have no impact; they only tantalize as 'prayers disappear into space.' Language issued by the powerful, however, can constitute a form of speech act, commanding performance" (Cheung, 1993, 128). For example, the Canadian government enacted official racism as a speech act; suddenly "Japanese" and "Canadian" were mutually exclusive terms, and internment camps and prisons were conveniently masked under euphemisms such as "relocation" and "evacuation" camps. Japanese-language newspapers and publications were censored, while Japanese Canadians, like Japanese in the United States, were stereotyped in official discourse as national threats and as a "yellow peril." Aunt Emily remembers, "None of us . . . escaped the naming. We were defined and identified by the way we were seen" (139). When other children at school call Naomi and Stephen "Japs," Naomi asks her father if that is what they are. He replies, "No. We're Canadian," to which Stephen suggests that it is a riddle, "We are both the enemy and not the enemy" (84). Here, naming, like vision, occupies a problematic primacy, thought to represent or reproduce the "truth." Thus, Naomi must constantly negotiate among multiple linguistic forms that attempt to narrate her into—or out of—existence. Cheung suggests that "words can liberate, but they can also distort and wound, and while silence may obliterate, it can also minister, soothe, and communicate" (128).

Many critics have interpreted *Obasan* using psychoanalytic frameworks and other white Western-centered paradigms, which privilege speech over silence and which equate the silences of characters (Naomi, Obasan, Naomi's mother) with denial of the "truth" and with a lack of subjectivity. As Cheung states, "Most reviewers . . . have applied the hierarchical opposition of language and silence to the very novel that disturbs the hierarchy" (1993, 126). Such Eurocentric models fail to examine culturally specific conceptualizations of language, speech, and silence. And while silence is understood in the English language as the opposite of speech, such is not the case in all languages. In both Japanese and Chinese, the ideogram for silence is understood to be opposite "noise," "sound," "motion," and "commotion" and synonymous with "serenity." Thus, while silence is generally understood in terms of passivity and absence in the United States, in China and Japan "it traditionally signals pensiveness, vigilance, and grace" (Cheung, 1993, 127).

Even Yamada's discussion of *Obasan* privileges speech over silence. Cognizant as she is of Kogawa's multiple ways of telling, still she argues that the novel is ultimately about the "miracle of breaking silence," as Naomi "comes to terms with her past when she breaks her own silence" (1996, 294). However, Yamada contextualizes Naomi's (and Kogawa's) breaking of silences against the larger silences exemplified by the mystery of Naomi's mother's disappearance and the "historical amnesia" of the Canadian government, the Christian Church, and the dominant culture (1996, 298). Arguing that *Obasan* represents one of the most forceful "indictment[s] of the Christian church's complicity in the persecution of the Japanese Canadians during this time" (1996, 302), Yamada commends Kogawa's willingness to tell the history of internment that she remembers.

Psychoanalytic analyses of the novel generally attempt to make meaning of Naomi's character through her relationship with her mother as representative of the pre-oedipal stage of childhood development.[24] Thus, her relationship with her mother signifies the dreamlike childhood bliss of silent communication, trust, and bonding. One site of conflict presented for Naomi is between symbolic and literal languages—a choice between the pre-oedipal, literal language of childhood that she shares with her mother and the symbolic (mature) language of the father (Goellnicht, 1991, 122). According to such an analysis, one could argue, as Jones does, that the narrative of the text is motivated by a desire for reunion with the mother (224). Also, psycholinguistic theorists have employed an interpretive model that emphasizes the novel's use of a "women's poetics."[25] Finally, most psychoanalytic criticism focuses on Naomi's experiences of sexual abuse during her childhood in Vancouver by a white male neighbor, Old Man Gower. Because the shame Naomi experiences caused by the sexual abuse parallels her subsequent shame during and after internment, and because Old Man Gower repeatedly warns, "Don't tell your mother," the secret of sexual abuse is understood by Naomi, during her childhood, to be related to the separation from her mother and her mother's disappearance during the war. According to Yamamoto, Gower's abuse "pushes Naomi into a realm where language is duplicitous, silence is the withholding of truth, presence is what renders one most vulnerable, and absence signifies both the erasure of self and the loss of the mother" (194). In Naomi's childhood nightmares during the time of the abuse, she is forcibly separated from her mother:

"The mountains yawn apart as the chasm spreads. My mother is on one side of the rift. I am on the other. We cannot reach each other. My legs are being sawn in half" (77). Her silencing, then—a silence that is not communicative with her mother, as previous silences between them can be interpreted—leads to Naomi's psychic disintegration. The sexual abuse she suffers results in the severing of the "umbilical cord between Naomi and her mother" (Goellnicht, 1991, 125).

In Goellnicht's study of the text, he critiques the Eurocentrism of French feminist theory, arguing that Lacanian psychoanalysis retains imperialistic tendencies and is therefore inadequate as a framework for a text such as *Obasan*. Because for an Asian North American girl there is more at stake in psychological development than simply a negotiation between the "subjective space of silent communication inherited from the mother" and "the symbolic language inherited from the figurative father," the trajectory of pre-oedipal to oedipal development must be recast in terms of a move between the old "mother tongue/culture" of Japan and the new "fatherland" of Canada (1991, 122). Thus, he argues, "the girl from an immigrant racial minority experiences not a single, but a double subject split: first, when she takes on the gendered position constructed for her by the symbolic language of patriarchy; and second, when she falls under the influence of discursively and socially constructed positions of racial difference" (1991, 123). He suggests that "this situation of potential double powerlessness—of being woman and minority—is brought home to her with the recognition that the 'fathers' of her racial and cultural group are silenced and degraded by the Laws of the Ruling Father (the white majority)" (1991, 123), as evidenced by the mistreatment and losses sustained in the novel by Naomi's father, grandfather, and Uncle Isamu, as well as the other Japanese Canadian men of Naomi's community.

The silence she experiences with her mother represents the one period in Naomi's life of trust and security. This meaningful silence, according to Goellnicht, is reproduced in her relationship with Obasan, for whom silence is also the primary method of communication. Yet, silence is figured in the text as both "escape and doom" (Goellnicht, 1991, 127). Because of its association with mother (culture), it represents disempowerment and debilitation at the same time that it may signify pride, empowerment, and love. Significantly, brother Stephen denies all aspects of the mother and motherland (Japan), assimilating as much as possible into Western culture, and Naomi, too, has assimilated into the mainstream by "becoming a good Canadian teacher" (Goellnicht, 1991, 127). However, throughout the novel, she struggles to negotiate her place as both Japanese *and* Canadian.

Tomo Hattori critiques Goellnicht's study as "orientalist" in its approach, arguing that in fact there is little in the text to suggest, as Goellnicht does, "that silent, pre-oedipal language is characteristically maternal or that figurative, symbolic language in the novel is paternal" (130). As Hattori points out, it is women in the novel, including Aunt Emily, Grandma Kato, and Naomi, who express both verbal and textual language, while "the men of the family are 'rendered voiceless, stripped of car, radio, camera and every means of communication' by the internment" (130). She writes,

> The commonplace orientalism of conveniently sexualized oppositions between the masculine West and the feminine East is especially out of place in a novel where all the living female characters are Canadian and where there are no functional living Canadian father figures worth mentioning (whether of Japanese ancestry or not). . . . [T]he novel's varied representations of gendered Japanese Canadian speech and silence do not definitively type pre-oedipal communication as feminine-Japanese and figurative language as masculine-Canadian. (130)

Also, Hattori critiques the interpretation of the characters of Obasan and Aunt Emily as dialectical signifiers of "recessive silence" and "sociopolitical fact" (130–131). While the two can certainly be said to represent different forms of discourse, Hattori is wary of Shirley Geok-lin Lim's argument that Obasan and Emily "[mark] the evolutionary progress of the Japanese Canadian female voice to the completed stage represented by Naomi, whose poetic language 'encompasses the two negative mirrorings of aunts Aya and Emily and exceeds them'" (131). Such a framework seems to suggest that Obasan's "muteness or aphasia" is associated with her status as first-generation Japanese, while Emily's "logocentric documentation" marks her identity as Canadian. In the words of Hattori,

> Emily's "limited and ineffectual mode" remains superior to Aya's "recessive silence" and shows that the ostensibly equitable multiculturalism of Naomi's finally achieved voice rests on a narrative of assimilationist progress. Emily,

with her allegedly "Canadian" habit of democratic self-assertion, is still higher on the evolutionary ladder of the Japanese Canadian subject-in-progress than Aya who, as the least assimilated Canadian, is the least progressive speaking-subject. (131)

Naomi, according to such an analysis, is not only seen as having a more evolved (more assimilated?) "voice" than her two aunts but a stronger capacity for language in general. According to Hattori, this fact marks Lim's ethnocentrism by establishing an opposition between (semiotic) Japan and (symbolic) Canada and by "narrowing the performance of subjectivity to the category of speech" (131). Such a move is orientalist in that it establishes Japan and the characters most closely associated with Japan as the "inscrutable, pre-Western (and therefore premodern) East" (Hattori 131). In their willingness to relegate the mother in Asian American literature to the "maternal, preverbal, pre-oedipal realm of the semiotic," Hattori suggests that critics display a psycholinguistic orientalism (133). Also, such interpretations, resting on assumptions that conflate speech and subjectivity, fail to recognize the limits of speech for marginalized groups of people and the complex meanings of silence.

Obasan, ultimately, is a text about history and fragmentation in relation to national discourse. My own interpretation focuses on the silences of the text, both internal and external, and the ways in which Kogawa deploys silence as a tool of unsaying the dominant historical narrative of internment. Like Yamada's *Camp Notes*, Kogawa's novel resists the totalizing tendencies of "master narratives" of history, choosing instead to depict a partial and fractured history of internment. The fragmentations are multiple: the narrative itself enacts a rupturing, as do its main characters. By reflecting on its own fragmentation, *Obasan* offers a good example of a marginalized historical discourse, attentive to its fragmented status and marking a refusal to demonstrate a false wholeness or seamless narrative of fixity. At the same time, *Obasan* as a text performs a gesture of doublespeak, an attempt to both say and unsay the history under consideration here. As Jones suggests, *Obasan* "'tells on' official history by revealing its guilty suppression of events in Canada (and similar events in the United States) during World War II, and by giving a version of history alternate in both form and content that draws attention to the inscription and/or suppression of difference" (215). According to Jones, both tellings of difference (e.g., historical accounts of marginalized groups) and different tellings (those "accounts that do not conform to the conventions of historical discourse"), which, she suggests, often co-incide, are elided by dominant histories, which seek to ignore and/or suppress inconsistencies and contradictions in favor of seamless, smooth narratives. These tellings rupture the dominant historical record and are therefore "relegated to the marginal realm of the incomprehensible, the foreign, the unfinished, the fundamentally unfamiliar" (Jones 214). Thus, different ways of telling risk incomprehensibility.

By focusing on the process of telling—the narration itself—Kogawa dismantles notions of innate, essential truths to be told. She does so not only with her use of unconventional form and displaced documents but also through an examination of the not mutually exclusive forms of com-munication: speech and silence. Such an examination is made most ex-plicit in the text with the two characters of Obasan and Aunt Emily. Na-omi, like the reader, must constantly negotiate between the positions of her two aunts and between how to both speak and unsay the history—and her (plural, often contradictory) memories of that history—into existence.

The two aunts of the novel differ significantly. Aunt Aya, a Japanese national, expresses herself most through her silences, which are described throughout the novel as rich and complex. Meanwhile, Aunt Emily, a Nisei and a Canadian citizen, is described as a "word warrior." Naomi narrates:

> How different my two aunts are. One lives in sound, the other in stone. Obasan's language remains deeply underground but Aunt Emily, BA, MA, is a word warrior. She's a crusader, a little old gray-haired Mighty Mouse, a Bachelor of Advanced Activists and General Practitioner of Just Causes. (39)

In fact, it is Aunt Emily's package of words that crashes into Naomi's life and complacence, forcing her to reexamine her history and that of her family and community. The parcel Aunt Emily sends Naomi includes letters, notes, newspaper clippings, and her journal from the 1940s—a collection of materials documenting the past and opening up the future, for to Aunt Emily, the past continues to shape the present and the fu-ture. In her painstaking attention to detail through letters and words, Emily asserts her identity and her place in Canada. As Naomi notes, "Wher-ever the words 'Japanese race' appeared [in the documentation], Aunt Emily had crossed them out and written 'Canadian citizen'" (40). To her family, she reports, "We're gluing our tongues back on. . . . We have to deal with this while we remember it. If we don't we'll pass our anger down in our genes. It's the children who'll suffer" (43). According to Gurleen Grewal, Aunt Emily's entire life is "consumed by her engagement with history" (146). It is through gathering the "facts," documenting the "truth" of what happened to her family and community, that Aunt Emily "finds and raises her voice" (Grewal 146).

Meanwhile, Obasan expresses herself most eloquently through her silences. While Naomi's brother Stephen felt "rebuke" in Obasan's silences and fled them, Naomi recognizes the multiple meanings of her aunt's silences. "The language of grief is silence. She has learned it well, its idioms and nuances. Over the years, silence within her small body has grown large and powerful" (17). Her steadfast silence keeps Obasan "inviolate" (270). As Cheung suggests, Obasan's attentive silence, "far from suggesting passivity . . . entails both mental vigilance and physical readiness" (1993, 147). Naomi herself recognizes that from Obasan and Uncle she learns that "speech often hides like an animal in a storm" (4). However, the silences frustrate Naomi. Obasan diverts her questions or ignores them altogether. About such silences that were used to shield her from knowing what was taking place in Canada during World War II, Naomi narrates: "The memories were drowned in a whirlpool of protective silence. Everywhere I could hear the adults whispering, 'Kodomo no tame. For the sake of the children. . . .'" (26). Such protective silence, however, is no longer necessary or effective. While Naomi has accompanied her elderly uncle to the same deserted prairie each August since 1954, she still does not understand the reason they come. She notes, "Whatever he was intending to tell me 'someday' has not yet been told . . . [though] at thirty-six, I'm hardly a child" (4). Thus, in the greater part of this novel, what Naomi needs most of all is for the words to be "made flesh"—for the silence to be broken and for the telling to matter. In her narration, there is recognition of the disempowering effects of being silenced:

> We are hammers and chisels in the hands of would-be sculptors, battering the spirit of the sleeping mountain. We are the chips and sand, the fragments of fragments that fly like arrows from the heart of the rock. We are the silences that speak from stone. We are the despised rendered voiceless, stripped of car, radio, camera, and every means of communication, a trainload of eyes

covered with mud and spittle. We are the man in the Gospel of John, born into the world for the sake of the light. We are sent to Siloam, the pool called "Sent." We are sent to the sending, that we may bring sight. We are the scholarly and the illiterate, the envied and the ugly, the fierce and the docile. We are those pioneers who cleared the bush and the forest with our hands, the gardeners tending and attending the soil with our tenderness, the fishermen who are flung from the sea to flounder in the dust of the prairies.

We are the Issei and the Nisei and the Sansei, the Japanese Canadians. We disappear into the future undemanding as dew. (132)

Rendered voiceless and stripped of all means of communication, Japanese Canadians here are figured as "despised," "fragment[ed]," covered with "mud and spittle," and "disappear[ing]." Speaking silences "from stone" suggests a physical pain associated with both speech and silence and indicates Naomi's need, at times, to break silences despite such pain. At the same time, the above quotation suggests that the silences themselves "speak."

Wary of stereotypes of inscrutable Asians and notions of silence as an innate Asian trait, Chua critiques the silences within the novel. He argues that Naomi achieves a more fundamental integration into Canadian society than her brother, Stephen, when she "breaks through the personal and cultural screens of silence and secretiveness that have enshrouded her individual, familial, and ethnic past and reintegrates herself within her history through the recuperation of that past" (101). Thus, it is through the breaking of silence that Naomi finds transformation and liberation. While Chua argues that the "stoical, unspeaking silence" of Obasan and other Japanese Canadians who have survived internment is a silence that comes from a "place of power of self-denial and a strength of love for the younger generation, which needs to be protected from unspeakable horrors," he also suggests that such silence is perilous to the younger generation: "Contrary to the ethic of strength in silence, the younger generation, in order to come into its own, must break the protective but petrifying silence and tell the unspeakable truths" (105). Only by doing so, he suggests, can they transform the silence of their victimization into a language of communication.

Indeed, most critics have equated the silences in the novel with denial and lack of memory.[26] In the character of Obasan, for instance, there has been a general consensus among the earlier critics that her silence represents her denial and her passivity. While some have attempted to reduce such silence to her status as a Japanese national who therefore enacts a peculiarly innate Japanese silence, there remains the notion that her silence is negative, representative of a void, a lack, an absence. In fact, Obasan's denial is separate from her silence. Obasan, who is often silent, remembers everything. Her refrain, *kodomo no tame*, is maintained *because* she remembers, because she is fully aware of what has taken place. Thus, her silence operates as a measure of protection and as a strategy, however misguided, of protection for the children in the novel, Naomi and Stephen. Also, her silence exists in opposition to the notion that speech will liberate, when she has yet to witness such "evidence for optimism."

The two aunts seem to represent various modes of speech and silence. However, even if we could interpret Obasan's actions as silence and Emily's language as speech, it is difficult to discretely categorize them as such. In fact, Obasan's silence speaks multitudes, and Emily's speech is complex and problematic as well. While some critics have interpreted this novel as being about Naomi's search for selfhood and journey into speech (as exemplified by her gaining access to the truth about her history, made available through Aunt Emily's papers), I believe it is more about her increasing awareness of the power of both speech and silence. On the subject, Grewal writes:

> The narrative oscillates between Aunt Emily's forthright and cleansing vociferousness, her "billions of letters and articles and speeches, her tears and her rage," and Naomi's quiet and haunting meditations on the past, informed by Uncle and Obasan's stoic language of silence. That is, the narrative moves between the documentary realm of public facts to the undocumented world of emotions, the shadowy world of memories, of the lived and livid history that eludes documentation. Registering the necessity of both facts and the subjective truths of memory—the novel alternates between these two modes of understanding the past—Kogawa clearly values and enacts the "drifting meaning" that evades speech. (147)

Thus, as she argues, "archival documentation" is different from "bodily remembering"—that "history that eludes documentation"—but both methods of personal history are necessary for Naomi, and both are strategic to the novel's account of the past.

To Aunt Emily's "materials of communication," which as McFarlane points out, resemble the form of the novel itself, Naomi is, at first, an "unwilling [communicant] receiving and consuming less than holy nourishment" (217). However, as the novel progresses, she begins to recognize the value of remembering and the power of telling her history. This recognition culminates toward the end of the novel in a passage in which Naomi finally learns the truth of her mother's disappearance. Finding a letter written in Japanese among the papers of Aunt Emily's package, which she, significantly, is unable to read, Naomi asks Obasan to translate it for her. Obasan, clinging to the practice of enduring silence "for the sake of the children," refuses to narrate the history represented by the letter.[27] Finally, upon Uncle's death, when Aunt Emily and Stephen return to Alberta to console Obasan, the letter is reopened. Nakayama-sensei, a family friend and minister who survived the internment with Naomi's family, reads the letter, saying, "Naomi, Stephen, your mother is speaking. Listen carefully to her voice" (279). The letter, written by Grandma Kato, describes her and Naomi's mother's experiences in Japan during the bombing of Nagasaki. In it, Grandma narrates the unspeakable horrors she witnessed in Japan and Naomi's mother's disfigurement and subsequent death. Kogawa writes:

> From this point on, Grandma's letter becomes increasingly chaotic, the details interspersed without chronological consistency. She and my mother, she writes, were unable to talk of all the things that happened. The horror would surely die sooner, they felt, if they refused to speak. . . .
>
> Mother, for her part, continued her vigil of silence. (282–283)

Naomi learns that her mother specifically requested that her children not be told of her fate. Also, she learns the reason that she and Uncle have visited the coulee each August—to commemorate the dropping of the atomic bomb on Nagasaki and to mark the event that caused the death of Naomi's mother.

Kogawa's focus on the processes of telling—of narrating—dismantles the notion of innate, essential truths to be told. Rather, her narrative style "[focuses] on the material 'documentation' of history and story, refusing to see either as simply 'pre-textual' events unconditioned by specific, contextualized 'tellings'" (Jones 214). It is the telling itself that creates the narrative. As Jones writes:

The novel thematizes and puts into play the narrative impulse both to search for a particular story and to search for an alternate, potentially redemptive form of telling that resists narrative closure, that both speaks out of historical silences and literally takes into account its own status as telling, as search grounded in historical/textual re-search. . . . The enigma [of Naomi's mother's disappearance] is a metonymy that draws attention to its metonymic status, to the fact that it "stands in for" what is not present, and in doing so conceals an absence. For both reader and narrator, "kodomo no tame," and the letter on the blue paper written in Japanese are "pure signifiers," mere markers. They foreground the fact that the concealment is accomplished by language. (223–224)

It is the negotiation of language with which Naomi continues to struggle. Upon learning of the reasons for her mother's disappearance, she encounters what is incomprehensible, beyond the limits of language and understanding. Yet, seeking some solace and some sense of comprehension, she knows to listen for what is not there: "Gradually the room grows still and it is as if I am back with Uncle again, listening to the silent earth and the silent sky as I have done all my life. . . . Mother, I am listening. Assist me to hear you" (288). As she remembers her mother's "voicelessness" over the years, her "remembered breath, a wordless word," she asks, "How shall I attend that speech, Mother, how shall I trace that wave?" (289).

Naomi both resists her mother's silence and, at the same time, acknowledges it as a form of speech and language in and of itself. Of this "powerful voicelessness," she narrates, "Gentle Mother, we were lost together in our silences. Our wordlessness was our mutual destruction" (291). And she reflects on the impact of her mother's silence on her own life: "Martyr Mother. . . . You wish to protect us with lies, but the camouflage does not hide your cries. Beneath the hiding I am there with you. Silent Mother, lost in the abandoning, you do not share the horror. . . . [A]m I not also there?" (290). Though the words have not been "made flesh," Naomi, finally, feels her mother's presence. To Nakayama-sensei's prayer, "Teach us to see Love's presence in our abandonment. Teach us to forgive," Naomi reflects, "I am thinking that for a child there is no presence without flesh. But perhaps it is because I am no longer a child I can know your presence though you are not here" (292). Her recognition of her mother's presence in her life—with or without conventional modes of speaking and communication—recalls a nightmare she had prior to hearing the letter. In the dream, a "Grand Inquisitor" demands to know the truth about what happened to Naomi's mother:

> The Grand Inquisitor was carnivorous and full of murder. His demand to know was both a judgment and a refusal to hear. The more he questioned her, the more he was her accuser and murderer. The more he killed her, the deeper her silence became. What the Grand Inquisitor has never learned is that the avenues of speech are the avenues of silence. To hear my mother, to attend her speech, to attend the sound of stone, he must first become silent. Only when he enters her abandonment will he be released from his own.
>
> How the Grand Inquisitor gnaws at my bones. At the age of questioning my mother disappeared. Why, I have asked ever since, did she not write? Why, I ask now, must I know? Did I doubt her love? Am I her accuser? (273–274)

Not only silence, but the demand for speech is problematized. The Grand Inquisitor, symbol of Naomi's need to know the "truth" about her mother's disappearance, "gnaws at [her] bones."[28] In fact, what is most urgent for her now is the recognition that her mother has been speaking to her all along, that her silences and absence, too, have presence and meaning. Her "mostly silent but relentless and accusing inquisition of her mother is over" (Grewal 153). Grewal suggests that Naomi, "the abandoned daughter[,] is able to transcend her personal pain only when she enters the grief of her absent mother. . . . The breaking of the long-held protective silence regarding her mother's terrible fate is what finally enables Naomi to come to terms with her past" (142–143). It is at this point in the novel that Naomi sees "how her own grief and hurt at being abandoned are surpassed by her mother's suffering and that of the other victims of the atomic explosion" (Grewal 153). Also, the above passage indicates Naomi's realization that silences result from multiple causes, that silence is part of the process of speech, and that to "attend her mother's speech," she must also listen to silences.

The novel's conclusion enacts both a series of resolutions and an undoing of the narrative. Mediating between the approaches of her two aunts, Naomi meets the challenge, as articulated by Grewal, of "how to

name that which is both unnamed and unnameable, how to mediate between silence and speech, and how to transform this wreckage into a
body of grace" (142). As Cheung states, "The ending of *Obasan* . . . enacts multiple reconciliations—between mother and daughter, past and
present, death and life, and above all, the nonverbal and verbal modes
of expression embodied in Obasan and Emily" (1993, 163). Reflecting
upon her history, Naomi narrates: "Once I came across two ideographs
for the word 'love.' The first contained the root words 'heart' and 'hand'
and 'action'—love as hands and heart in action together. The other ideograph, for 'passionate love,' was formed of 'heart,' 'to tell,' and 'a long
thread'" (273). Acknowledgment of love as both "hands and heart in
action together," symbolized by Obasan's form of love for Naomi, and a
process of telling, embodied by Aunt Emily's relationship to Naomi and
to the world, makes it possible for Naomi to accept both modes of love
as love and to acknowledge her mother's love for her, despite their
forced separation. By the novel's end, "Naomi learns that to attend both
the sound of Obasan's stony silence and Aunt Emily's linguistic rage demands a pathos capable of bearing witness to the loving intentions of
both. The two aunts . . . are united by the red, loving string of transcen-
dent empathy which conflates words and silence, presence and absence,
and testifies to the presence of an absent mother's nurturing love—
yasashi kokoro" (McFarlane 405). Finally, that the novel begins and ends in
silence indicates, for Yamamoto, that "this is not a novel about the at-
tainment of speech after its long repression" (190). Rather, the narrative
details Naomi's growing awareness of the various forms and meanings
of silence.

In her attention to the process of narration, Kogawa forces her readers to acknowledge processes of language and telling. As Cheung states,
"The voice of the narrator is undercut by her act of narration" (1993,
153). And, of the words her mother does not intend her to hear, Naomi
reflects on the process of delivery. "The letters take months to reach
Grandfather. They take years to reach me. Grandfather gives the letters to
Aunt Emily. Aunt Emily sends letters to the Government. The Government makes paper airplanes out of our lives and files us out the window. Some people return home. Some do not. War, they all say, is war,
and some people survive. No one knows the exact day that you die.
Aunt Emily writes and receives no replies. All that is left is your word,
'Do not tell. . . .'" (1993, 291).

It is the injunction to silence (which precludes memory) that is perilous, not the silence itself. Naomi's processes of remembering are crucial to the novel. Grewal calls *Obasan* a "ceremonial performance of memory" in which "remembering and mourning become signs of the subject's agency and recovery" (142, 170). Yet, she also notes: "When all is said and done, there is a reservoir of all that which remains unspoken, untouched. The gaps and the silences become quietly recriminating, refuting the possibility of any posthumous recompense that claims to be adequate to the past. All cannot be accounted for" (170). Thus, through her uses of both language and silence, Kogawa offers a counterhistory of Japanese Canadian internment and a powerful critique of the notion that there can be a simple, easily accessible window to such a complicated and painful history. As Naomi narrates, "The message to disappear worked its way deep into the Nisei heart and into the bone marrow. . . . The body will not tell" (219, 235).

McFarlane argues for the need to develop narratives in which Japanese Canadians are not inscribed as "already interned and already internable" (408). Internment, he suggests, is "a language in itself" whose grammar can be located in various racist cultural presuppositions and stereotypical representations about Japanese Canadians. Thus, he reads the internment itself as a text, and as a racist text, and argues for resistance through linguistic processes and oppositional language. In *Obasan*, Naomi resists having her history "told for her" by attempting to make meaning of her own (hi)story. Her methods for doing so are influenced by both Aunt Emily's quest for words and truth and Obasan's strategic silences. Reflecting on her social location as a Japanese Canadian, consistently having her identity as such undermined by questions such as "Where are you from?" she asks herself, "Where do any of us come from in this cold country? . . . We come from our untold tales that wait for their telling" (271). By asserting her history and national identity as *Canadian*, Naomi links both speech and silence to nation and memory. Her assertion of a Canadian identity articulates her demand for recognition of her lived history at the same time that she challenges notions of history (Quimby 271). In response to her above question, "Where do any of us come from?" Naomi also replies, "Oh Canada, whether it is admitted or not, we come from you, we come from you" (271).

In his book *Whispered Silences: Japanese Americans and World War II*, Gary Okihiro writes of his decision to pursue Asian American history: "Where were our stories within the master narrative of American history? And how were they told, from whose perspective? I remember how the silences of the past were deafening to us. I remember how the strident and subtle distortions filled us with rage. I remember how history's whispers sent us scurrying, searching for our identity, as Asians, as Americans, as Asian Americans" (91). Both Yamada and Kogawa engage the questions of history and silence, commenting on the ways in which histories of Asians in both the United States and Canada have been erased, specifically the history of the internment and dispersal of people of Japanese descent. In their texts, *Camp Notes* and *Obasan*, they also problematize notions of speech and silence against the context of such a historical silencing. In both works, silence emerges as nuanced and complex. Silences are tropes of difference, stereotypes, enforced erasures, and powerful strategies of resistance capable of evoking a doubly discursive voice. Such a form of silence attempts to correct the official historical record at the same time that it disrupts any notion that there can be such a construct. These discursive silences say and unsay the official history of North America, where Japanese Americans and Canadians are concerned. They suggest not only that some histories remain unspoken and unspeakable but also that silence "as a will not to say or a will to unsay" does, as Trinh suggests, sometimes provide a means to gain a hearing (1990, 373).

It murmurs inside. It murmurs. Inside is the pain of speech the pain to say. Larger still. Greater than is the pain not to say. . . . It festers inside. The wound, liquid, dust. Must break. Must void.

From another epic another history. From the missing narrative. From the multitude of narratives. Missing. From the chronicles. For another telling for other recitations.

Void the words. Void the silence. — Theresa Hak Kyung Cha, *Dictée*

four

Cartographies of Silence: Language and Nation in Theresa Hak Kyung Cha's Dictée

In this chapter, I focus on the theme of silence in relation to the work of Korean American woman writer, artist, and filmmaker Theresa Hak Kyung Cha. When I suggest a critical analysis of silence, in relation to Cha's work, what I mean is a reading of "silence" from at least two theoretical positions. First, I question the silencing of Cha's life and work within U.S. culture, especially in the context of a greater silence and invisibility surrounding the history and writings of Asian Americans, in particular Asia American women. Second, I look to the silences in Cha's work to explore the ways in which she herself makes use of silence — as a literary device, a method of historiography, and a feminist, postcolonial retelling and revisioning of her own subject position, experiences, and memories within U.S. culture. The complexities of multiple layerings of her text Dictée, as well as Cha's profound uses and questioning of language, engage the many ways silence operates at cultural, discursive, and political levels, as well as in and through historical and collective memory.

I am most interested in her experimental text, *Dictée*, first published in 1982 by Tanam Press.[1] However, I also attempt, to some degree, to contextualize my discussion of this text by considering other works by Cha: her shorter writings, conceptual art pieces, and film/video work.[2] While *Dictée* is Cha's most well-known work, and the majority of her other works are virtually unknown, I believe it is important to understand that Cha produced a great number of pieces, in various forms, and that many of them deal with themes similar to *Dictée*. I also heed the warning of Abdul JanMohamed and David Lloyd that "archival work is essential to the critical articulation of minority discourses" and that "theoretical and archival work of minority culture must always be concurrent and mutually reinforcing" (8). The point here is that we not canonize or focus exclusively upon one "minority" text, author, or group at the expense of other works, other writers, or other social groups, effecting a form of tokenization that fails to consider the complexities and richness of any "minority discourse." Thus, while emphasizing *Dictée*, I attempt to place my reading of this text into a broader interpretation of Cha's oeuvre.

I begin with biographical information about Cha and then proceed to a discussion of her work, primarily because her life and work have not, until quite recently, begun to receive the kind of critical attention they deserve.[3] For several years, *Dictée* was out of print, inaccessible, and virtually unknown outside of a small number of academic and artistic communities. Shelley Sunn Wong attributes the ten years of silence surrounding *Dictée* within Asian American literary communities to criteria within those communities that demanded the "representativeness" and authenticity of an Asian American text (103–104). For example, Lisa Lowe argues that the notion of Asian American identity has involved a homogenization and disavowal of "difference."[4] Not only are Asian Americans seen as "all the same," rendered interchangeable, but, as stated earlier, Asian American cultural politics have also created a specific, authentic, "Asian American identity"—one that presumes maleness, middle-class status, East Asian heritage, American birth, heterosexuality, and the speaking of English. Of the effects of such processes, Lowe writes:

The essentializing of Asian American identity also reproduces oppositions that subsume other nondominant groups in the same way that Asians and other groups are marginalized by the dominant culture: to the degree that the discourse generalizes Asian American identity as male, women are rendered invisible; or to the extent that Chinese are presumed to be exemplary of all Asians, the importance of other Asian groups is ignored. (1996, 71)

Such a construction, of course, must be contextualized against a culture in which Asian Americans have been rendered invisible or represented in stereotypical, demeaning ways. Thus, during the 1960s and 1970s, claiming an original, discrete, and authentic Asian American identity—one that could resist stereotypes of Asian Americans, claim status as American, and be properly situated within sociopolitical movement as well as discourse—was a significant part of the Asian American movement for liberation.[5] As Wong suggests, virtually all Asian American–authored texts that reached critical acclaim during and immediately after this period followed prescribed narrative structures that relied upon notions of assimilation and incorporation into American culture (105–106).[6] That Dictée, a text that refuses to conform to notions of representativeness or essentialist identity, was published during the historical period of reclamation for Asian American cultural and nationalist politics contributed to the silence surrounding its existence. In fact, Cha, with Dictée, questions the very ideas of fixed identity and universal history. Her text is marked by a non-narrative structure that calls into question any conventional bildungsroman, especially where marginalized social categories of identity converge.

The construction of such an Asian American identity, rendered "authentic," has also made possible the kinds of accusations leveled at Asian American women writers such as Maxine Hong Kingston and Amy Tan by Asian American male writers such as Frank Chin, Jeffery Paul Chan, and Ben Tong.[7] In his well-known essay "Come All Ye Asian American Writers of the Real and the Fake," Chin bitterly attacks Kingston and Tan, arguing that works such as The Woman Warrior and The Joy Luck Club, though popular among white Americans, are not "really" Chinese American or Asian American. The "fake" Chinese fairy tale that opens Tan's The Joy Luck Club is "not Chinese but white racist. It is not informed by any Chinese intelligence" (2). Rather, these women writers "boldly fake the best-known works from the most universally known body of Asian literature and lore in history" (3). In doing so, they "sell out" the Chinese community by perpetuating stereotypes of Chinese men in their writings. He goes on:

> To legitimize their faking, they have to fake all of Asian American history and literature, and argue that the immigrants who settled and established Chinese America lost touch with Chinese culture, and that a faulty memory combined with new experience produced new versions of these traditional stories. This version of history is their contribution to the stereotype. (3)

According to Chin, the stereotype involves casting Asian and Asian American men as more patriarchal than white European men and less civilized.[8] According to Lowe, Chin not only accuses Kingston of buying into the exoticizing of Chinese American culture, he suggests that she has "feminized" Asian American men and Asian American literature, stating that her work has "undermined the power of Asian American men to combat the racist stereotypes of the dominant white culture" (76).[9] His accusations that The Woman Warrior represents Kingston's attempt to "cash in on the feminist fad" thereby deepens the rift between mutually exclusive conceptualizations of feminism and nationalism (Espiritu 136–137) and robs Kingston of any agency or feminist subjectivity of her own. The claim that Kingston is merely attempting to "cash in on the feminist fad" suggests that a "real" Chinese American woman would not be feminist. It also resonates with Mitsuye Yamada's discussion of her experience speaking out against injustice within the academy, for which she was accused of "functioning as a 'front for those feminists'" ("Invisibility Is an Unnatural Disaster," 36) and therefore rendered invisible. In both examples, Asian American women are seen as incapable of espousing feminist ideals on their own, unable to make decisions for themselves. Clearly, stereotypes of Asian American women as passive, childlike, and incompetent influenced the ways in which Kingston and Yamada were perceived. Indeed, the writings of Kingston and Tan have included critiques of sexism and misogynist practices within Asian American communities. However, in their attempts to reclaim traditional forms of masculinity and heroism for Asian American men, writers such as Chin censure the writings of Asian American women.

According to Cheung, this positing of Chinese nationalism against

Chinese American feminism is dangerous because it reinforces racism against Asian Americans as well as sexism within Asian American communities. She writes: "If Chinese American men use the Asian heroic dispensation to promote male aggression, they may risk remaking themselves in the image of their oppressors—albeit under the guise of Asian panoply. Precisely because the racist treatment of Asians has taken the peculiar form of sexism—insofar as the indignities suffered by men of Chinese descent are analogous to those traditionally suffered by women —we must refrain from seeking antifeminist solutions to racism. To do otherwise reinforces not only patriarchy but also white supremacy" (1990, 244). She goes on to argue that instead of adapting to "white ideals," Asian Americans must work to develop new, alternative ways of envisioning masculinity and femininity. As Lowe and Yen Le Espiritu both suggest, a significant tension at work here for Asian American cultural politics is that between feminist and nationalist concerns, a point to which I shall return in the discussion of Dictée and in the following chapter.

As a text that refuses to be representative, and in fact calls the very notion of authenticity into question, Dictée, since its publication, was largely elided by scholars and critics of Asian American literature. More recently, however, there has been a resurgence of interest in the text among Asian American as well as postmodern and poststructuralist readers, a point not lost on Wong, who suggests that its emergence from obscurity is directly related to current struggles over meaning and interpretations in both Asian American and mainstream U.S. culture (104).

In the following pages, I offer a review of existing literature about Dictée, organized around four themes that shape my own analysis: 1) displacement; 2) questions of audience; 3) processes of translation; and 4) gender, nation, and the creation of a "third space." I attempt to further contextualize my discussion of Dictée by offering some general historical information and background about Korean history, the colonization of Korea, and the Korean language, issues that are central to Cha's work. Finally, I discuss silence as a primary theme within Dictée and within Cha's other works and attempt to make critical linkages between the historical and textual silences under consideration here.

Displacement and a Persistent Silence

Theresa Hak Kyung Cha was born in South Korea in 1951. Lawrence Rinder refers to her as "a refugee [even] before birth," noting the fact that Cha's parents left Seoul just ahead of advancing Chinese and North Korean armies, seeking refuge in Pusan, at the southernmost tip of Korea, where she was born (1990, 3). Her parents then sought to escape the repressive military rule imposed on South Korea after the 1961 anti-government demonstrations, so Cha's family immigrated to the United States in 1963, when she was twelve years old.[10] They settled first in Hawaii and then moved to San Francisco in 1964. Forced to adapt to a new language and culture, Cha developed a profound sensitivity to issues of language, communication, and translation. In an artist's statement, she wrote:

> The main body of my work is with Language, "looking for the roots of the language before it is born on the tip of the tongue." Since having been forced to learn foreign languages more "consciously" at a later age, there has existed a different perception and orientation toward language.[11]

Cha's positioning as a "1.5 generation" Korean American (someone born in Korea who immigrated to the United States as a child) contributes to "a spatial-temporal liminality [that] cannot be captured by the distinctions of native-born/foreign-born or Asian or American" (Kang, 2002, 216) and a "profoundly ambiguous relationship to both the country in which [she] grew up and the country of [her] birth" (Shih 146). Cha and her sister were the only Asian students to attend an all-girls Catholic school in San Francisco, the Convent of the Sacred Heart, and as Rinder notes, "the inscription beneath Cha's photograph in her High School yearbooks reads: 'there is only one thing I dread: not to be worth my sufferings'" (1990, 3).

Cha began college at the University of San Francisco in 1968 and later transferred to the University of California at Berkeley, where she studied ceramics, conceptual art, and French film theory, focusing on psychoanalysis and semiotics. She received her bachelor's degrees in comparative literature and art, and her M.A. and M.F.A. in art. Cha was drawn to a wide range of writings during these years, reading everything from Korean poetry to European modernist writing, and claimed as her influences the writings of Samuel Beckett, James Joyce, Stephane Mallarmee, Monique Wittig, Nathalie Sarraute, and Marguerite Duras (Roth 152). In the early 1970s, she worked as a performance artist in San Francisco, combining choreographed movement, images on video, film, and slides, various objects, and her own voice (both live and recorded), and began to produce her own films and videos. She was part of an artists community there, which included Yong Soon Min, Susan Wolf, Mark Thompson, Barbara Howard, and Reese Williams and emphasized challenges to traditional forms and narratives. In one of her performance art pieces, *Reveille dans la Brume* ("awakened in or under a haze," implying a state of being not yet awake or awakened), Cha stood in the center of a dimly lit room, lit a match, and circled her arm until it went out.[12] A recording began: "Now? Not now. Now? Not yet. Now? Not just yet. And now? Not quite yet. How about now? Not quite at this moment. What about now? Not right at this time. And now? Not this time." While the light in the room changed, Cha's voice continued: "Absolute silence. Reduced silence. Guarded silence. Bound to silence. To pass over something in silence. To pass under something in silence. . . . Be this word somewhere before this word between this word just before this word even before this word even before" (Wolf 11). According to Susan Wolf, Cha attempts to explore what is not there—"to locate some meaning in the in-between" (11)—the silence. In doing so, she questions notions of time and language and forces us to consider differences among silences (absolute, reduced, guarded), as well as different reasons for silences. This differentiation among modalities of silences resonates with Cheung's analysis of literary silences among Asian American women writers, in which she argues for an understanding of not only the different forms of silence but, more importantly, the different reasons for silences.[13]

Dictée is a multigenre text in which Cha includes images (including photographs of her mother, stills from two films by Carl Dreyer, and a rather well-known image of the murder of Korean resistance fighters by Japanese soldiers during the first years of the Japanese occupation) juxtaposed with documents, letters, Chinese calligraphy, writing in Korean, and French grammar exercises, among other seemingly incongruous textual forms. Her use of space, form, and poetry suggests narrative rupture and unfixed boundaries. In the text are representations of mythology (including the nine Greek muses around whom her chapters are structured), martyrdom, religious rituals, and love. Also in Dictée is an emphasis on speaking and silence, as we, the readers, are constantly made aware of the physicality of speech and the pain of speaking (or not speaking).

Displacement is a central theme within Dictée, especially juxtaposed with the history of exile from Korea. This history is central to Dictée, and Cha engages a consistent questioning of historiography itself. Rather than establishing any historical narrative of Korea, I propose here to think about what is already known about such history, its political possibilities, as well as its elisions. Moreover, I offer a brief reading of Korean social historical events in order to contextualize my reading of Dictée. As Kenneth Wells states in his introduction to South Korea's Minjung Movement, "a nation or class or individual has not just one but many histories, and one should assume the existence of as many histories as possible" (2). Directing himself (and the anthology) to the question, How many historical paths are there? Wells concludes that the histories of Korea are turbulent, often violent. Much like Elaine H. Kim's observation that Asian Americans bear a legacy of "'becoming American' through violent disenfranchisement,"[14] Wells suggests that for Koreans, a particular "minjung consciousness," or the development of a collective historical consciousness, is directly associated with violent episodes, war, and colonization (2–3), thus the need for the construction of a specifically Korean identity through oppositional political struggle and discourse. Citing the Japanese occupation of Korea between the years 1905 and 1945, the Korean War of 1950–1953, the "neocolonial economic predations," and imposed partition of Korea by Western capitalist powers (i.e., the United States), as well as various uprisings of the people (including the 1960 student uprising, the 1980 Kwangju uprising, and, I might add, the more recent student uprising at Yonsei University in the mid-1990s), Wells suggests not only competing versions of history but violent rendings of national identity for Koreans.[15]

The Korean peninsula was the target of a great deal of foreign intervention in the nineteenth and twentieth centuries, due in part to its location between Japan and Manchuria (Kang 79). Japan and the United States made a gentlemen's agreement (the secret Taft-Katsura Pact) that the United States would not interfere with Japan's colonization of Korea if Japan would stay out of the U.S. government's plans to colonize the Philippines. Such an agreement, however covert, points to the explicit if indirect involvement of the United States in the colonization of Korea.

Japan officially annexed Korea in 1910, ruling it as a colony until 1945, when World War II came to an end. The Japanese government ruled Korea by means of a military dictatorship, through the imposition of the Japanese language, land and property seizure, fragmentation of families, censorship of publications, and an educational system aimed at producing loyal subjects for the Japanese empire. The Korean national flag, language, and traditional customs were banned, and every Korean family was forced to take on Japanese names (Kang 79). As Lowe argues, "the education of Koreans in official Japanese culture . . . depended upon the erasure of native Korean cultural practices" (1994, 45).

These events exemplify the ways in which hegemony emerges from and subsequently informs the process of colonization and colonial society. Education and language are hegemonic apparatuses that supposedly socialize "subjects" into domination by attempting to produce consenting subjects. However, the fissures or "fault lines" existing in hegemonic apparatuses of colonization are apparent throughout Dictée, engaged in part by the silences and absences strategically deployed by Cha as a means of resistance—part of the will to unsay. As Kang points out, Cha attempts to reinvoke the history of Korea by confronting a representation system that has "facilitated its erasure":

> She presents provocative alternatives to remembering: a photo of a homesick message inscribed into the Japanese earth in Han-gul, the journal entries of a Korean exile in Manchuria, a picture of three crucified martyrs, a life story of a woman revolutionary, a photograph of a massive demonstration, the letter written by Korean exiles in the U.S. to President Roosevelt requesting intervention against Japanese colonial rule. (1994, 80)

Cha's direct confrontation with the totalizing histories of Korea, which elide and erase issues of power and domination in favor of a narrative of "progress," is evidenced by the frontispiece of Dictée, in which a visual text depicts Korean writing on the wall of a tunnel in Japan. While most readers unfamiliar with Korean language might simply skip over the photograph, it contains a significant message. Presumably written by a Korean migrant laborer in Japan during Japan's occupation of Korea, the writing translates to mean "Mother / I miss you / I am hungry / I want to go home to my native place."[16] As Eun Kyung Min comments, the writing enacts a secret, as it was written during a time of extreme physical and cultural displacement of Koreans, during which the

Korean language was forcibly outlawed. As she suggests, the text on the wall "does not transcribe the spoken, foreign, and mandatory tongue but rather writes the unspeakable, forbidden mother tongue—in the enemy's land" (313). The language recorded is not the official, public language but, she asserts, a secret and familial language. In not transcribing the message, Cha invokes silence. In her presentation of the "secret" passage, she alludes to its positioning within a history and context that would just as soon erase it.

Cha's use of the frontispiece is made all the more significant when we consider the traditional function of a text's frontispiece—to provide entry into the text. As Wong suggests, Cha's frontispiece and the Korean inscription (which is read vertically from right to left) effectively push the reader right back out of the text. In other words, this frontispiece functions "not to forward narrative, but rather, to forestall it" (Wong 107). With her use of such a device, Cha disrupts not only conventions of narrative structure but what Wong refers to as a discourse of wholeness, described as a "set of ideological assumptions which has historically framed [the traditional American] narrative apparatus" (108). Whereas discourses of wholeness are frequently enacted as uncomplicated and desirable narratives of progress, signifying resolution, Dictée contests such a framework, suggesting instead that "the Korean homeland that is longed for is neither recovered nor found" (Wong 109). Similarly, by its use of Hangul, the Korean language that was forbidden at the time, the frontispiece signals the displacement—cultural, physical, and linguistic— that continues to shape Korean American life.

Another passage in the text also suggests the possible, and powerful, consequences of displacement:

> From a Far
> What nationality
> or what kindred and relation
> what blood relation
> what blood ties of blood
> what ancestry
> what race generation
> what house clan tribe stock strain
> what lineage extraction
> what breed sect gender denomination caste

what stray ejection misplaced

Tertium Quid neither one thing nor the other

Tombe des nues de naturalized

what transplant to dispel upon (20)

As a "transplant," he or she who is displaced is constantly under interrogation. Of what nationality? Kindred and relation? What blood ties and ancestry locate the individual within a genealogy and a context? What "breed sect gender denomination caste," indeed. The entire identity of an individual comes under investigation, as her visible ties—to family, nation, or history—have been severed or complicated by colonial relations. The interrogative voice, too, which questions the protagonist's place in the world, resonates with other interrogative voices that, through inducement to discourse, subject those under interrogation to domination. Within *Dictée*, both interrogation and confession operate as tools of colonialist and neo- or postcolonialist power relations, which remain intact alongside displacement from the homeland.

Displacement is also a central theme within contemporary culture, at large. As Angelika Bammer suggests, "the separation of people from their native culture either through physical dislocation (as refugees, immigrants, migrants, exiles, or expatriates) or the colonizing imposition of a foreign culture—what I am calling here displacement—is one of the most formative experiences of our century" (xi). Bammer argues as well that the very notion of "family" is disturbed by cultural displacements (91). She notes the critical distinction between one's (literal) family and one's (more symbolic) nation and draws on Simone Weil's discussion of "grounding," an argument that "the strongest affective bond . . . has been transferred—or displaced—from the private level of domestic relations ('family' in the literal sense) to the public level of community and national culture ('family' in the symbolic sense)" (93).

As in *Camp Notes* and *Obasan*, the themes of family and lineage are crucial to *Dictée* and Cha's exploration of displacement. According to Rinder, *Dictée* articulates and enacts a genealogy that is central to the traditional Korean practice of Confucianism, in which "the most sacred tie is the tie among blood relatives."[17] This argument raises significant questions about family and genealogy, history and memory, and the politics of blood. Because the imperative to remember is evident but thwarted by Cha's family's exile from Korea, both the natural continuity and the memory (and processes of memory) of filial relations are disrupted. Thus, Rinder interprets *Dictée* as an attempt by Cha to recall this genealogy and resolve her sense of displacement, through the re-creation of "relatives":

> While certain sections of the book do indeed trace strands of a familiar lineage —for example, her mother's narrative, or the story of Hyung Soon Huo, who, like her mother was exiled to Manchuria during the Japanese occupation of Korea—other voices in the text carry us much farther afield. The chapters of the book, for example, are each assigned to one of the nine Greek muses. We meet other characters: Joan of Arc, St. Therese de Lisieux, Carl Dreyer's Gertrud, and a Mrs. Laura Claxton. . . . Optimistically, one might say that to accommodate for her displacement, Cha has created a new set of filial signifiers, new "relatives" held in place not by blood ties, but by ties of desire. (1990, 9–10)

According to this analysis, Joan of Arc, Therese de Lisieux, Gertrud, Yu Guan Soon, and others become Cha's "family," in addition to her own mother.[18] Interestingly enough, though the text includes an image of three Korean men who were martyred during the Japanese occupation of Korea (39), Cha's constructed "family" (if we follow Rinder's line of thinking) consists largely of heroic, exiled, and martyred women.

For example, Yu Guan Soon, a young revolutionary Korean heroine, is depicted in a brief history in the first section of *Dictée*, entitled "Clio/ History." Yu was a martyr of the March 1 Movement of 1919, a mass demonstration against the Japanese occupation of Korea, in which she resisted and was killed by the Japanese. In *Dictée*, an image of Yu faces the words on a page:

YU GUAN SOON
BIRTH: By Lunar Calendar, 15, March 1903
DEATH: 12, October, 1920. 8:20 A.M.
She is born of one mother and one father. (24–25)

On the following pages, written in calligraphy, are the Chinese characters for "woman" and "man." The attention paid her birth and her parents places her immediately within a familial context ("one mother" and "one father"), while the specificities of the lunar calendar mark the measure and passing of time and link this particular passage to a national historical event—the colonization of Korea. Yet, while it may appear that

Yu is inserted into a fixed identity and history of origin, reinscribed into a heterosexual familial context, Wong remarks that in fact Cha unsettles every notion of a "naturalized" identity and "undermines the idea of a universal history" (124–125). For example, Wong interprets Cha's use of Chinese characters delineating "man" and "woman," rather than Hangul (Korean), as invoking the legacy of colonization of Korea by China, which preceded that of the Japanese. She points to another section of the text entitled "Calliope/Epic Poetry" that details Cha's mother's experiences as a colonial subject. Wong suggests that this use of Chinese writing (which for centuries was the "official" language of Korean history and, as noted by Kim, was "off-limits" to women) refers to the hegemony of colonization and to the "inscription of the Korean woman within a patriarchal discourse" (126). Moreover, Cha's reference to the lunar calendar, "a system of measurement of Chinese origin which predates the Gregorian calendar which has become the standard measure in the West" (Wong 125), complicates the use of calendrical time in recording Yu's life and suggests a cultural specificity and history of colonization in processes as seemingly unmediated as the passing and marking of time.

In the continuing passage about Yu, Cha writes:

> She makes complete her duration. As others have made complete theirs: rendered incessant, obsessive myth, rendered immortal their acts without the leisure to examine whether the parts false the parts real according to History's revision.
>
> > Truth embraces with it all other abstentions other than itself. Outside Time. Outside Space. Parallels other durations, oblivious to the deliberate brilliance of its own time, mortal, deliberate marking. Oblivious to itself. But to sing. To sing to. Very softly.
>
> She calls the name Jeanne d'Arc three times.
> She calls the name Ahn Joong Kun five times. (28)

While marking Yu's displacement and subsequent death, Cha's words also suggest immortality and martyrdom. To be "outside time" and "outside space" is to be rendered incessant, obsessive myth and to "make complete her duration." Later in the text, Cha writes of Yu, "The only daughter of four children she makes complete her life as others have made complete" (31). Again, her location within a family is suggested simultaneous to her dislocation from history, time, and space. As Eun Kyung Min suggests, the space occupied by martyrs is paradoxically one of both absence and presence, fractured by processes of self-erasure and sacrifice, yet bound together by memory—the Mnemosyne of the nine muses around which the text is structured (315–317). The tension lies between memory (represented most conventionally by language) and forgetfulness, linked to unspeakability (and silence). However, Cha's usage of absence and silence complicates any easy correlation between memory and language. Yu, for example, exists outside of time and space, rendered immortal by her heroic acts. Yet her relationship to representation (or lack thereof, in Korean history) is complex.

According to Kim, Yu is a central figure of *Dictée*:

> [Cha] reclaims Yu's story from official Korean History, which emphasizes the details of her torture and death, probably to underscore the virtue of individual female self-sacrifice for the benefit of the group while encouraging Korean nationalism. Cha recasts the story by emphasizing instead Yu's agency—her leadership of the "resistance group" she formed, her refusal to be pushed aside by movement activists because she was young and female, and courageous "backtalk" to the Japanese captors who eventually murdered her. Thus Cha's story has an ambivalent relationship to the Korean nationalist narrative. (16)

Yu's history is clearly one of nationalist pride within Cha's narrative structure. In the section "Clio/History," Cha writes, "There is no people without a nation, no people without ancestry. There are other nations no matter how small their land, who have their independence. But our country, even with 5,000 years of history, has lost it to the Japanese" (28). Nationalism, then, engaged in an explicit relationship with history, is represented in *Dictée* by the heroic figure of a young woman whose biography comes to stand in for the biography of the nation itself: "She is given seven years prison sentence to which her reply is that the nation itself is imprisoned. Child revolutionary child patriot woman soldier deliverer of nation. The eternity of one act. Is the completion of one existence. One martyrdom. For the history of one nation. Of one people" (37). By relating the life of Yu Guan Soon to the history of Korea, Cha emphasizes the colonization and containment of both bodies and suggests that the history of Korea is intrinsically tied to the history of this "child revolutionary." In recasting the familiar nationalist narrative in terms of women's agency and resistance, however, Cha not only refigures conceptualizations of nationalism but also disrupts common understandings of genealogy.

The history of Yu's resistance efforts, while "domesticated" through familiar Korean narratives that have emphasized her self-sacrifice and victimization, is essentially a history displaced from genealogy. As Kim notes, besides Yu, she can think of only one other woman in Korean history "whose heroism and self-sacrifice is not defined primarily through family relations" (16). Rinder's desire to place *Dictée* within a familial scheme might also be interpreted as a will to domesticate the text. Why, then, might Cha insert Yu's image and history within a framework that attends to her parentage, effectively placing Yu into a context of biological family relations? Perhaps to draw our attention to her subsequent dislocating and recasting within a tradition of other martyrs, including Joan of Arc, signifying, too, a refiguring of notions of martyrdom and historicity. In fact, by focusing on narratives of women in Korean history, Kim suggests, Cha disrupts established notions of history, while at the same time disturbing what counts as official nationalist Korean discourse.

On the one hand, Cha places Yu within a specific familial setting, emphasizing filial connection. On the other hand, she invokes women from history, not commonly associated with family relations, and in fact often remembered as exiled from home, family, and national contexts. That Cha draws on significant historical figures often elided from traditional histories is itself important to this analysis; she attempts not to simply add these women into official histories but instead explores their displacement—or their places within the "missing narratives" (e.g., the effects of their having been silenced)—relating their physical and psychological experiences of exile to their subsequent exile from history. By situating Yu within a familial context and then unsettling that context, Cha first links "family" to other themes—nation, language, time—and then not only demonstrates Yu's complex relationship to these themes but also sets out to disrupt any conventional conceptualizations of family and genealogy, suggesting the effects of colonization on family structure, psychology, and language. Yu's absence (from the struggle for independence, due to her death, from the narratives, from history itself) thus occupies a peculiar and unsettling presence. Our awareness of such absence suggests its presence. Cha writes: "Some will not know age.

Some not age. Time stops. Time will stop for some . . . not death, but the dy-ing. . . . The memory is the entire. The longing in the face of the lost" (37–38). Through her death and subsequent martyrdom, Yu's absence occupies a site not unlike that suggested by Gayatri Spivak's theory of writing "under erasure," whereby a word is written, crossed out, and then both word and deletion are printed. Spivak writes: "In examining familiar things we come to such unfamiliar conclusions that our very language is twisted and bent even as it guides us. Writing 'under erasure' is the mark of this contortion."[19] Thus, to write under erasure is to resist the silencing while also attempting to doublespeak—a precarious act at best. For Cha, this process involves recovering figures such as Yu Guan Soon from historical erasure while also exploring the processes of such erasure. It entails a process of recovery, marked as such, that must change the direction of its own speech so as to not simply reinscribe itself within the master narratives. Such a process is manifested, throughout Dictée, in Cha's strategic silences, her fractured narratives, and that which she leaves unsaid and unwritten. After her representation of Yu, she includes segments of her own handwriting, with words and passages crossed out, marked over, and/or amended (40–41). The physical appearance of these markings and unmarkings suggests the visceral quality of writing—and living—under erasure.

While experiences of material and psychological exile from Korea, recurring themes in Dictée, involve the disruption of familial ties, they also evoke and are intricately related to national and linguistic forms of displacement. As Bammer suggests, "one of the primary places where issues of national culture and family coherence come together is the question of language" (96). Similar to Rinder's description of Cha's invented relatives, Bammer explores Patricia Hill Collins's discussion of "fictive kin" among African American communities as functional responses to race and gender oppression and renegotiations of kinship structures (104). For Cha, displacement from family and nation is indeed linked to speech and language. But whereas Bammer poses the idea of language as a central, open question in various configurations among family, nation, and displacement, Rinder's analysis presumes an equation between displacement and silence, arguing that with the resolution of Cha's displacement comes speech. He interprets the following passage from Dictée as representative of Cha's displacement, thereby her inability to speak:

She mimicks [sic] the speaking. That might resemble speech. (Anything at all.) Bared noise, groan, bits torn from words. Since she hesitates to measure the accuracy, she resorts to mimicking the gestures with the mouth. The entire lower lip would lift upwards then sink back to its original place. She would then gather both lips and protrude them in a pout taking in the breath that might utter some thing. (One thing. Just one.) But the breath falls away. With a slight tilting of her head backwards, she would gather the strength in her shoulders and remain in this position. (3)

He writes that "it is through her *willful act of self-displacement*, of first becoming 'other,' that Cha regains her ability to speak . . . [thus] [b]oth the cause, and ultimately the resolution, of Cha's predicament stem from her displacement, physically and culturally, from the Confucian chain of being" (1990, 9, emphasis added). The resolution, in Rinder's interpretation, is evidenced by the following passage from *Dictée*: "She allows others. In place of her. Admits others to make full. Make swarm. All barren cavities to make swollen. The others each occupying her. Tumorous layers, expel all excesses until in all cavities she is flesh" (3). However, the image of the female figure gathering the strength in her shoulders hardly seems to represent simply an inability to speak. Rather, by implying her simultaneous strength and silence, this figure's position seems to represent a persistence and the moment prior to speech. Also, the very silence described in this passage represents an effort to speak.

Finally, that she "allows others. In place of her" seems hardly a resolution or a regaining of the ability to speak. Being spoken for does not constitute the power or agency presumed to exist in speech. Rather, it resonates with Trinh T. Minh-ha's warning and urging for the dislocated and dispossessed to unsay:

> You who understand the dehumanization of forced removal-relocation-reeducation-redefinition, the humiliation of having to falsify your own reality, your voice—you know. And often cannot say it. You try and keep on trying to unsay it, for if you don't, they will not fail to fill in the blanks on your behalf and you will be said. (1989, 80)

In contrast, Cha's text, while descriptive of the anguish of not being able to say—a process presented in such minute detail that its physicality become painful, even torturous—simultaneously invokes ways of unsaying that operate as subtextual means of resisting dominant narratives. At the same time, not all forms of speech, or saying, operate as liberatory gestures. Consider the very act of dictation, the theme of the text's title. While dictation implies a passive translation from speech to writing, or from one language to another, it also suggests a translation in which he or she who takes dictation may unsay or unname that with which he or she is presented. Eun Kyung Min suggests that dictation begins with "a primary denial, a disowning of originality and of ownership" (310); in Cha's text, the process of dictation is represented repeatedly through "unfaithful" translations that result in entirely new, different narratives.

Also, as Kim suggests, "the racial, ethnic, female, and colonial selves in *Dictée*, though 'occupied,' invaded, inhabited, dictated to, 'by law tongue tied forbidden of tongue,' are by no means passive receptacles waiting to be filled. Just as martyrdom signifies choice, not passive resignation, being occupied does not imply a prior void" (17). Rinder misses the fact that immediately after the first passage he quotes, Cha writes: "It murmurs inside. It murmurs. Inside is the pain of speech the pain to say. Larger still. Greater than is the pain not to say. To not say. Says nothing against the pain to speak. It festers inside. The wound, liquid, dust. Must break. Must void" (3). And later, in a passage to/about her mother, she writes:

> Still, you speak the tongue the mandatory language like the others. It is not your own. Even if it is not you know you must. You are Bi-lingual. You are Tri-lingual. The tongue that is forbidden is your own mother tongue. You speak in the dark. In the secret. The one that is yours. Your own. You speak very softly, you speak in a whisper. In the dark, in secret. Mother tongue is your refuge. It is being home. Being who you are. Truly. (45–46)

Speech and language, then, are never simply liberatory or oppressive. Cha's mother's usage of Japanese is a product of colonialism and the occupation of Korea by Japan. However, her secret use of Korean, in whispers, in the dark, represents her resistance and her refuge. Likewise, one's silence as a response to interrogation during colonization may also represent a form of resistance as a will to not participate in the hegemonic, dominant narrative of events. As Foucault suggests, the will to power operates both through the production and the repression of discourse. The inducement to speak does not necessarily lead to liberation or freedom—as evidenced by the mode of confession, so dominant in Western discourse and history and deployed as well in Dictée as a signifier of the speaking subject, a point to which I will return—while silence need not represent repression and/or censorship.

Finally, as Kang suggests, Cha's exile is figured in terms of her language. In the passage in which she writes, "I speak in another tongue now, a second tongue, a foreign tongue" (1994, 80), Cha designates the English that dominates her text as a language that is alien to her (Kang, 1994, 84). Neither a return to Korean language—the "mother tongue" of the text—nor a return to the homeland is possible. In both attempts, the protagonist is thwarted by the fact that language and nation are not fixed, stable entities but are transformed by time and relations of power.

Rinder's thesis focuses on displacement as the central theme in Cha's work. He considers Dictée in the context of her other work, cataloguing her oeuvre and attempting to demonstrate how displacement, linked to speech and language, operates as a central theme in all of her works. In particular, Rinder notes Cha's linkages between her own struggles with speech and memory and the history of Korea in the early part of this century, during Japanese occupation. He attempts to locate her writing within a tradition of Korean Symbolist poetry, "influenced by the spare, melancholy verse of Mallarmé, Verlaine, and Baudelaire . . . [and] inspired by a lack of faith in the ability of words to convey meaning" (1990, 12). As Rinder notes, because of increasing restrictions placed upon Korean language and education, "such speechlessness was rapidly becoming an everyday rather than merely philosophical reality" (1990, 12). Rinder also comments on the process of learning English, for Koreans, and its relationship to displacement and loss. He draws our attention to the words, by Cha, in her slide installation It Is Almost That (1977), in which she writes: "these words / (not living / not having leaved)."[20] His analysis focuses on the juxtaposition of "not living" against "not having leaved." Rinder suggests that this wording is not simply a grammatical or phonetic error; he suggests instead that "for a Korean immigrant, and metaphorically for any displaced person, who must learn a new language, it is indeed one and the same 'to live' and 'to leave'" (1990, 16). He goes on to read Cha's language use—and slippages—within the context of Freudian psychoanalytic theory, whereby displacement, or the substitution of one term for another, may represent an unconscious drive or humorous play with words. Rinder suggests that it is characteristic for Cha to "take thematic and formal approaches developed in one medium and reinterpret them in another" (1990, 1), thereby complicating notions of, for instance, visuality and speech, in textual form.

Rather than a willful act of displacement, I interpret *Dictée* as an attempt to resist both the official histories of the United States, which ignore the history of Korea, and Korean nationalist writings, which often elide the roles of women. If there is indeed a willful "othering," it is the othering of the text, resisting categorization and conventional classification. Through a willful loss of genre, and a disavowal of conventional categorization, *Dictée* represents Cha's attempt to unsay and her "refusal to partake in the story." Through her refusal to work and write within existing genres and conventions, Cha's text enacts a form of resistance to being said.

Audience, Distant Relative

In 1976, Cha studied in France with film theorists Christian Metz, Thierry Kuntzel, and Raymound Bellour and became involved with an international group of artists in Amsterdam. In 1980, she edited a film anthology called *Apparatus, Cinematographic Apparatus: Selected Writings*, including writings by theorists such as Roland Barthes, Jean-Louis Baudry, Maya Deren, and Christian Metz. As Wolf suggests,

> [A] major focus of their work is the analysis and undermining of the traditional narrative, which creates a passively perceiving subject. They attempt to disrupt the passive, dreamlike state by altering the structure of the narrative and exposing the very apparatus of cinema itself, including the technical aspects of the camera, film, and projector, and the viewing experience in a darkened theater. (12)

Cha's emphasis on the audience, their perceptions, understandings, and interpretations, is a prominent theme in all of her works. In her artist's statement, she writes: "The audience/spectator is a major consideration, from conception to realization of a piece. She/He holds a privileged place in that She/He is the receptor and/or activator central to an exchange or dialogue. . . . The audience is the subject to whom the narrative is being transmitted." In her work "Audience, Distant Relative," Cha explores the relationship between the writer/artist and the reader/viewer.[21] She concludes the piece with the following:

you are the audience
you are my distant relative
i address you
as i would a distant relative
as if a distant relative
seen only heard only through someone else's
description

neither you nor i
are visible to each other
i can only assume that you can hear me
i can only hope that you can hear me

With these words, Cha projects a crucial relationship between herself and her audience, making the audience more family members, albeit distant ones. To address an audience as one might a distant relative is to assume a connection based on shared history, familial status, or memory (presumably of shared family members or family history). Such a relationship implies a common understanding of what may go unspoken. However, a distant relative is also perceived as one who is not a close family member and therefore not someone with whom one would share intimacy or closeness. Rather, the audience is separated from Cha by a barrier that makes neither her nor the audience visible to one another. Yet, with the possibility and wish that the audience (distant relative) might hear her comes the hope that there will be mutual understanding.

Finally, the mapping of distant-relative status onto an audience member resonates with the theme of displacement, whereby families are commonly fractured, and once close family members often become distant relatives. Through separation and loss, those with whom one should share intimacy become distanced. Similarly, through constructions of performance and print media under capitalism, as well as conventional modes of readership and viewing that assume passivity and a lack of engaged interaction, a producer of art is distanced from her audience. Cha, however, as I discuss here, consistently attempts to disrupt such conventions between artist and viewer/reader. Using innovative methods, she seeks to actively engage her audience.

Questions of audience are central to Dictée, both because of Cha's own insistence on the significance of the audience and because of the attention by critics of Dictée to the identities and subject-positions of readers. Also, current debates about representation, especially about race and representation, have shifted, as Richard Fung points out, from emphases on images to "discussion[s] about appropriation and control of production and distribution" (1996, 191)—who produces, who controls, and who consumes the work. As he suggests, "much depends on who is constructed as the audience for the work" (1996, 191).[22] For the most part, earlier critics of Cha's work failed to address issues of race, ethnicity, and national belonging; specifically, they failed to address Cha's identity as a Korean American woman. As Elaine Kim notes in her introduction to Writing Self, Writing Nation, an anthology she and other writers intended as a form of intervention, "the published conversations about Dictée just beginning among a number of contemporary critics . . . largely ignored or sidelined Korea and Korean America in their discussions of the book" (ix). Kim goes on to explain the "sense of urgency" she and other writers felt about the need to bring Dictée to the attention of Asian Americans. She writes:

> We wanted our reconsideration of Cha's Dictée to address the absence of interpretations of her text both in terms of the specific histories it represents and the material histories out of which it emerges: Japanese colonialism in Korea, Korean nationalist movements (official and unofficial), Korean feminism, the Korean War, and Korean immigration to the United States. Moreover, we felt that a materialist reading of this sort, sensitive to the issues of colonialism, nationalism, race, ethnicity, gender, and class, was especially urgent. (ix)

Additionally, Kim notes in the essay she wrote for the anthology that she is far less troubled by Korean and Korean American responses to Dictée, which emphasize references to Korea to the point of perhaps missing some of the other themes, than the critical arguments of those poststructuralists and postmodernists, who ignore Cha's Korean American identity, heritage, and gender. Kim suggests that these latter omissions are meaningful and result not only in the depoliticization of the text but also enact a kind of "reverse Orientalism"—"according to which we are all the same (white) people" (1994, 22). This solipsistic gesture on the part of predominantly white Western critics reinforces the dominant cultural choice in the United States for people of color—"a mutually exclusive choice between inferior difference and invisible sameness" (1994, 22). Instead, Kim states, "I want to be able to appreciate her work in terms of her Korean American identity" (1994, 23). Kim argues for recognition of the specificities of Cha's own social location and the references and histories chronicled within *Dictée*.

At the same time, some Korean American readers of *Dictée* have expressed anxiety and frustration over their own initial readings of the text. Laura Hyun Yi Kang, designating herself a "non-innocent" reader of the text, expresses feeling a "crisis of inaccessibility/incomprehension" upon first reading *Dictée*. Bringing with her a great investment in the text and its author, as a Korean immigrant feminist writer-scholar, she recalls frustration and anger over the "slipperiness" and inaccessibility of the text and writes:

> It angered me that the text was not always accessible, that it seemed to speak to a highly literate, theoretically sophisticated audience that I did not identify with. Most of all, Cha herself remained elusive. . . . I believed that I, as a Korean/American woman, should be able to immediately understand and identify with the work of another Korean/American woman, and since that instant mirroring/attraction did not happen, either there must be something "wrong" with me or with her. (1994, 76)

Similarly, Kim writes:

> The first time I glanced at *Dictée*, I was put off by the book. I thought that Theresa Cha was talking not to me but rather to someone so remote from myself that I could not recognize "him." The most I could hope for, I thought, was to be permitted to stand beside her while she addressed "him." (1994, 3)

However, as both Kang and Kim point out, such initial conflict soon came to be recognized as relevant to the very issues surrounding questions of authenticity, identity, and language engaged by Cha in the text. Central to such issues are further questions: What does it mean to be Korean American? What are the specificities of being a Korean American woman? Is such a category homogenous and fixed, or can we imagine a destabilization of any notion of an authentic Korean American woman speaking as the representative voice?

By moving among multiple voices, Cha troubles any expectations on the part of readers of a conventional relationship between writer and reader. In fact, Cha occupies such disjunctive sites within *Dictée* as storyteller, scribe, transmitter, translator, revisioning historian, Catholic penitent, student reciter, and camera lens (Kang, 1994, 78). Her refusal of any neat or fixed relationship between herself and her presumed audience forces us, the members of her audience, to rethink our own subject positions and localities in relation to the text. Furthermore, by juxtaposing unofficial historical narratives—of Korea and its colonization by Japan, of immigration to the United States and its subsequent struggles, and of the lived experiences of Korean and Korean American women —with the more "official" histories of the United States, Cha highlights what Kang refers to as the "history-making narrativizing apparatus" regarding such events and subjects (1994, 80). Similar to the ways in which her consistent emphasis on language and the processes of speaking and writing refuse to let us forget that the text—and thus all writing, all speaking, all narration, in fact—is a cultural production, her constant focus on the audience of Dictée never lets us off the hook. Rather, our attention is drawn to the social and political processes of narrative, its visceral qualities, and again, our own subject positions in relation to the text, language itself, and contemporary understandings and norms of English language in the United States. Kang argues that Cha's "unsettling of the reader's own ethno- and logocentric notions of linguistic proficiency" is central to the text (1994, 83).

Kang goes on to argue that certain sections of the text are, indeed, written for specific audiences, for example, Korean-speaking and bilingual readers. She points out the function of the frontispiece, which is neither translated nor explained in the text and therefore, as mentioned earlier, probably ignored by a vast majority of readers who are unfamiliar with Korean language and historical context. I read Cha's employment of language and images that may be inaccessible to some readers as a further method of unsettling her audience. Being confronted by a language one cannot read produces illegibility and may result in similar feelings of linguistic displacement that a Korean immigrant experiences upon arrival to the United States. The insertion of photographs of Korean martyrs, with whom most American readers will be unfamiliar, unsettles a reader and may perhaps force one to critically interrogate the absences within one's own cultural historical narratives and frameworks. Cha's methods frustrate any attempts on the part of readers to easily know Dictée (and Cha) and to passively consume the text. Rather, we are forced to question whether it is ever now possible to simply understand and easily grasp the contents of a text, its author, and its historical contexts and meanings.

At the same time, however, Cha herself remains uneasy about her audience's reactions to Dictée. She displays an anxiety about a potentially passive, unresponsive audience. In fact, the letters written within the text—including a plea for intervention written by Koreans residing in Hawaii in the early part of the twentieth century to the president of the United States, in protest of Japan's occupation of Korea, a letter by an unknown male writer to a Mrs. Laura Claxton, and a handwritten letter to Laura Claxton signed by "A Friend"—never receive responses, never spark dialogue and engagement between two parties. Rather, as unidirectional letters, whose requests for assistance seem to go unanswered, they mirror Cha's anxieties about her own text:

> This document is transmitted through, by the same means, the same channel without distinction the content is delivered in the same style: the word. The image. To appeal to the masses to congeal the information to make bland, mundane, no longer able to transcend their own conspirator method, no matter how alluring their presentation. The response is precoded to perform predictably however passively possible. Neutralized to achieve the no-response, to make absorb, to submit to the uni-directional correspondence. (33)

To be "neutralized to achieve the no-response" is to be silenced, to be conditioned into silence. Cha, while invoking the possibilites of silence in her own work, nevertheless expresses anxiety about the potential silence surrounding Dictée. Clearly, while speech is neither guaranteed nor necessarily liberating, silence also has its pitfalls. Silences as nonresponses fail to engage. Unidirectional letters, like those of Kogawa's Aunt Emily, disappear into space. Current discussions about Dictée, however, participate in a critical discourse that, in addition to addressing the themes of the text, must also believe in keeping the work alive. As Barbara Smith suggests in her essay "Toward a Black Feminist Criticism," "for books to be real and remembered they have to be talked about. For books to be understood they must be examined in such a way that the basic intentions of the writers are at least considered" (169–170). To understand Dictée, we must address Cha's intentions and concerns. To keep it alive as a text, it is crucial that readers continue to engage in discourse about Dictée's multiple meanings. And to fully appreciate the text, according to Kang, "the reader/audience must endeavor to see and hear beyond the surface words, to imagine the unspoken and the unspeakable" (1994,

96). Thus, even her silences must be adequately acknowledged and explored; otherwise, they are simply "more point given to the silencers" (Trinh, 1989, 83).

Unfaithful to the Original

Much of the more recent (and Asian American– or Korean-centered) work about Cha, and especially about Dictée, seems to pivot around notions of translation and the idea of being "faithful to the original," both in terms of Cha's deployment of dictation as a failed translation within the text and in terms of the ways in which criticism of the text is or should be structured. Thus, Dictée engages its readers—"audience"—in questions of the dynamics of translation and in debates about ownership of and accessibility to its pages, including the very ways in which we speak and write about it.

Some writers engage questions of translation in relation to Dictée by attempting to reproduce the style and spirit of the text. For example, Walter K. Lew, in his text Excerpts from DIKTH/DIKTE For Dictée, referred to as a "critical collage," reproduces Cha's form as well as her critique of boundaries of genre. In a form that attempts to be true to the style and tone of Dictée, Lew offers a response to the "original," as well as critical homage to Cha's work. Similarly, in her essay "'Transform this Nothingness': Theresa Hak Kyung Cha's Dictée," Juliana Chang makes use of quotations from the text in an experimental work that attempts to mirror Cha's style and form.

Theories of translation studies have generally been structured around two basic, often contradictory, principles: that of being faithful to the "original" in a literal, word-for-word manner, and that of being faithful in a figurative manner—more to the spirit of the original—rather than attempting to produce an actual verbatim translation. As Lowe suggests, "at the root of most translation polemic is the ideal of equivalence, whether literal, spiritual, or cultural, which serves to hold up translation as an emblem for the ethos of fidelity" (1994, 42; emphasis added). As she points out, what are made invisible are the actual power relations at work in any cultural, linguistic relationship: "the power of one nation state to determine not merely the language but the material conditions of another people" (1994, 42).

Translation as a practice and a concept highlights conditions of inequality, especially within colonial and postcolonial settings. The asymmetrical relations of power underscored by translation are evident when we examine the history of translation and its assumptions. According to Tejaswini Niranjana, the necessity of translation, in the case of England's colonization of and linguistic control over India, relied on three assumptions: 1) that Europeans required translations of Indian texts because the natives were "unreliable interpreters of their own laws and culture"; 2) that European rulers, as lawgivers, desired to "give the Indians their 'own' laws" and therefore needed to adequately understand them; and 3) that translation could "'purify' Indian culture and speak on its behalf" (13). Thus, loyal subjects to the empire desired to learn English (which provided new ways of seeing the world and themselves), and English administrators and lawgivers desired to possess knowledge of Indian languages in order to better rule and govern their subjects (and, as Niranjana points out, because they could not trust the "natives" to translate "faithfully") (16).

Niranjana suggests that a large component of the oppressive nature of translation, as it has been conventionally understood, involves the assumption that it can represent reality and that such representation "provides direct, unmediated access to a transparent reality" (2). In fact, translation "is always producing rather than merely reflecting or imitating an 'original'" (81). Not only, she argues, is translation never a neutral process, but its reliance on notions of fidelity and betrayal preclude questions about the historicity of translation. She writes, "The colonial subject is constituted through a process of 'othering' that involves a teleological notion of history, which views the knowledge and ways of life in the colony as distorted or immature versions of what can be found in 'normal' or Western society" (11). Thus, through colonialism's deployment of the technology of translation, the "Hindu"—or, more broadly, the "Oriental"—is rendered a discrete, exoticized creation—essentialized, decontextualized, and fixed in time and place. Such a subject (or nation) is placed in direct opposition to the "emancipated" Western subject (or nation). Translation as a process, then, operates alongside other colonial projects in establishing a hierarchical binary opposition between the West and the so-called Third World. Chandra Talpade Mohanty argues that one of the basic (and most instrumental) premises of hegemonic imperialism involves the distinctions established between "us" and "them"—social, political, economic, cultural, and discursive. To say that translation operates within such systems of nonequivalence is to acknowledge its complicity within systems of domination.

Similarly, while the topos of dictation suggests an even process from one mode (speaking) to another (writing) and an equivalence between the two, Cha's text disrupts any such notions. Instead, in Dictée, as Lowe suggests, students fail to obey the rules of dictation and translation; the colonized subject expresses antagonism to the empire to which it is socialized *as* subject; the religious subject fails to measure up to God, in whose image he or she is supposedly created; and the racialized citizen embodies "discontinuous"—even contradictory—ideologies and politics to the state. Translations fail. Scribes do not obey the rules of dictation. And we are left with an incommensurability suggestive of the unequal relationships between dominant and subordinate groups.

While both translation and dictation are processes through which the student presumably learns the rules and language of another, usually dominant group and is expected to reproduce in such a manner that is considered not only "faithful" but uniform, dictation is, as Lowe suggests, "at once a sign for the authority of language in the formation of the student, a model for the conversion of the individual into a subject of discourse through the repetition of form, genre, and example, and a metaphor for the many regulating reproductions to which the narrator is subject in spheres other than the educational" (1994, 39). In Dictée, the process of dictation is internally contradictory, as evidenced by the "deviations from the model." Lowe writes: "The subject of Dictée recites poorly, stutters, stops, leaves verbs unconjugated. She fails to imitate the example, is unfaithful to the original" (1994, 39).

An example from the text serves to illustrate this point. In the first section of Dictée, "Clio/History," Cha juxtaposes two paragraphs, one in French, the other in English, as a response to the query, "How was the first day?":

Aller à la ligne   C'était le premier jour   point   Elle venait de loin   point
ce soir au dîner   virgule   les familles demanderaient   virgule   ouvre
les guillemets   Ça c'est bien passé le premier jour   point d'interrogation
ferme les guillemets   au moins   virgule   dire le moins possible   virgule   la réponse serait   virgule   ouvre les guillemets   Il n'y a q'une
chose   point   ferme les guillemets   ouvre les guillemets   Il y a
quelqu'une   point   loin   point   ferme les guillemets

Open paragraph   It was the first day   period   She had come from a far

period   tonight at dinner   comma   the families would ask   comma

open quotation marks   How was the first day   interrogation mark   close

quotation marks   at least to say the least of it possible   comma   the an-

swer would be   open quotation marks   there is but one thing   period

There is someone   period   From a far   period   close quotation marks.

(1)

According to Kang, the question "seeks an account of the beginning of
immigration and resettlement . . . [and its interrogator is] foiled by the
striking absence of an 'I' in the response" (2002, 220–221). Rather,
Cha suggests an incommensurability between the spoken and the written and between two unequal subjects, where the translating "student"
repeats even the punctuation of the passage, reproducing verbatim each
spoken word. In addition, the sentences are literally translated, resulting in an awkward, stultifying, and somewhat confusing translation. By
translating not only the verbal text of the "teacher's" instruction but also
the punctuation and grammar commands, the student fails the task and
simultaneously disrupts the lesson, enacting, in Lowe's words, a "failed
subjection" (1994, 41). In addition, as she writes:

> Ironically, "faithful" verbatim translation does not "say it as simply as pos-
> sible," and is often the least exact in transmitting the contextualized mean-
> ing of a phrase. Thus, the nonequivalence of the French and English text . . .
> thematizes the failure of translation as a topos of faithful reproduction. The
> discontinuity of the two examples evinces not merely a disjunction in the
> process of translation, but the choice of English as the translating language
> further registers the increased suppression of the Korean language with the
> imposition of each Western colonial language. (1994, 41)

Lowe contextualizes this example within the history of French Catholic missionary colonialism in Korea beginning in the early nineteenth
century and American imperialism in Korea more recently. By addressing the influence of French language and linguistic rule with another
"foreign" and imposed language—English—Lowe suggests that Cha
marks the site of Dictée as a "layered and shifting configuration, unevenly
'dictated' by several Western colonial languages, French, as well as English" (1994, 40). In other places, Japanese language and colonization of
Korea is called up to engage issues of American occupation and impe-

rialism and vice versa. Thus, not only does Cha suggest multiple levels
—and layerings—of colonialism in Korea's history, but she also ties
such histories to the acts of dictation and translation.

As a central theme of the text, evinced by its title, dictation calls up
multiple meanings as well. To dictate is to speak or read aloud something that is to be written by another, but it is also to rule, to command,
and to impose authority over another (person or nation). Thus, dictation
is hardly a process removed from unequal power relations. Also, because
the text's title is "dictée," a French word (rather than its equivalent in
English or Korean), the reader is immediately engaged in the very process Cha wishes us to examine—that of transcription or translation. As-
sociating Japan's political colonization of Korea to its linguistic domination, she writes: "Japan has become the sign. The alphabet. The vocabulary.
To this enemy people. The meaning is the instrument, memory that pricks
the skin, stabs the flesh, the volume of blood, the physical substance
blood as measure, that rests as record, as document. Of this enemy people" (32). In her attention to the particularity of the experiences of Koreans under domination, she emphasizes the physicality of the events.
It is the blood of the people that documents their history. And (Korean)
language has all but disappeared, as Koreans—the unnamed referents to
Japan's "sign"—are rendered invisible. The imposed vocabulary is thus
a language of repression and domination.

Simultaneously, Cha embeds the nonequivalence of translation in the
relationship between history and History. In her thematization of Japan's
colonization of Korea, Cha demonstrates the impossibility of equivalence
between "official" versions of history and the material and physical realities faced by those who survived (Japanese) annexation and continue
to live under (U.S.) occupation. For example, according to Wong, Cha
suggests that "History" with a capital "H" glosses over and elides the
specificities of particular histories (111). Juxtaposing such histories, Cha
insists on specificity in the accounts, noting that to outsiders, this history
has been "neutralized to achieve the no-response." Its translations gloss
over relations of domination and subordination, erase the physicality of
the violence used to maintain such inequality, and render the history ab-
stract and unfathomable.

> To the other nations who are not witnesses, who are not subject to the
> same oppressions, they cannot know. Unfathomable the words, the terminol-

ogy: enemy, atrocities, conquest, betrayal, invasion, destruction. They exist only in the larger perception of History's recording, that affirmed, admittedly and unmistakably, one enemy nation has disregarded the humanity of another. Not physical enough. Not to the very flesh and bone, to the core, to the mark, to the point where it is necessary to intervene, even if to invent anew, expressions, for this experience, for this outcome, that does not cease to continue.

To the others, these accounts are about (one more) distant land, like (any other) distant land, without any discernable features in the narrative, (all the same) distant like any other. (32–33)

Yet Cha remains steadfast in her objective, not necessarily to "tell the truth of what happened," as if there can be one truth to be exposed and known, but to examine the ways in which History has elided relations of power and processes of oppression. She writes: "Why resurrect it all now. From the past. History, the old wound. The past emotions all over again. To confess to relive the same folly. To name it now so as not to repeat history in oblivion. To extract each fragment by each fragment from the word from the image another word another image the reply that will not repeat history in oblivion" (33). To not "repeat history in oblivion," that history—all the histories—must be named, resurrected from the past, and extracted even in its fragmentation. Cha never proposes a master narrative, an unfragmented History. Rather, in her refusal of such a construct, she suggests that total and totalizing histories are themselves part of the dictation that she attempts to disrupt and challenge. Thus, historical silences are marked by Cha as dangerous and totalizing. According to Kang, Cha "draws critical attention to the writing of history as a discursive production that illuminates and occludes certain details. . . . Dictée foregrounds the historiographical dilemma of attempting to access the past by way of previously written accounts" (2002, 225). Thus, in a context in which speech is so often controlled, permitted only in the language of the dominant group, silences—and acts of unsaying—serve as strategies of disruption.

One of the primary vehicles for such disruption in Dictée is the figure of the "diseuse." This figure, the fortune teller, seer, speaker, and scribe "thwarts authoritarian beginnings and endings" (Wong 121) through her failed translations and dictations. "She mimicks [sic] the speaking," a mimicking, as Wong states, "'that might resemble speech' (3) but which does not quite reproduce the original. Her method seems always to be that of unfaithful translation" (Wong 121). In fact, she is often silent. Such processes of disruption serve to "unname" and unsettle. Because translation "always proposes an original only to insist on a simultaneous departure from the original" (Wong 119), Cha's deployment of it suggests its complicity in the reproduction of systems of dominance. In the section of her text in which she engages the act of confession and the observation of Catholic rituals, in particular the dictation of the catechism, Cha again juxtaposes a version of the "original" with its failed translation in order to demonstrate a nonequivalence:

Q: WHO MADE THEE?

A: God made me.

To conspire in God's Tongue. . . . Accomplice in His Texts, the fabrication in His Own Image, the pleasure and desire of giving Image to the word in the mind of the confessor.

Q: GOD WHO HAS MADE YOU IN HIS OWN LIKENESS.

A: God who has made me in His own likeness. In His Own Image in His Own Resemblance, in His Own Copy, in His Own Counterfeit Presentment, in His Duplicate, in His Own Reproduction, in His Cast, in His Carbon, His Image and His Mirror. Pleasure in the image pleasure in the copy pleasure in the projection of likeness pleasure in the repetition. Acquiesce, to the correspondance [sic]. . . . Theirs. Into Their tongue, the counterscript, my confession into Theirs. Into Theirs. To scribe to make hear the words, to make sound the words, the words, the words made flesh. (17–18)

Juxtaposing the original—God—with the variants of reproduction, including "resemblance," "copy," "counterfeit," "duplicate," "cast," "carbon," and "mirror," Cha demonstrates the nonequivalence of God, the ruler, with those who are expected to be faithful translators of "His" image and message. Created to "conspire in God's tongue," Catholic subjects are expected to reproduce faithfully. Yet, the adjectives Cha uses imply neither equivalence nor faithful translation. Rather, they articulate the "sins" that distance and remove her from "God the creator": sins of "female otherness, racial and ethnic Korean alterity, colonial difference" that adulterate the catechism and parodically thematize the presumption of faithful religious subjection through equivalence (Lowe, 1994, 58–59).

In addition, Cha offers a challenge to the forced fluency implicit in her words "Acquiesce. . . . Theirs. Into Their Tongue" (18). Inducement into a language that dominates presents a problem for the narrator, who has already, in her image, failed the task of translation. Speaking, in this context, is marked as acquiescence and signals one's subjection. What might silence symbolize? As Lowe argues, Cha makes use of "tongue" in multiple and distinct ways throughout the text, as both organ and language, linking linguistic domination to physical, material violence and rupturing. She writes:

> Throughout *Dictée*, the processes of coming to speech in the imposed language of French, Japanese, or English, are thematized as simultaneously both a "forced fluency" that obliterates and silences differences, and the instrumental means of voicing an oppositional utterance: moving through those forced fluencies—naming them through parody, disrupting signification, and composing coherence through fragmentation—she articulates a hybrid, nuanced, "unfaithful" voice. (1994, 47)

Such a process of oppositional utterance is demonstrated in the section of the text entitled "Calliope / Epic Poetry." In this section, in which Cha addresses her mother, she notes that during the Japanese colonization, when her mother was eighteen years old, Koreans were forced to speak Japanese:

> You speak the tongue the mandatory language like the others. It is not your own. Even if it is not you know you must. You are Bi-lingual [sic]. You are Tri-lingual [sic]. The tongue that is forbidden is your own mother tongue. . . .
> They seek you, inhabit you whole, suspend you airless, spaceless. They force their speech upon you and direct your speech only to them. (45, 50)

Not only was her mother forced to take on Japanese language, but as a teacher she was also expected to reproduce faithful compliance in her students in order to socialize the Korean children into Japanese language and colonial rule, to prepare them for their subjection to the empire. Yet she resists, secretly, by retaining her own language and by claiming her "mother tongue" as refuge and as home:

> You speak in the dark. In the secret. The one that is yours. Your own. You speak very softly, you speak in a whisper. In the dark, in secret. Mother tongue is your refuge. It is being home. Being who you are. Truly. . . .

You write. You write you speak voices hidden masked you plant words to the moon you send word through the wind. (45–46, 48)

When she is unable to speak her own language "in the secret," she relies on silence. Thus, the dictation is incomplete, and the subject—Cha's mother, Huo Hyung Soon—fails the task of "faithful" translation. Her voice, enacting a gesture of doublespeak, represents both the forced fluency and the oppositional utterance, however furtive, described by Lowe.

As dictation, translation requires of students a submission to the realm of the knowable or what is considered knowable. As such, the student is required to "submit to prohibitions against what cannot be said and consents to closures that eliminate the unsayable, which refuse the indeterminate and inadmissible. That uniformity of genre depends upon regulated omissions" (Lowe, 1994, 40). Dictée, with its parodies of fidelity, its consistent rupturing of "master" and totalizing, whole narratives, and its critique of translation, engages its readers in examinations of the parameters of language. Of such parameters, Kang writes: "The systematic suppression of the native language in favor of the colonizer's lagnuage, the patriarchal idealization of female silence, the racist devaluation of 'pidgin' English, the religious obligation to make a true confession, and the classroom exercises for inducting students into normative grammar and spelling are all invoked as instances in which language is a formidable medium of social, political, and psychic subjection" (2002, 220). Speaking from a subject position of liminality, Cha not only questions any assumptions of equivalence but also suggests that we explore what is not spoken or written, what can never be faithfully translated. It is in the silent spaces, alluded to throughout her text, that we gain access to that which has been effaced from history and discourse.

Gender, Nation, and the Third Space

Kim suggests that Dictée, in its refusal of the narratives of both Korean nationalists and Western feminists (at least as they are commonly interpreted, as mutually exclusive), celebrates a kind of "third space":

> An exile space that becomes a source of individual vision and power. Indeed, far from dropping a specific identity in favor of endless difference, she predicts the breakdown of binaries that are part of the logic of domination. She

foregrounds a highly specific cultural context, inserting Korea, Korean women, and Korean Americans into the discourse, thereby opening the space for an individual search for selfhood as a non-reified, non-essentialized collectivity. (1994, 8)

Cha's text, then, fits well with Kim's own search from a "space where 'woman' and 'Korean' might work together" (1994, 7). In fact, Kim's personal history and identity are central to her critical analysis. She explains in a footnote by writing: "I insert myself into the picture that is supposed to be 'about' Dictée because it, unlike other texts, gives me multiple points of entry and feelings of ownership. It is mine and not mine at the same time. Besides, I have concluded from reading many other critiques of Asian American writings that we are mostly just pretending not to be writing about ourselves in our critiques" (1994, 23, fn. 2).

Cha's creation of a "third space" must be critically examined also within a context of erasure and invisibility of Korean and Korean American history, culture, and identity. Kim establishes this notion of an exile space within such a context—a significant point to make regarding Dictée. As Kim points out, little is known of Korean history, culture, and language outside of Korea, and even great inventions and achievements of Koreans —sources of pride and accomplishment—have been appropriated by other, dominant cultures.[23] Even though the United States and other Western powers have been crucial to the subordination of Korea and have negatively affected the nation's autonomy and history, these nations fail to recognize their own role in Korea's colonization and remain unaware of the nation's context. Kim notes that the two martyred Korean patriots named in Dictée, Yu Guan Soon and Ahn Joong Kun, "are familiar to virtually everyone in North and South Korea, but they are completely unknown in the West, where little is known even about the Japanese colonization or the national division, two events that shaped the lives of millions of people from the turn of the century to the present, despite the fact that the U.S. played a crucial role in both. Dictée suggests that this effacing of Korean history in the West may be the result of the willful indifference often exhibited by the powerful in colonial and neo-colonial relations" (1994, 10). In contrast, Dictée insists on the reality and cultural history of Korea and Korean Americans in opposition to their absence and/or erasure from Western historical discourse and consciousness.

Similarly, while the text, as Kim puts it, is in many ways a contradictory one, "its paradoxes rooted in Cha's location in the interstitial outlaw spaces between Korea and America, North and South, inside and outside, and between the world of the Western *artiste* and the specific Korean nationalist impulses she inherited from her mother. . . . [and] she focuses on the 'in-between'—the cracks, crevices, fissures, and seams that, when revealed, challenge hypnotic illusions of seamless reality— Cha insists on the specificity of her Korean American identity" (1994, 21). The writing is always rooted in her multi-varied, yet specific subject position. In her reclamation of liminal and interstitial spaces, she points not only to the fracturing of the historical record but also to the power of silence as a will to unsay and an intervention into the dominant narrative.

With its emphasis on spatial relations, border crossings, and the partition of Korea, *Dictée* does indeed evoke a sort of "third space." In its refusal to partake in dominant narratives, Cha's "third space" uses silence and rupture as forms of discourse and resistance. Similar to other liminal zones, such as the site of lesbianism suggested by Wittig, the frontera of Anzaldúa's *Borderlands*, the "very house of difference" articulated by Lorde, the gendered and sexualized "space off" of Teresa de Lauretis's "technology" of gender, and Chela Sandoval's theory of "oppositional consciousness,"[24] Cha's strategies rely on spatial and visual epistemologies as well as gaps, absences, silence(s).

The third space of the text provides a site in which to examine the ways that Cha invokes silence in *Dictée*. Critical disruptions within the text, characterized not only by a lack of formal structure and narrative but also the absence of comprehensibility and conventional "readability," serve to unsettle the reader. Jarred out of complacency, members of Cha's "audience" are forced to reexamine what we know of history and what "counts" as history, as well as notions of visibility, visuality, language, and translation. She changes her language(s); she disrupts the structure time and time again. She decenters and undermines the "I" of *Dictée* while constantly foregrounding her own subject-positionality.

Cha structures a liminal space along boundaries of citizenship and borders like that created within Korea to partition the North and the South. To "become American" is to cross over, to be "uni formed" as a singular, discrete subject, and to be made over into the image of what is considered truly American. Furthermore, to be American requires proof of existence in the official—documented—narrative. Cha writes:

> I have the documents. Documents, proof, evidence, photograph, signature. One day you raise the right hand and you are American. They give you an American Pass port. The United States of America. Somewhere someone has taken my identity and replaced it with their photograph. The other one. Their signature their seals. Their own image. And you learn the executive branch the legislative branch and the third. Justice. Judicial branch. It makes the difference. The rest is past. (56)

American status is evidenced by visual documentation. In this scenario, "they" have replaced the speaker's image and identity with their own.[25] Not only must she sacrifice her previous identity, but she is also required to be educated in the language and narrative of this new, more powerful, government that refuses to acknowledge her presence before becoming American. As Priscilla Wald suggests, the passport itself makes apparent and visible the fact that the transformation (into American identity) is incomplete, as her documentation is absolutely required as evidence of her status as American. Also, the narrator experiences her identity as both stolen possession and estrangement. Her induction into a new, legislated (and selective) narrative that passes over the "rest," to Wald, suggests the clear distinction made between the stories "that can be told and those that cannot" (301). Thus, Cha examines the processes —and limits—of narration.

Similarly, the return "home" is also marked by a border crossing that transforms both sides of the border.

> You return and you are not one of them, they treat you with indifference. All the time you understand what they are saying. But the papers give you away. . . . They ask you identity [sic]. They comment on your ability or inability to speak. Whether you are telling the truth or not about your nationality. They say you look other than you say. As if you didn't know who you are. You say who you are but you begin to doubt. They search you. They, the anonymous variety of uniforms, each division, strata, classification, any set of miscellaneous properly uni formed. They have the right, no matter what rank, however low their function they have the authority. Their authority sewn into the stitches of their costume. . . . The eyes gather towards the

appropriate proof. Towards the face then again to the papers, when did you leave the country why did you leave this country why are you returning to the country. . . .

Not a single word allowed to utter until the last station, they ask to check the baggage. You open your mouth half way. Near tears, nearly saying, I know you I know you, I have waited to see you for long this long. They check each article, question you on foreign articles, then dismiss you. (56–58)

The "return" signals a return home, experienced as both anxiety and longing by the narrator, who has "waited to see you for long this long." But she is no longer "one of them." The same papers that grant entry on one side of this imaginary border preclude belonging on the other side. Not only the documentation but language and appearance, too, mark one as insider or outsider. The "uni formed" border guards who question and doubt her identity force her to do the same. While their authority is "stitched" into the fabric of their uniforms, they also dominate the situation by virtue of their unquestioned belonging and her desire to belong. Near tears, she seeks their acceptance of her, their acknowledgment that she is "one of them." Yet they refuse to see or hear her; they dismiss her. Wald suggests that it does not matter whether we view this particular crossing as a return to the birth country of Korea or the adopted home of the United States. Either way, she argues, its tensions expose the contradictions of national narratives. She writes,

> For American border guards, she [the narrator] embodies a particular anxiety. If she is one of them, then they become unrecognizable to themselves. If she, an American, is excluded, then she embodies a displaced person—the consequences of not belonging and the possibility of their own exclusion as well. The narrator of Dictée confronts the contradiction of national narratives at cross purposes; an inclusive narrative comes into conflict with a competing exclusive narrative that brings a nonwhite, foreign-born American's identity into doubt [which is] contagious and destabilizing. (302–303)

Yet it seems that the narrator's exclusion, as a displaced person, serves also to reinforce the inclusion of the border guards. Her status as outsider reinforces their location within the parameters of the hegemonic norm. As Mohanty indicates, it is the margins that, in their boundedness, establish the center of power and the significance of belonging

("Under Western Eyes," 73–74). In addition, I read this particular border crossing as a return to Korea and suggest that it *does*, in fact, matter where this incident takes place. To have waited "this long" and to desire recognition suggests a return "home" that is no longer possible. Significantly, at this border crossing, she is not permitted to speak. Her words, "I know you I know you," are never uttered. "They" do not know her and refuse to hear what is unspoken (unspeakable?). Leaving the nation of origin, Cha seems to suggest, situates her narrator in perpetual displacement and exile. A return to Korea is marred by the events surrounding the original departure, and thus, "home" itself has been transformed, both materially and psychologically.

Cha suggests as much when she reflects on the time period of the narrator's original departure from Korea. In the section "Melpomene/Tragedy," she includes a map of Korea, with the DMZ border between North and South Korea boldly demarcated (78). This visual image of the partition of Korea precedes a letter to the narrator's mother, written during the return visit to Korea. She writes:

> Our destination is fixed on the perpetual motion of search. Fixed in its perpetual exile. Here at my return in eighteen years, the war is not ended. We fight the same war. We are inside the same struggle seeking the same destination. We are severed in Two by an abstract enemy an invisible enemy under the title of liberators who have conveniently named the severance, Civil War. Cold War. Stalemate. (81)

Cognizant of the fact that the United States, her new "home" and nation, was the imperial power responsible for partitioning her own country, she relates the fracturing of Korea to her own internal fragmentation. The dramatic splitting of Korea, as a nation broken apart by external forces and remembered as a betrayal and a tragedy, is reflected in Cha's language when she writes, "*Imaginary borders. Un imaginable boundaries.* / Suffice more than that. SHE opposes Her. SHE against her" (87). The partition, represented as a self divided, "SHE opposing Her," is likened to war and to an "insect that eats its own mate":

> Others anonymous *her* detachments take her place. Anonymous against *her*. Suffice that should be nation against nation suffice that should have been divided into two which once was whole. Suffice that should diminish human

breaths only too quickly. Suffice Melpomene. Nation against nation multi-
plied nations against nations themselves. Own. Repels her rejects her expels
her from her own. Her own is, in, of, through, all others, hers. . . .

Violation of her by giving name to the betrayal, all possible names, interchangeable names, to remedy, to justify the violation. Of her. Own. Unbegot-
ten. Name. Name only. Name without substance. The everlasting, Forever.
Without End.

Deceptions all the while. No devils here. Nor gods. Labyrinth of deceptions. No enduring time. Self-devouring. Devouring itself. Perishing all the
while. Insect that eats its own mate. (88)

The partition, remembered by Cha's narrator and other Koreans as a violation, is incomprehensible to "anonymous" though powerful outsiders,
who view the splitting as remedy, justify it with their own notions of
progress and reform, and, in the end, have difficulty distinguishing Korea and Koreans from other "foreign" places and "foreigners." These
places and people are seen as simply interchangeable. Yet the unending
violent intervention, enacted in the name of assistance, continues to
plague the nation. "Perishing all the while," the nation—and *Dictée*'s
narrator—eats at itself with internal contradiction, division, and deceit.
A narrative of wholeness is envisioned as both positive resolution and
impossibility.

Cha's narrator also remembers a simultaneous, more personal tragedy
—the death of her brother, who was part of the student demonstrations
that took place eighteen years earlier:

My brother. You are all the rest all the others are you. You fell you died you
gave your life. That day. . . . After it was all over. You were heard. Your victory mixed with rain falling from the sky for many days afterwards. I heard
that the rain does not erase the blood fallen on the ground. I heard from the
adults, the blood stains still. Year after year it rained. The stone pavement
stained where you fell still remains dark.

Eighteen years pass. I am here for the first time in eighteen years, Mother.
We left here in this memory still fresh, still new. I speak another tongue, a
second tongue. This is how distant I am. From then. From that time. (85)

The brother, figured as the whole ("You are all the rest all the others are
you"), is martyred for the cause. His blood stains still, and he was "heard,"
finally. Yet, Cha's narrator, having become an American, is distant from

that time and place now. Speaking another language, having had her identity replaced by "their image," she struggles to find herself back in the memory of this tragic event. The blood of her brother, affirming his identity as forever Korean, reminds her of her own exile, which she contextualizes against the partition of Korea. As Chungmoo Choi suggests, nationalist movements in Korea focus on issues of national unification, and in the minjung consciousness, national reunification is "coterminous with decolonization" (1995, 105). To point repeatedly to the partition of Korea, then, is to refuse any denial of the colonization of Korea by both Japan and the United States. To be located within the "third space" of a specifically gendered and racialized body is to inhabit a subject position that has become representative of both American colonizer and resistant Korean subject of colonialism. Cha claims all of these so-called contradictory spaces through memory and discourse, making meaning of silence through the "in-between," the interstitial and "outlaw" spaces that force recognition of the fissures within dominant and totalizing narratives. Cha's juxtapositioning of her own specific histories with national, totalizing histories of both Korea and the United States suggests the instability and inability of hegemonic narratives to contain the unofficial stories that continue to "bleed" through.

Cha produced more than a dozen films and videos, including *Passages Paysages*, *Re Dis Appearing*, *Exilée*, and the unfinished *White Dust from Mongolia*. She created dozens of writings and works on paper, including art books such as "Pravda/Istina," "Markings," "Tongue Tied," and "Chronology." In 1981 she was appointed instructor in video art at Elizabeth Seaton College in New York. In 1982, the year she died, she published *Dictée*. At the time of her death, according to Moira Roth, Cha was working on a piece about the representation of hands in Western painting, "[a] study of cultural differences using hands as a metaphor" (157).

Dictée is a text often referred to as unclassifiable. It engages issues of language, memory, time, visuality, history, and autobiography. It combines several different writing styles, different voices, and different kinds of narrative strategies and devices. The wide range of Cha's work speaks to her desire to question and cross established boundaries as well as her interest in the theoretical implications behind the problematizing of existing genres. As Wolf points out, "we are constantly made aware of the process of writing in explicit ways: pages of rough draft are included, as is a handwritten letter; punctuation is spelled out at times; exercises in

French grammar are used to illustrate the imposition of a foreign culture and way of thought and being, and some passages are printed in both English and French" (13). The relationship and distinctions between writing and speaking are central to *Dictée*, as are critical distinctions between the writer (scribe) and the speaker or "teller" (*diseuse*; fortune-teller, truth-teller, soothsayer). To form letters or characters, to inscribe the memories, parallels the pain and necessity of utterance, verbalization and language, while at the same time representing a completely different mode of communication and historicization. In *Dictée*, Cha experiments with form and genre to engage questions about historicization, nation, genealogy, immigration and transmigration, and the losses and ruptures of translation. How is it possible to express and inscribe a history of a nation —of Korea? How are we to tell the history of Yu Guan Soon, young Korean woman revolutionary? How is it possible to convey one's own experience of immigration to and naturalization within the United States? What is involved and what gets lost in the process of translation?

Language provides a method of expression and communication, but it is closely circumscribed by colonialism, racism, and male dominance. In addition, the dominant narratives of the United States fail to recognize unofficial histories that point to its violence against and domination of other nations, including Korea. Such narratives also leave little room for persons who are not part of the hegemonic and "uni formed" structure of its establishment and institutions. As such, "Korean" and "American" are rarely seen as equivalent or coterminous. While language marks identity and belonging, it, too, is marked by borders such as those of history, nation, and citizen.

In *Dictée*, Cha problematizes both speech and silence. Like Kingston, Yamada, and Kogawa, she does so in order to question the dominant historical narratives that have excluded her. While silencing has been a negative and oppressive force for Asian American women, Cha argues that speech, too, is complicated by relations of power and nonequivalence. Though silence risks dismissal and erasure, Cha suggests that it also operates as a form of language and a means of resistance. In her essay about *Dictée*, Kang discusses her own multiple relations to language and silence, writing about the increasing significance, for Asian Americans, of discussions about silence. As noted in this book's introductory chapter, a central theme within Asian America has revolved around "breaking silence" and "coming to voice." In a context of deliberate political suppression and historical censorship of Asian American writing, as well as a proliferation of stereotypes about Asian Americans, such a move makes sense. However, like Kang, I, too, am troubled by questions of power. While language can be a site of resistance and empowerment, she notes, "I am troubled by the questions of who is served and who is excluded from its discursive field" (1994, 74). Commenting on her own ambivalent relationship to language, she writes:

> I am evaluated, misunderstood, affirmed, ignored, congratulated, disdained depending on shifting and often contradictory combinations of how I look, in what language(s) I speak, whether I am silent or surprisingly eloquent, how I talk (with or without an accent), who I may be speaking to/with. Knowing these things about how I am (un)seen and (un)heard, I do not delude myself into thinking that I live within easy and immediate grasp of such a thing as "My Authentic Voice," which, only if it were allowed—by whom? —to be freed from the secret shame and powerlessness of its long suppression, would find some appropriate outlet and common audience in an impartial and unmediated language. (1994, 73–74)

Language and discourse enable communication and provide a significant site from which to challenge narratives of exclusion and violence. However, forms of language are not equivalent in the current social and political context, as evidenced by the intense silencing experienced by Asians in the United States. Through her experiments with varied forms of discourse, including silence, Cha suggests critical distinctions among processes of speaking, (un)saying, and "being said." She writes: "Being broken. Speaking broken. Saying broken. Talk broken. Say broken. Broken speech. Pidgon [sic] tongue. Broken word. Before speak. As being said. As spoken. To be said. Then speak" (161).

This night will forever remain outside articulation. . . .
—Hershini Bhana, "How to Articulate the Inarticulable I, II, and III"

five

Silence and Public Discourse:
Interventions into Dominant National and
Sexual Narratives in Nora Okja Keller's
Comfort Woman and Anchee Min's *Red Azalea*

Women's sexuality has been conceptualized as a site of and for both pleasure and danger. In recent years, feminist theorists have attempted to interrogate the multiple roles sexuality perform in women's lives in relation to categories of identity as well as social, historical, political, and economic contexts and transitions. As Carole Vance suggests, "Sexuality is simultaneously a domain of restriction, repression, and danger as well as a domain of exploration, pleasure, and agency" (1). To focus on either pleasure or danger at the exclusion of the other leaves women at risk of overlooking either the oppressive, patriarchal contexts of their lives or the ways in which women demonstrate agency as well as resistance to oppression.

For Asian American women, sexuality must be contextualized against a history of denigrating stereotypes about Asian women's deviant sexuality, erotic sensibilities, and exotic sexual practices.[1] Linked to these images are representations constructed by Western feminist writers, in which Asian and other Third World women are conceptualized only as victims, especially where sexuality is concerned.[2] Also, globally, Asian women bear a unique relationship to prostitution and the sex industry not only because of stereotypes but also through imperialist and capitalist expansion into Asian nations, United States and other Western powers' occupation of and subsequent demand for prostitution economies within Asian countries, and the nineteenth- and early-twentieth-century U.S. history of unequal sex ratios, bachelor communities, and enforced prostitution among, especially, Chinese immigrant communities. Given such histories, it is hardly surprising that there exists a highly publicized market for the sexual services of Asian women, both in the United States and abroad, comprised of mail-order bride businesses, massage parlors and brothels, and racialized pornography, in which Asian women are most often portrayed as victims of abuse and torture.[3]

In a context in which Asian and Asian American women's subjectivity is consistently questioned and/or undermined, Asian women have attempted to resist notions of passivity and to assert their own sexuality in multiple ways. At the same time, they have also examined the ways in which sexuality has been a site of victimization and pain. In acknowledging such histories and in claiming the "pleasures" of sex and sexuality, Asian American women pose significant questions about the interactions of race, gender, and sexuality. In this chapter, I interrogate the role of historical and textual silences regarding Asian American women's narratives of sexuality, specifically the textual ways in which sexual silences are reproduced and/or transformed in cultural spaces.

In Nora Okja Keller's Comfort Woman (1997), silence is used both thematically within the narrative and as a literary device by the author to highlight ways in which sexual oppression and victimization have been treated in public discourse. More specifically, Keller explores the historical role of silence surrounding the "comfort women" system in Japan, Korea, and other parts of Asia during World War II and the silences deployed by comfort women themselves, in this case through the character "Akiko" Bradley. Anchee Min, in her autobiographical work, Red Azalea (1994), also problematizes the silences surrounding sexuality, but she is most concerned with the issues of sexual desire, pleasure, and same-sex intimacy between women contextualized against China's Cultural Revolution. Her own use of silence, when it comes to description and terminology for women's same-sex desire, offers both reinforcement and an implicit critique of the dominant narratives of heterosexuality, Western discourse of same-sex sexuality, and Cultural Revolution–inspired nationalism.

In both Comfort Woman and Red Azalea, silence offers a means through which the authors may problematize sexual relations, sexual identities, sexual violence, and sexual desire. Also, Keller and Min both explore the role of sexuality in contained and confined spaces. In Comfort Woman, "Akiko's" sexuality is controlled (along with her body) during World War II within the parameters of institutionalized rape in a military "comfort" camp. In Red Azalea, Min's sexual desire for another woman is awakened while she is confined at a socialist labor camp, Red Fire Farm. In both texts, protagonists confront issues of sexuality within contained camp settings during times of political upheaval for their nations, respectively Korea and China, suggesting the limited range of sexual choices experienced by Asian and Asian American women in recent and current global and political contexts and drawing attention to the relationships between sexual and national subjectivities. In both texts, silence is deployed as a means to refigure the sexual, including sexual experience, victimization, and desire. For Keller, it emerges as a way to retell or re-imagine history, including histories of Korea and Korean nationalism. Also, it serves to link the systematic sexual abuse of Korean women with the feminization of Asia and the colonization of Korea. For Min, silence operates to disrupt conventional understandings of Chinese nationalism, as well as "homosexuality" and "heterosexuality" and other, parallel, binary oppositions (including East and West, and China and the United States).[4]

I am Korea, I am a Woman, I am Alive

Like Cha's Dictée, Keller's Comfort Woman employs an unconventional method of narration that relies, among other strategies, on multiple narratives in order to represent the fragmented status of Korea, the space that we call Korean America, and the actual women whose lives have been fractured under colonization, Western occupation, and other forms of oppression. At the same time, however, both Keller and Cha participate in the rewriting of history as part of a rewriting of self, a strategy of resistance and empowerment. *Comfort Woman*, like *Dictée*, utilizes postmodern, post-colonial, and feminist methods, centering the experiences of Korean and Korean American women in its narrative and offering critiques of histories that exclude such experiences.

Comfort Woman is told from the distinct perspectives of Beccah, a young woman of mixed heritage—Korean and white—and her mother, known to Beccah only as Akiko Bradley, a Korean immigrant.[5] Beccah's father was a minister who met Akiko in Korea while working as a missionary; he marries Akiko and they return to the United States. When he dies during Beccah's childhood, Akiko attempts to take her daughter "home" —to Korea. Because of poverty and a lack of resources, however, the two get only as far as Hawaii, the novel's setting.

Like Kingston's *The Woman Warrior*, *Comfort Woman* interrogates the meanings of history and truth, elaborating on the frustrations of a girl/child narrator who cannot know the truth of her immigrant mother's life.[6] In dreamlike trances (labeled "psychosis" by her daughter), Akiko is privy to the world of ghosts and spirits of the dead, with whom she communicates. As a medium, she connects her clients to those whom they have lost to death. When Akiko is "sane," she sings and tells her daughter stories of Korea and of the life she had before her immigration to the United States, stories of being a famous singer in Korea or helping Beccah's missionary father save orphaned children during the war, "stories," notes Beccah, "that began 'Once on a time' [sic] but occasionally hinted at possible truths" (3). When her mother's stories change, contradicting previous tales, Beccah grows frustrated, shouting at her mother, "Wait! That's not what you told me before! What's the truth?" (32). Realizing that she cannot trust her mother's stories, Beccah determines to remake herself and her mother, telling herself new stories, inventing a life without the shame and loss evoked by her relationship with her mother.

In her narration, Akiko rarely speaks and is largely silent. Her past is reconstructed through her memories, structured around the frameworks of living and dying and centered around the first "death" that occurred when she was twelve years old. Although, as she narrates, "[her] body moved on" (15), her connection to material reality was severed by the extreme, severe violence she was forced to endure. At times, her silence signifies this connection as well as her conscious attempt to sever herself from the world of the living. As she tells Beccah, her searches through the spirit world involve the search for something she has lost, implying a loss of subjectivity and self.

At the center of the narrative lies a secret of sexual shame so powerful its effects have transformed Akiko and must be hidden from her daughter. Sexuality represents threat and danger, and as the incidents of Akiko's past have been virtually erased from historical accounts, so, too, have they been erased from her own stories to her daughter. Keller's narration of Akiko's private thoughts, however, provide an entirely different narrative than the one she presents to her daughter. Through her narration, we learn that her original name was Soon Hyo and that she was renamed Akiko in the "recreation camps" of World War II, where she was forced to service Japanese soldiers as a "comfort woman" after being sold by her oldest sister at the age of twelve. Upon first entering the camps, because of her youth, Soon Hyo is required only to clean the quarters and serve the Korean women, who were renamed and numbered by the Japanese: Hanako, number 38; Miyoko, 52; Kimi-ko, 3; and countless others listed only by imposed names and numbers, including Induk, who was called Akiko, 41. Yet when Induk resists the subjugation of her body and her country to the Japanese, Soon Hyo is forced to replace her. Remembering the night Akiko/Induk died, Soon Hyo questions the notion that Induk "cracked"; instead, she speculates, perhaps Induk was "going sane." On that night, after years of enforced silence, Induk would not stop talking. Soon Hyo remembers:

> In Korean and in Japanese, she denounced the soldiers, yelling at them to stop their invasion of her country and her body. Even as they mounted her, she shouted: I am Korea, I am a woman, I am alive. I am seventeen, I had a family just like you do, I am a daughter, I am a sister. . . .
>
> All through the night she talked, reclaiming her Korean name, reciting her family genealogy, even chanting the recipes her mother had passed on to her. (20–21)

Induk's words suggest both a reclamation of Korea and an indictment of colonization. When, at daybreak, the soldiers take Induk into the woods and murder her, Soon Hyo discovers that she is to take Induk's place. She states, "That was my first night as the new Akiko. . . . That is how I know Induk didn't go crazy. . . . She was planning her escape. The corpse the soldiers brought back from the woods wasn't Induk. It was Akiko 41; it was me" (21).[7] This is the night Soon Hyo recalls as her first death.

Though comfort women were predominantly young Korean girls and women, a smaller percentage were of other nationalities, including Japanese, Filipina, Chinese, Indonesian, Burmese, Vietnamese, and Thai women. Recruited (often under false pretexts of job opportunities) or coerced from Japan's colonies and occupied territories, approximately 80 to 90 percent of the women were Korean.[8] Having been kidnapped, sold, or tricked into servitude, they were contained in camps for the sexual gratification of Japanese troops. Until quite recently, the very existence of comfort women had not been acknowledged by the Japanese government; the atrocities suffered by more than 100,000 women had been denied, and the women who had come forward after many years of silence had been refused the compensation and public apologies they had demanded.[9] Thus, for nearly fifty years, as Hyunah Yang points out, "there was virtually no research, investigation, or discussion of the subject" (123). Silence, she argues, has been the key component of representations of comfort women (124). Indeed, the profound silence surrounding the history of comfort women operates as a deliberate and official construction (a silencing—influenced by nationalist discourse about the role of women's bodies and sexuality). Yet, "the comfort system consisted of the legalized military rape of subject women on a scale—and over a period of time—previously unknown in history" (Hicks 16). Considered essential to wartime success, comfort women arrived with (or even before) ammunition, food rations, and other supplies (16). Most researchers estimate that there were between 140,000 and 200,000 comfort women. The average ratio of Japanese soldiers to the comfort women who were forced to service them was 50:1. And, as George Hicks argues, each woman was forced, on average, to have sex with approximately thirty men each day (19). The institutionalized rape of so many women during war, according to Mary Ann Tetreault, is not only "an act of conquest and subjugation of whole societies, involving deliberate national humiliation as a means of suppression and social control" but also "an instrument of policy" (427). For this reason, rape has an unparalleled power to signify the subjection of one nation to another (428).

With her powerful statement, "I am Korea, I am a woman, I am alive," Induk also suggests a linkage between the subjection of her body and that of her nation. For her, and for Soon Hyo and other comfort women, the rapes of their bodies parallel the rape of their nation and homeland. The physical body becomes one with the social body, as the two are seen as interchangeable. Korean nationalism, too, is predicated on such a belief system. Yang suggests that nationalism upholds the notion that "We Koreans are one and the same body" (130), and that minjok, or the notion or quality of being Korean—part of the people—assumes that all Koreans constitute a homogeneous "self." "Invocation of this national self affirms unified identity, based on an unchangeable essence that is transmitted through blood and homogeneous culture. At the same time, this notion consolidates the Korean nation as a geographically and culturally fixed unit" (Yang 129). However, one of the primary assumptions of a unified Korean nationalism is that of maleness, and Induk and Soon Hyo (and other comfort women) are women, a fact that is highlighted all the more by the particular type of violation they experience. Thus, Keller, by equating comfort women with the national body, performs a double gesture, at once highlighting the ways in which women's bodies are central to their identities as national subjects, thereby consolidating women's identification with the body and implying a critique of Korean (masculinist) nationalism that posits women only as sites of contest between male national subjects (Korean, Japanese, and American, in this case). Representing Korea's "national body" with women opens up the possibility for women also to identify as national subjects.

The Japanese army equated Korea's women with the nation in its attempt to humiliate and subjugate Korean women as a visible signifier of its control over Korea. However, Keller's text enacts a challenge to the this nationalist model in that the central Korean women figures of the novel—Soon Hyo, Induk, and even Beccah—resist male-defined norms and paradigms, inventing their own women-centered models of Korean identity. For example, Soon Hyo throws a hundred-day party for Beccah, an event celebrated in Korea only for boys. She narrates, "I want my own child to know that I gave her a hundred-day celebration, that I love her and thank the spirits for her health, even though she is not a boy and not in Korea. Or perhaps I celebrate because she is a girl, an American girl" (119). Interestingly, it is the location of Korean America that provides space for Soon Hyo and Beccah to rework what it means to be Korean, as well as what it means to them to be women. Korean men in the text are hardly visible. In Comfort Woman, it is the women, living among only Korean women and Japanese men (and later, Americans in Hawaii), who come to stand in for their nation and homeland.

If the institutionalized rape of Soon Hyo represents the subjection of Korea to the violent forces of the Japanese, then the subsequent rape she experiences in marriage, perpetrated by her American missionary husband who purports to "rescue" or "save" her, could also be said to represent the domination of Korea by the United States. Such domination occurs not only through the military force the United States has exerted on Korea, resulting in the partition of the nation, but also the hegemony of colonialism (what some might refer to as neocolonialism) illuminated here through the spreading of Christianity and Western doctrine in a non-Christian, non-Western nation. *Comfort Woman*, like *Dictée*, incorporates a critique of hegemonic Western Judeo-Christian traditions imposed on Korean culture and people.

Also, Akiko's relationship with "the [American] husband" shifts the locale in which her body and sexuality are seen to belong. As Yang argues, chastity is a concept that circulates throughout discussions of comfort women, discussions suggesting that "chastity involves not virginity as such, but rather that there is always a proper place where female sexuality *belongs*" (131). Thus, some Korean men have expressed their anger over the fact that Korean women's sexuality—seen as rightfully belonging to them—has been seized by Japanese men, thereby robbing Korean men. Similarly, Akiko's American husband, believing in his own entitlement to her body and sexuality, expresses anger and frustration over his perception that she has "allowed" other (Asian) men to dishonor her. His shame signals the U.S. attempt to control and possess the bodies, sexuality, and subjectivity of Korean (men and) women.[10]

Significant to the hegemonic power of Japan and the United States over Korea is the control of language. Silence and the control of language are constant and powerful tools in acts of domination and colonization. As a comfort woman, Soon Hyo is not only forbidden to speak Korean, she is forbidden to speak at all, thereby becoming more and more dehumanized, responding, she says, only to the simple commands, "close mouth" and "open legs." In her marriage to an American, a husband she refers to only as "the husband," she is expected to speak only English, especially with their daughter. Of his language, which Soon Hyo links to imperialist conquests, she narrates:

My husband speaks four languages: German, English, Korean, and Japanese. He is learning a fifth, Polish, from cassette tapes he borrows from the public library. He reads Chinese.

A scholar who spends his life with the Bible, he thinks he is safe, that the words he reads, the meaning he gathers, will remain the same. Concrete. He is wrong.

He shares all his languages with our daughter, though she is not even a year old. She will absorb the sounds, he tells me. But I worry that the different sounds for the same object will confuse her. To compensate, I try to balance her with language I know is true. I watch her with a mother's eye, trying to see what she needs—my breast, a new diaper, a kiss, a toy—before she cries, before she has to give voice to her pain. (21)

After an enforced abortion in the camp, Akiko/Soon Hyo escapes. By the Yalu River, near a graveyard, she encounters an old woman who agrees to help her by taking her to the American missionaries in Pyongyang. Before leaving her, Manshin Ahjima warns Akiko that though they will save her from starvation, she should be prepared to be renamed by the missionaries. "I think they call all of the girls Mary," she says (58). For Akiko, who has already lost her name, this fact does not scare her. However, what she is not prepared for is her actual encounter with the missionaries who, to her, are not real. "What I came to find out was that Manshin Ahjima was talking about the Americans, the missionaries, not about real people" (60). And when Akiko/Soon Hyo arrives at the missionaries' headquarters, she is unable to speak: "They asked me—in Korean, Japanese, Chinese—where I came from, who my family was, but by then I had no voice and could only stand dumbly in front of their moving mouths as they lifted my arms, poked at my teeth and into my ears, wiped the dirt from my face. She is like the wild child raised by tigers, I heard them say to each other. Physically human but able to speak only in the language of animals" (16).

However, as long as she is silent, she is safe. The silence with which she surrounds herself during her stay with the missionaries, she narrates, grants her the hope that she will be overlooked and allowed to die in the darkness (65). But Akiko's future husband notices her and pursues her. He offers her salvation through Christianity, but Akiko sees the truth in his eyes:

I discovered his secret, the one he won't admit even now, even to himself, after twenty years of marriage. It was a secret I learned about in the comfort camps, one I recognized in his hooded eyes, in his breathing, sharp and fast, and in the way his hands fluttered about his sides as if they wanted to fly up against my half-starved girl's body with its narrow hips and new breasts.

This is his sin, the sin he fought against and still denies: that he wanted me—a young girl—not for his God but for himself. (94–95)

Offering her marriage and the chance for a new life in America, he takes Akiko/Soon Hyo home with him. His unreciprocated desire for her permeates their relationship. On their wedding night, he expresses pleasure in his assumption that she is sexually knowledgeable. He "cooed" and "petted," she remembers, then "grabbed and swore at [her], as he stripped the clothes from [their] bodies" (106).

His sexual advances, often forceful and sometimes violent, repel her. His voice and language are even worse. Of the songs he sings to their daughter, she says, "I hate them and I hate him. . . . I cannot sing to my daughter like that, in a voice full of laughter" (69). Having confronted the limits of conventional forms of language, especially official narratives, Akiko/Soon Hyo cannot and does not rely on it. Her chosen silence, however, is distinct from the enforced silences she has suffered, both in the camp, contextualized against Japan's rule, and in her marriage to an American (also contextualized against national domination). When the husband accuses her of having worked as a prostitute during the war, implying her complicity, she refuses to bow down for forgiveness. When she speaks out against the abuses she has suffered, he silences her by quoting the Bible and casting her in the role of a sinner. Forcibly pushing her to the ground, he physically covers her mouth, stating, "I ask you to protect our daughter, with your silence, from that shame" (196). His injunction to silence mirrors a larger Western Judeo-Christian silencing of Korean subjectivity, as well as discourse related to sexuality.

As noted in the previous chapter, silence operates metaphorically and historically, ideologically and as reality and lived experience. During the Japanese colonization of Korea from 1910 to 1945, one of the primary exercises of subjugation was the control of Korean language. Within the nation, Koreans were forbidden to speak their own language; they were forced to speak Japanese within schools, public settings, and official areas.

Korean-language publications were censored and then banned, and Japanese names were imposed on Korean subjects. As Lisa Lowe suggests, the "forced fluency in Japanese . . . silenced native Korean language and popular traditions" (1994, 45). Such a silencing was part of an attempt to eradicate not only Korean language and cultural traditions but Korean national history and Korean identity as it is understood in terms of national belonging and subjectivity. Furthermore, physical control over language was paralleled by ideological control that sought to instill in Korean subjects the internalized belief system that supported their own subordination. Similarly, in other parts of the world, the control of language is a primary apparatus of hegemonic power, made explicit in contexts of colonization and yet also insidious and threatening within postcolonial and neocolonial settings.

Thus, the character of Soon Hyo, having become Akiko, is alienated from herself. As such, she represents Korea in its subjection. Having become unrecognizable to herself, she mirrors the experiences of subjects of a dominated nation. And in her fragmentation, she parallels the fracturing of the Korean nation into two separate and unrecognizable countries, subject to Japan and the United States. Of this, Akiko/Soon Hyo herself notes, "It still seems strange to me to think of Korea in terms of north and south, to realize that a line we couldn't see or feel, a line we crossed with two steps, cut the body of my country in two. . . . [The people] will never be able to return home. . . . [T]hey are forever lost" (105). Likewise, the multiple narration of the novel, through the sometimes contradictory accounts of Beccah and Soon Hyo, involves the fragmentation of a family and identity against the disturbing backdrop of colonialism, war, and the exploitation of women's bodies and sexuality. The mother's secrets, madness, and lies become a powerful metaphor for the consequences of Japan's (and subsequently the United States') control and occupation of Korea. Beccah's pain and silence become symbols of a nation that cannot know its own history, all the while suffering the repercussions of that violent history. And Soon Hyo, having been made over into Akiko, can never return "home"—to a previous place or self.

Yet, Soon Hyo is not merely a passive victim, subject to Japan and the United States; likewise Korea cannot be viewed simply as a dominated nation. Rather, Korean nationalism represents a powerful force and means of resistance. However, that resistance, as I have argued, has been typically based on male experience and subjectivity. Keller places women at the center of Korea's fight for independence from colonization, similar to Cha's placement of Yu Guan Soon and other "heroic" women at the center of her text.[11] In doing so, she suggests the possibility of a specifically Korean female (feminist?) nationalist consciousness. As such, not only do women's bodies come to stand in for the national body, but women's subjectivity constructs and produces a form of national subjectivity, the results of which must be distinguished from what occurs when Asians nations are simply "feminized" by Western and/or colonial powers, as has been the case for both Korea and China.

The Outsider Within: Fragmented Narration and Double-Voiced Discourse[12]

The border crossings within Comfort Woman foreground Korean American women's experiences as diasporic and shifting. Because crossing borders often entails fluency in two or more languages, as border crossers, Keller's narrators possess the ability to both say and unsay, sometimes simultaneously, as demonstrated through the author's careful deployment of a multiple narrative style. Multiple and fragmented narrative styles recur among Asian American women's writings as well as within the writings of other marginalized groups in the United States, raising issues of voice, speech, language, and silence, issues of primary importance to all people subjugated by racism, sexism, colonization, homophobia and heterosexism, and other forms of domination. As Trinh T. Minh-ha writes, "Dominated and marginalized people have been socialized to see always more than their own point of view. In the complex reality of postcoloniality it is therefore vital to assume one's radical 'impurity' and to recognize the necessity of speaking from a hybrid place, hence of saying at least two, three things at a time" (1992, 140). Thus, speaking from two or more subject positions at the same time reflects the hybrid place inhabited by many colonized groups of people. Also, having one's speech limited or enforced only for the service of the ruling class enacts a condition of domination that actually transforms an individual's own understanding of his or her subjectivity. In other words, by controlling the speech and language of a group, processes of colonization are involved in the production of new forms of identity and subjectivity, thus enabling not only the creation of strategies of resistance to such domination but counternarratives and counterhistories that call official discourse into question. Hegemonic contexts always enable the production of counterhegemonies.

The use of multiple narrators is an effective strategy here, because it represents and articulates a reality for those living under colonization. Keller enacts the political conflicts at the heart of recent Korean history through her characters. Soon Hyo is telling a history of colonization, marked on her life and her body. In the retelling, her narrative is seamless; her English is "perfect"; she requires no translation. Yet, in her day to day life, as Beccah narrates is, Akiko/Soon Hyo speaks to Beccah in "broken" or "fractured" English, when she speaks at all. Other times, her language is unintelligible; when she communicates with the dead, Beccah finds her incomprehensible. To Beccah, her mother speaks like a foreigner, an outsider, an immigrant. To Beccah, Akiko/Soon Hyo speaks confusing and shameful half-truths and bizarre maniacal ravings of the dead or the insane, or she speaks not at all. To her own daughter, Soon Hyo cannot speak her history, but in Keller's narration of her thoughts, she is articulate, even eloquent. While Soon Hyo presents a narrative of history, names and dates and other "facts" and "truths," her story is an "unofficial" history, one not found in history books or official public records, unknown to the majority of the public, and one that is lost to her daughter. However, Soon Hyo is cognizant of her dissemblance.[13] She notes that these were lessons she learned early: "I was able to survive what eventually killed my mother. Hiding my true self, the original nature of my head, enabled me to survive in the recreation camp and in a new country" (153). Again, what she survived is not only the oppression of Japan's control but also that of the United States.

With the dead, including her own ancestors and Induk, Soon Hyo is communicative, but with so-called living people—first the Japanese and then the Americans of the novel—she is silent. In the United States, her silence is interpreted as an inability to speak English and as passivity. Yet, given the ways in which verbal language has been structured in her life, as exclusion, as ridicule, and as abusive rule, her silence enacts a direct refusal and rebuke of the dominant language form. Thus, her silence is expressive, a strategy for survival, a refusal to participate in the creation of dominant, exclusionary narratives, a response to paternalistic comments by rude Americans (including the husband), and a means of gaining quiet in her own head. To her daughter, she is unable to communicate freely in the language they share. Instead, she leaves Beccah a tape on which she records her truths, her memories and history. Only at her death, when she is presumably among the spirits with whom she is most at home, can Beccah hear her and know her.

To Soon Hyo, the shape of one's head determines his or her fate. As her own mother taught her, however, head shape is not fixed for life. She notes that the shape of her mother's head was changed forever by the Japanese control over Korea: "My mother's generation was the first in Korea to learn a new alphabet, and new words for everyday things. She had to learn to answer to a new name, to think of herself and her world in a new way. To hide her true self. I think these lessons, these deviations from the life she was supposed to lead, from the person she should have been, are what changed the shape of her head" (153). Similarly, Soon Hyo attempts to teach her own daughter that fate is not scripted but affected by circumstance and will. While she attempts to shield her daughter from "death thoughts" and arrows, it is Beccah who, ultimately, becomes the "guardian" of her mother's life (125). The relationship between Soon Hyo and Beccah is complex. While Beccah is convinced that Soon Hyo must have been a better daughter than she is a mother, Soon Hyo draws her strength as a mother from her memories of her relationship with her own mother.

Recounting her own deaths, Soon Hyo realizes that her mother, too, was no stranger to death. Soon Hyo's own silences can be traced to her mother's silence and her mother's first "death." As a young woman, Soon Hyo's mother survived the 1919 revolutionary uprisings in which her lover—a fellow demonstrator—was murdered by soldiers. She was then forced to fake her own death to save her life. Soon Hyo retells the story: "In order to protect her, my grandmother killed her daughter off. She sent my mother north, to Sulsulham, to marry my father. . . . My mother never heard her name again" (179).[14] After the arranged marriage to Soon Hyo's father, her mother was referred to only by her husband's name or as Omoni, "mother." Realizing that she never knew her own mother's name, Soon Hyo decides her daughter must know hers:

I try to think of the words to a prayer I can offer for my mother. I cannot. Instead I will tell my daughter a story about her grandmother. I sift through memory, and this is what I say: She was a princess. She was a student. She was a revolutionary. She was a wife who knew her duty. And a mother who loved her daughters, but not enough to stay or to take them with her.

I will tell my daughter these things, and about the box that kept my mother's past and future, and though she will never know her grandmother's name, she will know who her grandmother is.

Later, perhaps, when she is older, she will sift through her own memories, and through the box that I will leave for her, and come to know her own mother—and then herself as well. . . .

I start with our names, my true name and hers: Soon Hyo and Bek-hap. I speak for the time when I leave my daughter, so that when I die, she will hear my name and know that when she cries, she will never be alone. (182–183)

Like Cha, Keller highlights the demonstrations of March 1919 in Korea's struggle for independence. The March 1919 revolt represents a turning point in terms of the production of nationalism and national consciousness and identity for Koreans. For Soon Hyo's mother, it also represented the solidification of her dissemblance, a strategy she would pass down to her daughter. Soon Hyo is convinced of the power of multiple forms of expression: She resolves that her daughter will one day know her name. At the same time, she is cognizant of the power of the unspoken. Recalling the ways in which her mother used to touch her lovingly, she reflects on her relationship with her own daughter during the time that Beccah is a baby:

I touch my child in the same way now; this is the language she understands: the cool caresses of my fingers across her tiny eyelids, her smooth tummy, her fat toes. This, not the senseless murmurings of useless words, is what quiets her, tells her she is precious. She is like my mother in this way.

Because of this likeness, this link to the dead, my daughter is the only living thing I love. . . . What are living people to ghosts, except ghosts themselves? (18)

As a "ghost," Soon Hyo claims her mother and her daughter in a family of unrest. Silence in the present material reality is juxtaposed against speech in other forms (in death, in the spirit world, even in the textual narration). As mentioned earlier, Soon Hyo is eloquent in her narration. Also, she expresses herself in the tapes she makes, as a medium for the dead. As a "dead" person herself, she is unable to communicate using the medium through which she has been destroyed.

And Beccah, who is silent at first when it comes to her mother, begins to speak. An aspiring writer, she notes, "I wanted to believe that my voice would rescue me, transport me to a new world" (27). Yet rather than writing the news she wants to record, she becomes a writer of obituaries—documenting lives, sorting chronologies, and recording death. When her own mother dies, she is unable to record a single fact that she knows to be "true" and suggests that her own mother is a *yongson*, "the ghost of a person who traveled far from home and died a stranger" (140). Discovering that her mother has recorded her own history for her daughter, Beccah wonders how she should remember her mother's life, narrating, "my mother once belonged to a name, to a life, that I had never known about. . . . [M]y mother, once bound to others besides myself, had severed those ties—my lineage, her family name— with her silence" (173). Realizing this, Beccah determines to remember her mother, to know her name, and to speak the history that she shares with her mother.

When she listens to the tape, Beccah hears her mother's anguish over "so many true names unknown" (192). Even after death, leaving the recording for her daughter, Soon Hyo's story is unintelligible. Linked to no known histories, Beccah finds the tape at first incomprehensible. She narrates:

> Just as when I was a child listening in on my mother's sessions with her clients . . . I heard, when I first began playing my mother's tape in the apartment I had chosen for myself, only senseless wails, a high-pitched keening relieved by the occasional gunshot of drums. Still, I listened, but only when I stopped concentrating did I realize my mother was singing words, calling out names, telling a story. (191)

It is only when she gives herself over to the power of her mother's words that she begins to comprehend that there is a story hidden under layers of confusion and silence. Beccah must replay the tape many times to make meaning of her mother's words—words, she notes, "connected to blood and death" (192). Also, she must rely on her Korean-English dictionary, translating words she does not know, sounding out "rough, possible translation[s]" (193). For *chongshindae*, she translates "battalion slave." In fact, as Dai Sil Kim-Gibson suggests, the term, literally translated as "'Voluntarily Committing Body Corps,' a Japanese-coined term meaning devoting one's entire being to the cause of the emperor" (177), denotes the complexities of hegemonic domination. The term implies the willingness of comfort women as well as their duties to the empire.

Significantly, as a writer of obituaries, Beccah is inspired by her mother's death to produce a narrative of her life. She realizes, however, that the "blood and death" associated with her mother's words signify the ways in which death is bound up with narration and both personal and collective histories. In fact, as noted earlier, Soon Hyo bears a special relationship with themes of death and dying, as the daughter of a woman who falsified her own death and as someone who has experienced at least two deaths and who communicates mainly with the dead. For Beccah to understand her mother's actual death, she must make sense of the circumstances surrounding her first (spiritual) death.

As Beccah listens to her mother's voice on the tape recording, she hears Soon Hyo speak of the chongshindae, her language for what has been done to her:

> The Japanese believe they have destroyed an entire generation of Koreans. That we are all dead and have taken the horrible truth with us, but I am alive. I feel you, knowing you wait by my side until the time comes for me to join you across the river. I offer you this one small gesture each year, worth more than the guilt money the Japanese offer to silence me . . .
>
> I rewound the tape where my mother spoke of the Chongshindae, listening to her accounts of crimes made against each woman she could remember, so many crimes and so many names that my stomach cramped. Without reference, unable to recognize any of the names, I did not know how to place my mother, who sounded like an avenging angel recounting the crimes of men. . . .
>
> I clawed through memory and story, denying what I heard and thought I remembered, and tried to pinpoint my mother's birth date, her age during World War II. (193–194, 196)

Without context or reference, Beccah is unable to "place" her mother's experiences or her mother. She realizes, however, that though the tape is meant for her, it is addressed to her grandmother—Soon Hyo's mother; to know her own place in the world, Beccah must find a way to understand the struggles of her mother and other women ancestors. To do so, she is required to "claw through memory" and history.

Soon Hyo, too, emphasizes the power of memory and links resistance with remembering. To never forget means to stay alive, though life costs Soon Hyo more than she can express to her daughter. She envies the women in the camps who chose death, remarking that she herself is a coward. Yet her words and subsequent actions suggest otherwise. Comparing the Induk she knew in the camp to the figure who haunts her in the present time of the novel, she writes:

> When she was alive, she did not seem so impatient. But then I knew her only at the comfort stations, when she had to hide between layers of silence and secret movements. I want to say that I knew she would be the one who would join me after death. That there was something special about her even then . . .
>
> But I am trying not to lie.
>
> There was nothing special about her life at the recreation camps; only her death was special. (143)

While Soon Hyo pronounces her intentions to remember events accurately and to tell the truth, Beccah is not always so sure. As noted previously, her mother's stories often change. The truth of her mother's history, to Beccah, is largely untold. Soon Hyo's reliance on dissemblance offers her a measure of protection, as it did in the camps, where the women employed "layers of silence and secret movements" to guard themselves from the Japanese soldiers, but makes it difficult for her to communicate with Beccah.

What made Induk's death special, to Soon Hyo, is that Induk chose it herself. To die as Induk did was to die heroically. Incidentally, it is through her breaking of silence that she chooses death. Soon Hyo, on the other hand, remains silent for many years to come, believing in its power to protect her from even worse danger. To Soon Hyo, who courts death in her life after the camp, choosing life during her ordeal seemed cowardly and shameful. She feels that she has the obligation, if not the right, to kill herself. To remain alive, she implies, is a selfish and shameful choice, yet she feels she must do so for her daughter's sake. Having been abandoned through death by her own mother, she acknowledges that Beccah is a thread that keeps her in this life, at least physically. As her grasp on life loosens, Soon Hyo moves more frequently between the living and the dead. Also, she uses language and truths to find release. Through her narration and final words to Beccah, she demonstrates her resistance to the violence enacted against her body, spirit, and nation.

Through her silences, she counters the narratives that occlude her memories of her own experiences. And through the conscious act of remembering, Soon Hyo enacts a will to make her truth known, at least to her daughter.

Suggesting that after leaving the camps, she was unable to hear for a period of time, Soon Hyo remembers when her ears "opened," and she heard singing:

> In that song I heard things that I had almost forgotten: the enduring whisper of women who continued to pass messages under the ears of soldiers; a defiant Induk bellowing the Korean national anthem even after the soldiers had knocked her teeth out; the symphony of ten thousand frogs; the lullabies my mother hummed as she put her daughters to sleep; the song the river sings when she finds her freedom in the ocean. (71)

Soon Hyo's narrative marks and is marked by her physicality and her spirituality. It is bodily and spiritually that she experiences the abuse of conquest of Korea and herself. Thus, Keller equates Korea not only with Soon Hyo's body (the national body) but also with her spirit and selfhood (the national subject). In *Comfort Woman*'s nationalist narrative, Korean women heroically assert their identites as Korean *and* women. They refuse the easy equation of femininity with weakness, and they narrate alternative histories, using methods such as silence, multiple narration, and distance (through a displaced or exiled narrator). In suggesting the transformative power of unconventional strategies of resistance, Keller forces us to view the character of Soon Hyo not simply as a victim but as a woman who struggles against oppression, even when her strategy for survival is her silence, a strategy that enacts a "will to unsay" and a language of resistance. Her silence is never absolute. Even when she dies, an ultimate form of silencing, her words and memories live on through her daughter and her recorded message for Beccah. Soon Hyo's silence operates as part of a discourse surrounding the history of comfort women. Likewise, her death (and relationship to death) is a part of her life, neither outside of nor in opposition to it.

Finally, Soon Hyo finds strength through other women, including the memories of her mother, Induk, and, Beccah. Induk, or the "Birth Grandmother," as Soon Hyo teaches Beccah to refer to her, is Soon Hyo's mother figure, caregiver, and eventually, lover. After following Soon Hyo to the United States, where she watches over her, Induk begins to visit more and more frequently. When Induk is with her, Soon Hyo feels pleasure in her body for the first time. Her (imaginary?) fingers and lips caress Soon Hyo's body, and, repeatedly, they have sexual encounters. Soon Hyo narrates, "I open myself to her and move in rhythm to the tug of her lips and fingers and the heat of her between my thighs. . . . I see only the blackness of my pleasure. My body sings in silence until emptied, and there is only her left, Induk" (145). Again, silence for Soon Hyo is a significant mode of expression, in this case, of her pleasure.

While the love and sexual pleasure Soon Hyo shares with Induk offer the only respite in her life, her actions are viewed as "sinful" by the husband. Unaware of Induk's presence, he believes he has caught Soon Hyo masturbating and warns of the evils of self-fornication and sexual pleasure for women (145–146). While Soon Hyo laughs, wondering, "How could he compare what went on between men's and women's bodies with what happened spiritually?" (146), she also notes the fear in his eyes. To her, the relationship represents no sin. It is a relationship in which she engages sexually with herself as well as her historical memory, represented by Induk. It is through her relationship with Induk, however obscure, that she attains power in her relationship with the husband, vowing now that he will never be able to use her sexually again. Her relationship with Induk symbolizes her claiming of subjectivity and embodiment, simultaneously.

While sex and sexuality operate predominantly as sites of pain and victimization in Comfort Woman, Keller also introduces the possibility of sexual pleasure and fulfillment with Induk, a ghostlike woman lover. Thus, in Comfort Woman, same-sex desire among women is emphasized as a means of sexual exploration as well as the questioning of authority. Throughout the novel, Soon Hyo's experiences are conceived not as discrete facts or truths so much as a mystery and an "open secret" of sorts —a past that cannot be spoken, even in Korea, and as a tactic of intervention into official discourses of Japanese rule, Korean masculinist nationalist efforts, and U.S. imperialism and occupation of Korea. The already fragmented narrative is further disrupted by Beccah's constant questioning of her mother, by Soon Hyo's memories of another time, and by the plot's movement back and forth between Korea and the United States. Sexuality as a social and discursive construct, inhabiting distinct meanings across time and place, offers multiple meanings, as do speech and silence.

Women's Bodies and the National
Body in *Red Azalea*

In *Red Azalea*, author Anchee Min remembers her life in China during the Cultural Revolution. Identified by some critics as part of an "escape from Asia" tradition of writing (Chen), *Red Azalea* further complicates notions of heroism and nation, for women. Raised, as she writes, on the teachings of Mao and the operas of Madame Mao, she becomes a leader of the Little Red Guards while she is in elementary school. Her narrative of pride in being a leader in the "Great Proletarian Cultural Revolution" is contextualized against the downward mobility of her family and the increasing terror of those around her. Her family of six is forced to move from a four-room apartment of their own into a cramped two-room apartment shared with two other families over a noisy hardware shop. Her educated, intellectual parents are stripped of their academic positions and "reeducated" by being moved into hard labor. Her mother, who is forced to work in a shoe factory, eventually develops tuberculosis. Meanwhile, Min, an aspiring writer, notes that all her compositions for school were party slogans and that the people were allowed to listen only to the same eight operas over and over again. Yet, she remembers, "Not for a day did I not feel heroic. I was the opera" (26). Locating herself within the scripted role she was made to perform, Min suggests that for a time, this role was comfortable for her, and she played it well. Of her preparation for her journey to a labor camp, Min writes: "It was in the shadows that I began my heroic journey. The officer passed me back my family's resident registration book. I saw my name blotted out by a red stamp. The red stamp, the symbol of authority" (41). Thus, her heroism implies her departure from Shanghai and her family, marked by both rebirth and the erasure of her previous life by those in authority.

Her experiences existed, as she recalled, in opposition to Western influence and imperialism; in fact, she repeatedly implies a critique of American imperialism. At thirteen, Min is forced to denounce her favorite teacher, Autumn Leaves, who was born and educated in America, the child of a Chinese American who remained in the United States. Secretary Chain, the school's Communist Party secretary, refers to Autumn Leaves as a "hidden class enemy, an American spy" (27). While Autumn Leaves is a beloved teacher, Min realizes that she must denounce her as an enemy of the people or risk being denounced herself. In a public meeting, she gives a speech in which she accuses Autumn Leaves of attempting to brainwash her into becoming a "running dog of the imperialists" (34).

When Autumn Leaves stands accused of being a traitor to Mao, she refuses to speak:

> Secretary Chain shouted at her. The crowd shouted, Confess! Confess! Secretary Chain took the microphone and said that the masses would not have much patience. By acting this way Autumn Leaves was digging her own grave.
>
> Autumn Leaves kept silent. When kicked hard, she said that she had nothing to confess. She said she was innocent. Our Party never accuses anyone who is innocent, said Secretary Chain, and yet the Party would never allow a class enemy to slip away from the net of the proletarian dictatorship. He said now it was time to demonstrate that Autumn Leaves was a criminal. He nodded at me and turned to the crowd. He said, Let's have the victim speak out! (33)

For Autumn Leaves, as Min recalls, silence signifies refusal. Having nothing to confess, she says nothing. However, Min, who also has nothing to confess, is induced to speak, realizing that her speech costs her the first real teacher she has had. Acknowledging that it was Autumn Leaves who forced her to look critically at the world around her, bestowing on her the pride and expectations of a good teacher, she claims, "I had not realized the true value of what all this meant to me until I lost it forever that day at the meeting" (36). In a subsequent passage, Min disrupts the flow of time in her memoirs, writing:

> I was never forgiven. Even after twenty-some years. After the Revolution was over. It was after my begging for forgiveness, I heard the familiar hoarse voice say, I am very sorry, I don't remember you. I don't think I ever had you as my student.
>
> It was at that meeting I learned the meaning of the word "betrayal" as well as "punishment." (38)

Such a passage jars Min's readers into the present, reminding us that she is a writer who currently lives in the United States, the locale that now shapes both her memory and her narrative, and that her autobiography has been written in English. The interruption in the text reminds us of "the paradoxical space of the U.S. from which she now writes. Whereas she once evoked this space in opposition to her identity as a revolutionary, she now evokes it as an enabling limit for telling her story" (Somerson, 106). Her position as a Chinese woman in the United States signifies a specifically liminal position from which to describe her history and life.

In her essay "Agency via Guilt in Anchee Min's *Red Azalea*," Wenying Xu describes this precarious position for recent immigrant writers from the People's Republic of China. To articulate their own victimization during the Cultural Revolution risks a disavowal of any sort of agency, thus robbing them of subjectivity in their new homeland. But confessing their complicity with the actions of the Revolution, including the denunciation of others, while it may empower them within the United States as subjects, renders them guilty in the eyes of their other mainland Chinese immigrants. According to Xu, Min is one of the few Chinese immigrant writers who focuses not solely on her victimization but also her agency (and guilty complicity) during the Cultural Revolution. Because Min narrates her denunciation of Autumn Leaves, when, according to Jung Chang, "silence would have been perfectly possible" (quoted in Xu, 211), Min simultaneously articulates her own subjectivity and foregrounds the complex relations between speech and silence.

At seventeen, Min is categorized as a peasant, an "unalterable decision" (39), and sent to do hard labor at a farm near the East China Sea. It is at Red Fire Farm that Min meets Yan Sheng, the commander of the Advanced Seventh Company and a formidable presence. It is also during this time in her life that Min begins to question and challenge existing cultural gender norms. As Wendy Somerson suggests, during the Cultural Revolution, China engaged in a massive process of reconceptualizing its nation's gender norms. Citing Lisa Rofel and Lydia Liu, she explains that China's re-gendering process constituted a challenge to Western imperialist ideology that feminized China as a weak nation compared with the masculine and "heroic" nations of the West.[15] The equation of China with femininity or women, who were subjugated in China, necessitated a strengthening of the position of women in China in order to strengthen the position of China itself in the global context. Thus, the Chinese Communist Party promoted raising the status of women in China. Its main vehicle for accomplishing such an objective was the enforcement of women's participation in the public sphere of labor. Also, though men and women were officially declared equal, such equality was premised on the erasure of women's difference from men. Thus, "women were expected both to look and behave as men did at that time. By encouraging women to wear the same dark clothes as men, short hair, and no make up, the official doctrine suppressed women's traditional 'femininity'" (Somerson 104). Women, then, were officially "de-gendered," while sexuality was virtually erased from public discourse. Non-normative (in this case, traditionally feminine) gender expressions and sexual transgressions posed a threat to the official, dominant discourse of the time.

Min's friend and comrade, Little Green, however, disturbs conventions of gender within the camp setting. Her explicit performance of femininity exists in opposition to the gender code established for women in the camp. Min remembers that Little Green was "daring":

> [She d]ared to decorate her beauty. She tied her braids with colorful strings while the rest of us tied our braids with brown rubber bands. Her femininity mocked us. I watched her and sensed the danger in her boldness. I used to be a head of the Red Guards. I knew the rules. I knew the thin line between right and wrong. I watched Little Green. Her beauty. I wanted to tie my braids with colorful strings every day. But I did not have the guts to show contempt for the rules. I had always been good. . . .
>
> Little Green upset me. She upset the room, the platoon and the company. She caught our eyes. We could not help looking at her. The good-for-nothings could not take their eyes off her, that creature full of bourgeois allure. (51–52)

Min is both attracted to and disturbed by Little Green. She regards her with contempt at the same time that she is forced to acknowledge her own desire to tie her braids with colorful strings, markers of traditional ("bourgeois") femininity. Here, Little Green's femininity is linked to class status, signifying a betrayal of the goals of the Revolution. She is eventually destroyed by her illicit sexual relationship with a man, as she is forced to accuse him of rape in order to save herself. Her lover is put to death, and she, in her grief and subsequent madness, commits suicide. As the only woman in the camp who dares to break the rules, she symbolizes the implicit threats posed by both femininity and women's sexuality. "By emphasizing the transgressive nature of Little Green's excessive femininity, Min exposes how official ideology's claim to 'de-gender' women actually gendered them according to a traditional male standard in an attempt to utilize their labor without disrupting this masculinist norm" (Somerson 107). The severe consequences of Little Green's transgression exemplify the extreme threat such a transgression posed to the dominant discourse surrounding gender and sexuality.

Yan Sheng, however, is masculinized, and Min begins to model herself after Yan. Upon her first meeting with Yan, Min writes, "She had the look of a conqueror. . . . When her eyes focused on mine, I trembled for no reason. She burned me with the sun in her eyes. I felt bare" (48). Min goes on to describe her growing self-awareness of feelings for Yan. While Min notes that she has intense feelings for Yan that go beyond friendship, she also finds it increasingly difficult to put into language any expression for those feelings. Comparing her feelings for Little Green with the feelings she has for Yan, she writes, "I adored Little Green as a friend, but I needed Yan to worship" (56). As a figure worthy of worship, Yan becomes Min's heroic object of inspiration: others speak of Yan "as if Yan were a god" (55); Min notes that Yan "was worshiped [sic]. She was more real than Mao" (55); Yan inspired Min and "gave significance to [her] life" (56).[16] Relying on the medium through which she first learned of heroism, she writes, "Yan had become the protagonist in my opera. . . . I was singing the song of Yan. Yan was the heroine in real life. In singing I wanted to reach her, to become her. I wanted to become a heroine" (56). Yet, of all these emotions, Min realizes, "I found it hard to comment on Yan. I was unaware of when I had become Yan's admirer" (54).

Yan and other women in the camp assume positions traditionally reserved for men. As Min's attraction to Yan develops, she begins to imitate Yan's way of walking, dressing, and talking. She attempts to impress her by giving speeches in the evening self-confession and criticism meetings and competes with her in her labor in the wheat fields. Yan rewards her by making her the leader of a platoon and moving her into the bunkhouse with other platoon leaders, in which she is to share a bunk bed with Yan. As their relationship develops, they take turns assuming the traditionally masculine role within a conventionally defined heterosexual narrative. Because they both disrupt traditional norms of masculinity and femininity, their usurping of the so-called male prerogative of sexual love for a woman redefines sexual desire itself. At the same time, Min also locates her love for a woman within other ideologies, including the dangers presented by men, as exemplified in Little Green's downfall. Of disgraced women, she writes, "I learned to never put myself in their position, to stay clear of men. . . . The heroine in my life, Yan, did not seem to have anything to do with men either" (65–66). Thus, their love for one another is figured as both acquiescence and resistance to official discourse. As Somerson argues, "Min's desire to be Yan is partially produced from the rhetoric of strong, revolutionary, sexless women, yet it reinterprets that discourse when it turns into sexual desire for Yan" (107).

Min's difficulty with language, in relation to her feelings for Yan, is punctuated by the absence of any specific terms or phrases to describe her relationship with Yan. Indeed, her silence on this matter is provocative, both in terms of cultural differences in signification and Min's deliberate uses of strategic silences. Describing her growing desire for Yan, she writes, "I spent the night of my eighteenth birthday under the mosquito net. A nameless anxiety had invaded me. . . . I was restless" (63). In the only private space allotted her, a bed enclosed by a mosquito net that she describes as a grave, Min recalls an unnameable presence invading her body. Employing the reeds growing under her bed as a metaphor, she notes that they were "excessive" and "indestructible"; causing her great discomfort, "they grew from nowhere" (63). Of the growing restlessness, she writes:

> [It] overtook me like the growing back of the reeds, from nowhere. It was the body. That must be it. Its youth, the salt. The body and the restlessness working hand in glove. They were screaming in me, breaking me in two. . . .
>
> The body demanded to break away from its ruler, the mind. It was angry. It drove me to where I did not want to go: I had begun to have thoughts about men. I dreamed of being touched by many hands. I was disgusted with myself.
>
> It was violent. My body was in hunger. I could not make it collaborate with me. . . . I could feel a monster growing inside, a monster of desire. (64)

Sexual desire for Yan is translated into sexual desire for men, the only option within the sexual discourse available to Min. Yet, any desire at all is experienced as both monstrous and alien. Her feelings are not of the mind, equated with her "true self," but "the body," a space deemed unfamiliar territory. In fact, her body itself is marked as alien and separate from herself. Such a body is linked throughout the text to notions of the public body—the people supposedly represented by the Communist

Party. Worried about her seeming loss of control over her mind—and recalling the fall from grace she witnessed among girls in middle school who apparently became sexually experienced—she narrates: "My mind was no longer the mind I knew. It was no longer the perfect stainless mind. . . . These girls had no self-respect. . . . They had no future. They were garbage. Placing them next to me showed the generosity of the Communist Party. The Party abandoned no sinners. The Party saved them. I represented the Party" (65). Min's body and mind are conceptualized as "the body" and "the mind," detached from herself. Yet, they also stand in for the social body and its collective "mind" or ideology, just as she represents—in fact, is—the Party.

In *Red Azalea*, Min links women's bodies, including her own, to social, national bodies. By emphasizing women's bodies in her narrative, and by linking her own body to those of other women, Min refuses to individualize her situation or her desire. Rather, she relies on a collective sense of the social body as well as a discourse of dualism, in which the mind and the body are seen as separate, even oppositional spheres. Such a dichotomy necessitates a hierarchy in which the mind is privileged over the body and, as Somerson argues, becomes emblematic of official discourse that "suppress[es] bodies that might resist or disrupt its doctrine" (108). However, in *Red Azalea*, women's bodies, representative of the social body, encompass sexual desires that cannot always be contained through "recourse to official ideology" (Somerson 108). As Min develops a sexual relationship with Yan, she writes: "The restlessness came back. It stirred me deeply. I felt my mind and body separating themselves. My mind wanted to force sleep while my body wanted to rebel" (109). The body rebels through its desire (located in a physical, material realm) for another woman. Pointedly, Min suggests a symbolic rebellion of the (social) body against the official and dominant discourse of the time. Somerson writes: "Min and Yan reclaim the passion encoded in revolutionary language by redefining what 'the war' is about. Here the role of the war against reactionaries in communist discourse gets rearticulated as the war against the official discourse itself which disallows a private sphere or expressions of sexuality" (109). The cultural space that set out to limit the production of desire among women actually contributed to such desire in its transformation of both gender and sexual norms. Thus, the official discourse surrounding gender during the Cultural Revolution, while attempting to degender women, not only masculinized them but transformed the meanings of masculinity and femininity, producing new ways to be both men and women.[17]

As in *Comfort Woman*, women's bodies here are equated with national, social bodies, a reversal of conventional understandings of both gender and nation. However, the national body represented by women such as Min and Yan exists in opposition to the national ideology. Thus, once again, women as (heroic) national citizens problematize the relationship between national embodiment and national subjectivity/consciousness, suggesting reconceptualizations of nationalist discourses and insisting on women's roles in shaping such discourses.

In *Red Azalea*, as mentioned earlier, Min discloses details of her relationship with Yan but leaves the terms of their relationship uncertain and unnamed. As she narrates, her ("the") body has become increasingly restless; she "developed a desire to conquer Yan" as a means, she states, of conquering herself. She writes, "Yan symbolized my faith. . . . I wanted her to surrender. I was obsessed" (70). Indeed, her vivid descriptions of her feelings for Yan exemplify this obsession, which parallels her growing discontent with the promises of Communism and the labor camp. With Yan, she feels "awakened," "frustrated," and increasingly "restless." To tell the story of her relationship with Yan, Min relies on what Julie Abraham refers to as the "heterosexual plot," consisting of specific formulaic conventions and plot twists.[18]

According to Abraham, the heterosexual plot, in which female characters are constructed *as women* according to certain norms of femininity (and their main concern is generally represented as love, fulfilled through romantic and sexual relationships) also constructs heterosexuality as the social norm (3, 12). Thus, the heterosexual plot is intricately connected to gender prescriptions as well as sexual norms. Abraham argues that "within the heterosexual plot, femininity and masculinity are ensured by heterosexuality, and ensure heterosexuality" (3). This convention of the heterosexual plot has also often been the means through which narratives of lesbians have arisen. As Abraham suggests, certain strategies recur among "lesbian novels," strategies she refers to as formula fictions.[19] One such strategy worth consideration in *Red Azalea* is that of "triangulation," in which three characters become involved in a struggle, usually over one of the three (5). In *Red Azalea*, the "triangle" consists of Min, who loves Yan; Yan, who loves Min yet also desires Leopard Lee, a man in another company; and Leopard, who, after some time, returns Yan's attention. Having begun their intimate relationship around the disclosure of a secret—Yan's illicit love for Leopard—Min and Yan grow closer because Min, using Yan's name, begins to write love letters to Leopard for her. Min writes, "Blushing, she told me that she had something to confess. . . . I said I had closet-thoughts too. She said that's different. Hers was a monster. . . . A man, I said, looking straight into her eyes. She lost her calm" (101). Min's own "closet-thoughts" differ from Yan's, however, as she realizes she is falling in love with Yan. Indeed, her use of the term "closet," a term with significant impact in Western queer politics, signifies her double meaning. Yet, writing the letters that will inevitably bring Yan and Leopard together is her only means, at the time, of securing Yan's attention. By writing the letters, she recalls, "Her intimacy belonged to me" (107).

Their growing feelings for one another form the center of the narrative about Min's growing social, political, and sexual awareness. The two become more and more involved in their intimate relationship, all the time making sure to carefully hide their feelings for one another while in public, a difficult task in a labor camp in which workers had few entitlements to privacy. Of their need for hidden, silent forms of expression, Min writes, "Yan and I betrayed no intimacy in public. . . . We became accustomed to each other's eye signals" (99). Both Min and Yan are aware of the potential danger of their relationship. When Min hears Yan playing an erhu at the brick factory at the edge of the camp, she recognizes the melody from a banned opera about two lovers, Liang and Zhu, "who committed suicide because of their unpermitted love" (86). Of their subsequent meeting, she narrates:

> She sat down on the stool and motioned me to sit next to her. She kept smiling and said nothing. I wanted to tell her that I had not known she played erhu, to tell her how beautifully she played, but I was afraid to speak. . . .
>
> I felt her true self through the erhu. I was awakened. By her. In a strange land, faced by a self I had not gotten to know and the self I was surprised, yet so glad, to meet. . . .
>
> We talked. A conversation I had never before had. We told each other our life stories. In our eagerness to express ourselves we overlapped each other's sentences. (87–88)

Their conversation is like none Min has experienced before. For the first time in her life, she feels "awakened" and deeply connected to another person. Min develops a relationship with Yan at the same time that she begins to express disillusionment with the camp and with China's Communist regime. Feeling angry about Little Green's suicide, an event for which she blames the company and herself, she begins to view the camp as "[a] complete darkness. A hell" (91). As Somerson suggests, "Yan's articulation of her desire [for Min] forces her to question her persecution of Little Green, and thus to begin questioning official ideology; desire becomes resistance" (108).

It is at this time that Min begins stealing food from the fields, a crime she would have reported in her earlier days as a "guard" for the people. Because she realizes that her salary is inadequate to meet her hunger, she becomes a thief along with several other soldiers, demonstrating her lack of loyalty to the system she previously upheld. Yan, too, grows disillusioned with the farm and with the present system after Little Green's death, for which she also feels responsible. Min's desire, too, forces her to question the events around her. When she goes home to visit her family, she witnesses their increasing impoverishment and her younger sister's fear of being sent to a farm. Coral refuses to see a doctor although she has severe dysentery, hoping that if her intestine is permanently damaged, she might claim disability and be able to remain in Shanghai (125). Unhappy with the state of the Revolution and increasingly restless, Min experiences a growing sense of transgression.

Min describes the further rebellion of the body against the mind by linking her love for Yan to both social transgression and her challenges to the authoritative narrative of the Cultural Revolution. Another device elaborated by Abraham in the heterosexual plot involves the use of masculine/feminine distinctions between two women. She writes, "lesbian stories could also be superimposed over the heterosexual plot, with one of the women in the central couple represented as 'really' male" (6). This strategy is also employed in *Red Azalea*, with Yan and Min alternately taking the "male" role. However, Yan, who is older and higher ranked in the camp, is often portrayed as the more masculine one. Desiring more intimacy but fearful of the repercussions of a watchful bunk mate, Lu, the two pretend to be cold one night by coughing and sneezing until Lu impatiently suggests that they share blankets. Within Yan's mosquito net, which they stop washing so that it will become opaque, they begin to spend their nights together. After this point, their relationship becomes explicitly sexual, characterized by a growing restlessness and sense of frustration. Assuring Yan that Leopard will soon respond to her advances, Min writes, "I told her that he would fall in love with her. . . . If I were a man, I would" (108–109). When Leopard fails to respond, Min worries about Yan's depression, writing, "I could not bear her sadness. It haunted me when she said that she had nothing except the Party titles. She had me. . . . I was unable to say anything. I wanted to say: You are very very beautiful. I adore everything in you. If I were a man, I would die for your love" (120). Though Min is clear about her feelings for Yan, she is capable neither of expressing such feelings directly nor of envisioning such a relationship without placing herself or Yan in the role of a man. Her silence in outward expression, regarding her love for Yan, is tied to her inscription of that love into the heterosexual narrative of a masculine/feminine dichotomy. This silence also relies on a mind-body split in which "the mind" represents the previously "perfect, stainless" promises of communism and "the body" represents the social/ national body—the people.

By reconstructing their relationship in terms of Yan's not being "allowed to have a man to love," Min reinscribes herself and her relationship with Yan back into the conventions of the heterosexual plot. Similarly, in a public reading in the United States after the publication of *Red Azalea*, Min opened with the words, "There were no men there." While her explanation of her relationship with a woman rests on an assertion of the absence of men in the labor camp, thereby reaffirming "the U.S. tradition of positing China as a space of repression," Min's interpretation of her relationship with Yan also "marks this space as productive of desire" (Somerson 98). In other words, Min's text enacts both a reinforcement of heterosexist, orientalist beliefs about the United States and China and a challenge to them.

Thus, their desire for one another, enabled by official national discourse, transforms the discourse and offers a counternarrative of resistance. When Min is chosen to go to Shanghai to participate in a filmic portrayal of the life of Madam Jiang Ching, she realizes that both Yan's commitment to communism and her own are faltering. Lu attempts to sabotage Min's chances of leaving the farm by opening an investigation of Min and Yan. To save Min and allow her to leave the farm, Yan casts herself as being in a sexual relationship with Lu, sacrificing her own career and future. And when Min develops stage fright and panics during her audition, Yan enables her to continue by silently mouthing the words of Mao's poem with her. Somerson suggests that this "doubly voice recital by two women restructures the ideological discourse of Mao's poem, even as their desire for each other is partially structured by this discourse" (98). Significantly, such a transformation relies partly on Yan's silent discourse—her soundless mouthing along with Min of Mao's poem. However, Min is able to leave the dark "hell" of the labor camp only by also foregoing her relationship with Yan. Yan, who is demoted within the ranks of the camp, encourages her to go in order to save herself. In the typical fashion of lesbian narratives, the two central women characters are unable to remain together.

In her essay "Violence in the Other Country," Rey Chow argues that China's marginalization in the West constructs it as a "spectacle," in opposition to the United States; U.S. viewers of this spectacle engage in "China watching," a product of their own making in terms of media culture. While Western reporters, film people, and academics participate in speaking of and for the Chinese, they also "try to make them talk," regardless of the dangers in their doing so (83). China, then, is represented as the "other" country, while Chinese people are viewed in terms of their absolute difference from (white) Western people. Furthermore, ideology is presumed to exist only in China (or the "other" country), while the Western world is maintained as the norm. "This China becomes, in its relation to the West, 'woman': in the sense that it is the 'Other' onto which the unthinkable, that which breaks the limits of civilized imagination, is projected" (87). As uncivilized, monstrous, and debased, China bears the burden of a presumed backwardness, in the words of Mohanty, a "Third World difference" in which all women are represented as oppressed and voiceless. Real women disappear, as do matters of their gender and sexuality, which Chow argues, might provide "challenges to the bases of traditional authority . . . which would provide the genuine means for undoing the violence we witness today" (88).[20]

As China represents the "other," it also represents the other space in terms of sexuality. Somerson suggests that "the U.S. as spectator secures its normative boundaries by projecting onto China a connection between political repression and repression of 'natural' (insistently hetero) sexuality" (103). Through her disruption of U.S. media constructions of

the Cultural Revolution, resulting in an undoing of public/private dichotomy, Min both sustains and challenges the U.S. construction of China
as a space of (sexual) otherness. Her statement that "there were no men
there," in Somerson's words,

> echoes the strand of U.S. reception that equates the separation of men and
> women in forced labor camps with "unnatural" acts between women. . . .
> Enforced labor enforces homosexuality; China bears the burden of linked
> labor, sexuality, and ideology, while sexuality in the U.S.—governed by free
> will—is configured as separate from the public sphere of politics, ideology,
> and capitalism. Reviewers construct Min's "escape" to the U.S. as a rescue
> mission; the role of the U.S. is to deliver Min from repressive sexual condi-
> tions to freedom—freedom to chose a heterosexual narrative. (103)

China, as the other country, is figured, then, as an "'anachronistic space'
where racial, sexual, and gender degenerations converge" (Somerson 103)
in a nation bound to an immovable, ahistorical past (juxtaposed against
a "modern," progressive, free United States in which non-normative
sexualities are happily tolerated?). Thus, China is linked to homosexuality and to degeneration.[21]

When Yan arrives in Shanghai to visit Min, the two share a romantic and sexually charged afternoon at the bathhouse, marred by Yan's
subsequent request that Min cover for her while she meets with Leopard
Lee. Min agrees to allow Leopard and Yan to spend the afternoon in her
parents' apartment, while, at Yan's request, keeping watch over them.
Remembering Lee's earlier lack of response to Yan's letters, Min narrates,
"I remembered my disappointment, Yan's disappointment. Her lovesick-
ness. I could not forgive Leopard. Yet, I forgave him. For he once was
the reason Yan needed me, for he had made us two one" (216). Leopard's central role in their relationship is acknowledged by both women
as a necessary element of their connection, as his presence enables and
legitimizes their relationship to one another. Fighting her desire to watch
the two of them have sex, she writes, "Can he read the poetry of her
body like I do? Can he understand the way her heart sings like I do?
. . . But Yan kept throwing me into reality. She knew I could not stop
watching her. She wanted to put my heart to death" (219, 221). Min
both wants Yan and identifies strongly with Yan, "her other self." She
longs to be connected to both Yan and Leopard, imagining "three instead of two people on the porch"; yet also finds herself increasingly

jealous of Leopard. He is conceived as a threat, as competition, and as someone who will never be able to "read the poetry of [Yan's] body" or "understand the way her heart sings" like Min can. The ways in which Min imagines herself capable of knowing and loving Yan depend on acts unrelated to speech. "Read[ing] the poetry of her body" and "under-stand[ing] the way her heart sings" do not rely on conventional language. Furthermore, the feelings Min experiences for Yan during this passage are expressed only in her writing—not directly to Yan. Saying "I will always love you" only in her heart emphasizes her own lack of trust in putting such feelings into language. Upon her departure, Yan makes clear what Min has suspected. Saying "I am sorry to do this, but I just have to. I think we are now ready to go on with our own lives. You are done with Red Fire Farm" (220), she reveals her intentions. She has "murdered [their] love" to make it possible for both women to go on with their lives knowing that they will not be able to be together. In the above passage, how are we to make meaning of Min's interpretive ability to "read" Yan's body and desire? Where does such an ability come from? In the context of China as "other" and as degenerate (a place of "enforced" homosexuality), this "ability" is both naturalized and provocative.

In the final section of the book, Min is trained to participate in the filming of *Red Azalea*, celebrating the life of Madame Jiang Ching. "To me," she narrates, "it was not only about the past wartime, about history, but it was also about the essence of a true heroine, the essence of Yan, the essence of how I must continue to live my life" (174). Committed still to her ideals of Yan's heroism, Min embarks on a new love relationship. During her time at the film studio in Shanghai, she begins a relationship with the Supervisor, a shadowy figure who arrives from Beijing sent by Jiang Ching to supervise production of the film. Meeting in a dark closet where they both go to smoke, Min is both attracted to and repelled by the Supervisor. She writes, "Staring at his painted face, my mind was oc-cupied by a strange thought: Was he a woman or a man? He seemed to be both. He was grotesquely beautiful. He lowered his head, then looked away, almost bashfully. Lifting his robe carefully, he walked to-ward the door like a swinging willow—he was wearing costume boots with four-inch heels" (236). The Supervisor is strangely feminine, and Min cannot determine "his" actual gender.[22] In fact, as Somerson points out, "the Supervisor appears to be Jiang Ching in disguise" (110). She argues,

Although it is established that he is the Supervisor in charge of the production, nobody knows his name, and when he tells Min his life story, it shares many of the same elements as Jiang Ching's story: they both played Nora in productions of Ibsen's *A Doll's House*; they both share an obsession with Western movies and a love for beautiful things. (110)

He describes himself as being able to understand women because he "carrie[s] a female part in him as well" (286), and notes that Madame Jiang Ching could also not always "tell if she was a man or a woman" (291). Also, when Min talks with him in their closet, she notes that "his smile carried a message. The message was written in an unbreakable code which I could not interpret. How strange, I started to think, a supervisor who has no name, who swims in and out of the studio at will, who rounds his tongue with the country's most powerful names" (248). Though she considers the Supervisor a mystery, they begin an affair and he secures for her the starring role in the filmic portrayal of Red Azalea.

Becoming Red Azalea casts her again in the role of both desiring and desiring to *be* her lover, exemplified most cogently in her transition into the character of Red Azalea, presumably based on the life of the Supervisor. She finds the Supervisor's femininity "beautiful" and his mystery "intriguing" (262). The Supervisor's desire, like both Min's and Yan's, also produces a critique of official ideology. When the Supervisor and Min meet to make love in a public park, the "forest of masturbators" (264), the Supervisor is thrilled by the discovery of other people in hiding for their forbidden desires. He exclaims:

> I can see them groaning silently, their fronts and rears exposed like animals in mating season, begging for touch and penetration. I see the hills of youth covered with blood-colored azaleas. The azaleas keep blooming, invading the mountains and the planet. The earth is bitten and it groans, wailing nonsensically in pleasure-drive. Do you hear it? The passion they had for the Great Helmsman has been betrayed. Oh, how grand a scene! I wish our greatest Chairman could see it. He would be shocked but impotent. (263)

The Supervisor "describes the people's physical passion as resistance enacted because Mao has betrayed their revolutionary passion, and Mao is stripped of sexual/political power" (Somerson 111). Min links political power with sexual power, once again suggesting resistance in desire. The repression of desire is symbolized by silence, while silence also signifies "unofficial"—or illicit—forms of desire. In the preceding passage, Mao is emasculated because of the uprising of the people ("the body"). Joined to the "social body," the two become one with the people, and Min invokes the blooming azaleas to signify the growing threat to official discourse posed by her transgressive desire. Later in the text, when Mao dies and Jiang Ching falls from the people's favor, the film production is canceled. The Supervisor asks Min if she will forgive Comrade Jiang Ching. "I said I did not know her. He insisted that I did. He said that Comrade Jiang Ching had been a spectator of my passion. She was proud of you and, at the moment, she is counting on you. Because she herself is going to be hung by her Long March comrades one of these days and she must count on her Red Azalea. She must see her ideal passed on" (299–300).

In her autobiography, Min employs formulaic strategies of the heterosexual plot, as delineated by Abraham, such as triangulation and a masculine/feminine distinction; however, she also employs an alternative device by turning to "history." As Abraham argues, "lesbian writers in particular turned to 'history' as a source of narrative alternative to the heterosexual plot. . . . To choose history as a framework for fiction was to gain access to an already established narrative" (30). But, as she goes on to suggest, "women were always at a disadvantage when the 'history' that provided these identifications was a record of political or cultural authority: it is logically a male character who provides the historical reference, even in a lesbian novel. . . . [Thus,] history did not offer any substantial solution to the limits imposed by the heterosexual plot on the narrative representation of lesbians" (31). Incidentally, as is the case for Min in particular, the "identification of 'history-proper' with masculinity meant that modern lesbian writers who turned to history as a source of narrative alternative to the heterosexual plot were directed away from female subjects and towards male subjects" (Abraham 32). However, in *Red Azalea*, gender transgressions abound. Yan's heroism is superimposed over the heroism of Chairman Mao; the Supervisor as love interest is decidedly feminine, even female.[23] And Min, the narrator of her own memoirs, however fictionalized, retains some grasp of history as providing a space for possibilities, even reconfigurations of official discourse. As such, she follows a tradition of "lesbian" writers in claiming history as her subject and in "rewriting the accounts of past and present that would erase [her]" (Abraham xix).

In the text, it is the Supervisor who enjoins Min to remember the power of history and retain some hope in its potential. For the Supervisor, history is based on will. When he invites her to his home, he shows her a historical film. Of his screening room, he says, "It's a screen on which history is performed and reperformed. . . . It is all in our will" (273). He subsequently translates for her a movie, *The Battle of Ancient Rome,* about the fall of an empire and the suicide of its princess (274–275). As the tragedy unfolds, his interpretation becomes "fragmented" and his breath quickens until he is unable to continue speaking. His invocation of history within a text that also invokes the meaning and power of history, placed within the historical setting of China's Cultural Revolution, further reinforces Min's deployment of history as a tool providing access to the official narratives of a nation, thus enabling her to reconfigure such histories.

In a passage near the end of the book, Min brings together history, betrayals, revolution, and her desire for both the Supervisor and Yan. She claims the historical space of the Cultural Revolution as both repressive and productive of desire. Desire is seen as a potential source of resistance. And language—and silence—are signifiers of both repression and resistance. Repeatedly, the Supervisor reminds Min to remember her obligation to history, stating:

> From this moment on, I want you to forget your family name. You are Red Azalea now, said the Supervisor. . . . You are creating an image which will soon dominate China's ideology. You are creating history, the proletarian's history. We are giving history back its original face. . . .
>
> You see, we are going to go through a forest of guns and a rain of bullets to pay respect to our mothers. Mothers who, for thousands of years, lived their lives in shame, died with shame, were buried and rotted in shame. We are going to tell them, Now it is a new world. A world where being born female merits celebration and value. A world where a woman who is forced to marry a pig can have an affair. (280–281)

The Supervisor claims history as a site in which to celebrate women's agency. Not only has history been appropriated from men, but historical discourse, too, is now the domain of women as well as men. This world of equality enjoins desire to both mind and body and signifies the "possibility produced by the Revolution that was never realized" (Somerson 112). Again, it is the Supervisor who encourages Min not to forget the radical potential of history when he tells her "I lose to history, not to them. . . . Tell me you know you are a heroine. Promise me you can bear it. Don't you disappoint me" (300). Min recalls: "He asked me to remember the darkness of the night, to watch the marching steps of history, to watch how it was altered, to see how the dead were made up and made to speak, how they never complained about what was put in their foul mouths. He said that it was this power of history that had charmed him. He asked me to admire history" (301). Of himself, he tells her he never trusted Chinese history books "because those books were written by people who were impotent of desire. . . . We held each other. I felt Yan—we were walking out of the darkness" (302). To the Supervisor, "Chinese history books"—the nation's official historical narratives—are not to be trusted. Yet history itself cannot be relinquished as a liberatory tool. He therefore implores her to transform the discourse, and thus the effects, of history.

Neither of the two central relationships around which this narrative is structured is clearly delineated in terms of gender or sexuality, at least in terms of the Western binarily opposed categories of man/woman and heterosexuality/homosexuality. Min's implicit critique of such binaries replicates Chow's critical stance in regard to the West/East dichotomy, whereby China is produced as the "other" country in relation to the United States. Min's "coming out" narrative, by no means a conventional formulaic story, must be seen in relation to her own inscription of herself as part of—in fact, one with—the social body. Her resistance embodies the people's resistance. Her sexual desire evokes a national, public reclamation and subverts the existing order for gender and sexuality in China. Finally, her official silence and unwillingness to name either herself or her narrative as "lesbian" perhaps signifies not an intention to remain in the "closet" but a refusal to partake in such conventional methods of naming, tied as they are to other binaries implicated in Western imperialism and the brutalities of dominant discourse both in China and globally. I read her silence, then, neither as a fear of "coming out" nor as the backwardness often attributed to Third World people, especially in terms of gender and sexuality, but as a carefully delineated form of resistance to any official, dominant discourse that upholds the rights of the elite while eliding those of others. For Min, made invisible within the historical setting she describes, except as a degendered, desexualized being, naming a relationship or individual according to Western sexual categories is not necessarily empowering. Thus, her reliance on particular forms of silence with regard to such categories suggests her critique of the categories themselves, as well as the meanings attached to them.

To apply Western theories of gender and sexuality to texts produced in interstitial spaces between the West and the so-called Third World is, of course, problematic. Equally problematic, however, is the assumption that the West and the non-West are hierarchically dichotomous and essentially, absolutely different, a point, I argue, Min makes with *Red Azalea*. While any analysis of a text produced by a member of a marginalized group must be adequately contextualized, the analysis applied must also be grounded in our own contexts as writers and scholars. Chow discusses her own reaction to questions such as "Why are you using Western theory on Chinese literature?" and "Why are you using Western feminist theory on Chinese women?" (90). She writes:

> The point that we must not be trapped within dichotomies is a familiar one, [however] many of us, especially those who experience racial, class, or gendered dichotomies from the unprivileged side, are still within the power of dichotomization as an epistemological weapon. The above kind of interrogation slaps me in the face with the force of a nativist moralism, precisely through a hierarchical dichotomy between West and East that enables my interrogators to disapprove of my "complicity" with the West. Such disapproval arises, of course, from a general context in which the criticism of the West has become mandatory. However, where does this general critical imperative leave those ethnic peoples whose entry into this culture is, precisely because of the history of Western imperialism, already "Westernized"? For someone with my educational background, which is British colonial and American, the moralistic charge of my being "too Westernized" is devastating; it signals an attempt on the part of those who are specialists in "my" culture to demolish the only premises on which I can speak. (91)

To suggest that the literature and histories of Chinese women and other Third World people should remain "uncontaminated" by Western methodologies implies their relegation to an absolute, ahistorical, and timeless place—what Johannes Fabian, according to Chow, refers to as the "culture garden." Chow goes on to argue that those of us who occupy this particular site—the space of the "outsider within"—do so through "naturalization" and learn to speak the "oppressor's language" fluently. She writes: "The task of the Westernized feminist is not to unlearn that language but to ask that her accented interventions be understood properly, not as an excuse for nativism but as the demand, put to feminism, for a 'willingness, at times, to shred this "women" to bits'—so that other histories can enter" (98, citing Riley, 1988, 114). Thus, revisions of history, where women are concerned, necessitate critical interventions into the very notions of what "women" entails and how our varied subject positions, even as women, produce and transform our relationships to various social processes, categories, and institutions.

Min's location and status, as a Chinese woman living and writing in the United States—in English, about her experiences in China—provide a significant site in which to explore such questions. Somerson suggests that "through her translation of the Chinese Cultural Revolution into a story told in English for the 'West,' Min negotiates a space of resistance where, in Homi Bhabha's terms, cultural difference is 'inscribed in the "in-between" in the temporal break-up that weaves the global text'" (100). As a text that crosses "West" and "East," Red Azalea refuses classification as American or Chinese but claims both locations, "articulat[ing] a specific interstitial space on the borderland of discourse between the two countries. . . . Min disrupts both the U.S. Orientalist discourse about the Cultural Revolution and Chinese masculinist national discourse to envision a different version of both the past and the future" (Somerson 100). As an inhabitant of the "borderland" between the two, Min disrupts the binary itself and speaks both the language of her homeland and that of her adopted land. Similarly, Min offers a critique of the binary between homosexuality and heterosexuality, disrupting the heterosexual narrative even as she reinscribes it.

Min, for whom official discourse once provided the only means of expression—the same eight operas heard over and over again, her well-memorized poems by Mao, the party slogans written rather than essays—longs to overcome such prescriptions, though risky to herself and others. Not only might such speech threaten her life, but the language she wishes to speak is the same language that has become increasingly associated with oppression and the repression of desire. Thus, she chooses silence as an alternate, differently meaningful form of expression. Within the narrative, certain things are presented as unsaid, even unspeakable. Silence operates as a powerful metaphor for what is beyond or outside of language, and in Min's narration, she seems acutely aware of such silences and gaps. Red Azalea signifies Min's resistance to official Chinese narratives of the Cultural Revolution and Western orientalist assumptions. She inserts desire into the ideology of the Revolution at the same time that she rewrites women's same-sex desire. As the protagonist of her narrative, Min represents both body and mind; she is the embodiment and the consciousness of the people and the nation. Through her reworking of sexuality and sexual silences, she manages to disrupt conventional, male-centered narratives of Chinese nationalism and the Cultural Revolution, as well as understandings and meanings of the heterosexual plot. Thus, in both Comfort Woman and Red Azalea, the authors explore sexuality as representative of both pleasure and danger, especially in relation to narrative of nationalism and national belonging. Through their deployment of heroic women as national subjects, Min and Keller disrupt and contest both the feminization and implied degeneration of China and Korea, inscribing resistance through multiple forms of silence and placing their own lesser known narratives at the center of discourse surrounding gender, sexuality, and nation.

There is something incendiary in me and it has to do with being female, here, now, in America.

—Meena Alexander, *The Shock of Arrival*

She says to herself if she were able to write she could continue to live.

—Theresa Hak Kyung Cha, *Dictee*.

Conclusion.
Tell This Silence: Asian American Women's
Narratives, Gender, Nation, and History

During one of my first years of teaching, I had a team-teaching experience with the course Introduction to Women's Studies. I was distressed to witness, from the beginning, the silence of certain students in the classroom. A small cluster of Asian American women students, in particular, sat together and rarely spoke during class discussions. Expressing my concern to my fellow graduate student instructors, I confronted their attitudes that such silence was somehow "normal"—they attributed the silence to cultural differences and argued that there was nothing we could or should do about it. Such terms seem to me problematic when they are conceptualized as though "culture" is somehow an essential, static way of being, and such assertions suggest that Asian American women are inherently silent. Other (non–Asian American) students in the class seemed to interpret the silence of these Asian American students as signification that they did not understand the material or could not speak English, neither of which was true. This example made me begin thinking of all the meanings silence may carry—stereotypes of the "inscrutable Asian," the submissive and obedient "model minority"—at the same time that silence, of any student, can also signify shyness, fear, disagreement, refusal to participate, hostility or in other cases, agreement, respect, and acceptance. It may be related to the content of the class (or lack of content) related to an individual student's experiences. Silence, like speech, is a form of discourse and can communicate various thoughts or emotions. Speech and silence are, of course, always socially and culturally constructed; they may have less to do with innate cultural values than with current social and cultural contexts.

In *The Woman Warrior*, for example, as noted in my first chapter, Maxine Hong Kingston demonstrates the silences—and silencing—concurrent with that mysterious process of "becoming American" for a young daughter of Chinese immigrants in the United States. Immigration to the United States for Asians has involved an erasure of histories that may never be fully "recovered." Paralleling the exclusionary practices of U.S. immigration policy have been the exclusions enacted against Asians from full participation in U.S. culture. When Asian Americans claim status *as* Americans, questions such as Where are you from? act as constant provocations to jar them back into their prescribed roles as foreigners, guests, and "outsiders within." Always there is the reminder that Asian Americans (and other people of color) are not *American*, certainly not in the ways that Americans of European descent may be perceived to be. Somehow, the official narratives of North America remain reliant upon principles that equate American identity with whiteness. Such ideologies have effectively maintained Asian Americans within the borders of America's historical discourse, while also rendering whiteness—as the unmarked, "neutral" racial category—invisible and therefore normative. While Asian Americans and other people of color have been silenced, they have neither wholly accepted this silencing nor necessarily agreed that speech fully represents their primary avenue toward liberation and social justice.[1]

In addition, Asian Americans have experienced radically shifting relationships to America. For Kingston's narrator, becoming American is always bound up with white, Western standards of femininity. Gender is thus racialized, while racial, ethnic, and national identities are shaped by gender and sexuality. As Rachel Lee argues, gender and sexuality, along with race and ethnicity, shape and complicate the ways in which Asian American writers conceptualize "America." While Asian American cultural nationalist critiques of America have posited a particular form of nationalism that, according to Lee, suggests that America is not commensurate with nationalism (5), such frameworks have also resulted in the pitting of nationalism against feminism (8). As Asian American studies shifts its primary focus away from a domestic cultural nationalism—a critical stance that enabled gender criticism—and toward more transnational and postcolonial emphases, Lee suggests that gender risks being considered irrelevant (10). She writes, "Asian American feminism risks renewed marginalization as Asian American cultural studies defines its more pressing concerns not through cultural nationalism but through alternative postcolonial and transnational convictions" (10–11). To press for the urgency of Asian American feminist analyses, it is vital to consider the ways in which gender and sexuality shape most, if not all, formations of Asian American identity, history, and subjectivity. In other words, as I have argued in *Tell This Silence*, Asian American histories have been dependent upon shifting notions of gender and sexuality, from the Chinese immigrant bachelor societies and prostitution houses of the early part of the twentieth century to the fragmentation of heterosexual Japanese American families during World War II, the racialization of Asians in America has always depended on conceptualizations of gender, sexuality, and desire.

In *Tell This Silence*, I have argued that silence has multiple meanings and that Asian American women writers have deployed silences in their texts as means of unsaying. In so doing, they suggest a great silencing of Asian Americans in general and of Asian American women in particular. Also, their writings protest their exclusion from official historical narratives and they transform discourse, at times offering critiques of oppositional frameworks in which Asian American women are generally marginalized or rendered altogether invisible, and often making use of silences to produce counternarratives of resistance. Silence, in such instances, operates as a strategy for Asian American women writers to retell narratives of nation, gender, race, and sexuality.

In the first two chapters, I discussed the "uses" of silence, suggesting that silence, too, operates as a form of discourse, a way of saying and, at times, unsaying. As such, silence, rather than being outside of or in opposition to speech, exists alongside it. Considering the history of Asian immigration to the United States and Kingston's writings, I proposed that silence is a powerful metaphor for the actual, material exclusion of Asians from the United States and is also often used to symbolize power-lessness and lack of subjectivity. However, for Asians in the United States, living in enforced servitude and silence, it has also come to signify a means of resistance. Choosing not to speak, when such speech is induced by oppressors, can be seen as a clear refusal to be dominated. Also, silence for Asian Americans has been neither monolithic nor static, but it shifts according to context and societal pressures and constraints. Writers such as Kingston have recognized the ways in which enforced silence is oppressive, yet they also suggest that coerced speech too, enacts domination. As Cheung argues, it is not just prohibition against speech but also the coercion to speak that obstructs or hinders articulation (1993, 169). Such coercion also encourages specific forms of articulation, for example, certain formulaic devices for "coming out." Such forms do not always allow subjugated groups of people to actually "claim their voices" or define their own experiences, as much as they enforce speech through the voice(s) and language of the oppressors. In fact, Foucault argues for recognition of what he calls a "'reverse' discourse," the means through which marginalized groups of people often are able to speak. Yet, according to his theoretical framework, such discourse often relies on the same vocabulary and the same categories by which it was disqualified in the first place. He writes:

> There is not, on the one side, a discourse of power, and opposite it, another discourse that runs counter to it. Discourses are tactical elements or blocks operating in the field of force relations; there can exist different and even contradictory discourses within the same strategy; they can, on the contrary, circulate without changing their form from one strategy to another, opposing strategy. (101–102)

Thus, speech does not necessitate freedom from oppression, and silence is not merely the absence or opposite of speech.

In this conclusion, I return to silence, as both theme and method in Asian American women's textual production. In specific cases, as with Joy Kogawa's Obasan and Mitsuye Yamada's Camp Notes, silences signify a rebuttal to conventional narratives of Japanese North American internment during World War II—narratives of exclusion and/or marginalization. In such texts, silences operate as powerful indictments of the historical record and a refusal to be erased from history. At the same time, both authors also critique any notion of a totalizing, master narrative of the United States, suggesting instead that histories are multiple, heterogeneous, complex, and interconnected. In Theresa Hak Kyung Cha's *Dictée*, silence emerges as a way of telling a different story, a method of unsaying. Juxtaposing discursive, textual silences with nationally endorsed forms of silencing, Cha demonstrates what has been rendered "unspeakable" and/or incomprehensible within the forms of language presently available to us. She places "Korean American" and "woman" into a third space, a narrative zone that is cognizant of the ways in which Korea, Korean America, and Korean American women have been pushed to the margins of language and discourse. As that which is outside of language, Cha's silences—similar to Irigaray's model of a closed signifying economy—are figured not as sites of repression but of unknowability within existing theoretical contexts.[2] To unsay, for Cha, involves a careful acknowledgment of the fact that she writes—and lives—under constant threat of erasure.

In the first three chapters, my focus is American history, Asian immigration to North America, and the experiences of Asian Americans in the United States and Canada. In the last two chapters, my emphasis shifts to understandings of nation and nationalism, especially within transnational contexts, heavily influenced as they are by U.S. ideology and historical sense. With this shift, I attempt to make the point that such histories are interconnected, a point that is made explicit by Cha, Min, and Keller. Min, in her autobiographical *Red Azalea*, proposes a breakdown among binary oppositions between East and West, China and the United States, woman and man, body and mind, and homosexuality and heterosexuality. Locating these configurations within a global context that exoticizes China while upholding the United States as part of the "free world," Min suggests that dualistic thinking not only maintains hierarchies and inequalities but also naturalizes difference and characterizes all "inferior" part of these binaries as deviant. She employs strategic silences in her discussion of a same-sex relationship in Cultural Revolution China in order to fracture the dominant narratives of Chinese nationalism and heterosexuality. Keller, on the other hand, through her character, Soon Hyo, evokes the subtle powers of silence, especially in contexts where enforced speech enacts violence. For both Min and Keller, silence operates as a tool to problematize sexuality and history. In their narratives, speech is not necessarily liberating, silences are often protective, and sexuality—figured as both pleasure and danger—relies on multiple methods of discourse to emerge into public consciousness.

However, critical questions remain. In *Comfort Woman*, Soon Hyo's silence, while clearly a tool of resistance, also enables her extreme victimization. Her act of speech, illustrated by the tapes she leaves for Beccah, functions only through a disembodied voice. Thus, her naming of herself through speech is possible only when separate from her body, and Keller suggests an inability to claim both body and voice in relation to nation simultaneously. In *Red Azalea*, Min also positions "the body" as separate and removed from the subjectivity represented by her mind. Absent speech acts that rarely effect change, do Asian American women's *bodies* represent the sole avenue for Asian American women writers to raise questions about nation and nationalism? And as the "national body," where/when can Asian and Asian American women claim status as national subjects? While Min hints that she and Yan accessed national subjectivity through their sexual desire, the other protagonists of *Tell This Silence* experience complex and conflicted relationships to nation and national belonging, evidenced by displacement, sexual violence, the rupturing of family structures, and the fragmentation of both individual and collective subjectivities.

As a specifically feminist method—and subject of feminist inquiry—silence serves as an intervention into contemporary feminist discussions in the United States. Such discussions have tended either to overlook the involvement of Asian American women in the history of feminist movements, or they have attempted to interpret the lives, actions, and experiences of Asian and Asian American women (and other women of color) according to disturbing stereotypes and/or categories framed in oppositional paradigms: "developed" vs. "underdeveloped"; complex, real, material subjects vs. monolithic, homogeneous, objectified nonsubjects; independent and empowered vs. oppressed, victimized, and dependent; capable of expression and possessing a feminist vision and voice vs. silent, unknowing, and unable to understand or analyze one's surroundings. Chandra Talpade Mohanty suggests that such Western feminist frameworks produce an image, or representation, of an "average third world woman" who "leads an essentially truncated life based on her feminine gender (read: sexually constrained) and her being 'third world' (read: ignorant, poor, uneducated, tradition-bound, domestic, family-oriented, victimized, etc.)" ("Under Western Eyes," 56). She notes that this representation contrasts the "(implicit) self-representation of Western women as educated, as modern, as having control over their own bodies and sexualities, and the freedom to make their own decisions" (56).

When Asian American women are represented, then, it is usually according to standards and paradigms that they themselves do not construct or choose. More often than not, however, Asian American women are simply excluded from feminist discourses, and white, Western feminist organizations have justified such exclusions by reliance on black/white racial paradigms, the conflation of African American women with women of color (and often the conflation of African American subjectivity with "race" itself), and statements such as "We did not know who to ask," or "There aren't any Asian American women we know who are feminists."[3] Thus, not only are Asian American women rendered invisible in mainstream feminist movements and writings, but "feminism" itself is defined as outside the parameters of Asian American women's lives and experiences, and vice versa. When an Asian American woman does take a stand, defining that stand as feminist, she may still be characterized as something other than feminist herself. For example, as I argue in chapter 3, stereotypes of Asian American women as passive, childlike, and incapable of thinking for themselves continue to limit the choices of Asian American women and affect the ways in which others perceive their actions. Asian American feminists are often dismissed with statements suggesting that they are not *really* feminists, that they are attempting to "cash in on the feminist fad," and that they are merely functioning as a front for "those [authentic (white?)] feminists."[4]

While there have always been Asian Pacific American women involved in movements for social change and justice in the United States, participating in activities that could easily be called "feminist" in nature, it has been the definition as well as common interpretations of feminism that have excluded them or made them invisible. In her essay "The Feminist Movement: Where Are All the Asian American Women?" Esther Ngan-Ling Chow argues that feminism, from its inception in this country, has been predominantly white and middle-class and that women of color for the most part have simply not joined white women and thus "have not made a great impact on the movement" (362). This "relative lack of political activism" on the part of Asian American women, she argues, "stems from cultural, psychological, and social oppression which historically discouraged them from organizing . . . result[ing] in their apparent political invisibility and powerlessness" (362–363). Her argument, however, fails to account for the many actions instigated by Asian American women, actions that, though espousing rights for women, have not been defined as "feminist." Because many of the social justice organizing efforts of Asian American women have included nationalist struggles, the fight for racial equality, and analyses of class oppression, they have often been referred to as other than feminist.[5] Moreover, Asian American feminists, like the feminists among other women of color and Third World women, have rarely attempted to exclude Asian American men and other men of color from analyses of oppression and have argued instead for collective action and struggle against all forms of domination.[6]

Ngan-Ling Chow's analyses of Asian American women's absence from feminism takes whiteness—and white middle-class women—as her point of reference. She attempts to explore the ways in which Asian American women fit—or fail to fit—models of white middle-class feminist norms, rather than centering the experiences and feminist histories and strategies of Asian American women. Also, her assertion that Asian American women's lack of political participation stems from cultural, psychological, and social oppression that has discouraged them from organizing comes dangerously close to blaming Asian American women for their own marginalization and exclusions from feminism. Rather, Asian American women have participated in multiple movements for social change, speaking out and breaking silence in various ways.

As early as 1902, Asian women in the United States attempted to fight for women's rights. That year, Sieh King King, an eighteen-year-old student from China living in San Francisco, gave a speech in which she linked women's oppression to the domination of China. Aligning herself with the "New Women" of the United States, she suggested that Chinese women, too, must redefine the meanings of womanhood and femininity (Yung 52–53). Other women in Chinatown devoted their energies to creating women's clubs, in particular the Chinese Women's Jeleab (Self Reliance) Association of 1913 and Chinese YWCAs, as early as 1916 (Yung 92–105). Linking their understandings of feminism to Chinese nationalism, they raised funds for disaster relief in China, organized child-care and education programs for new mothers, provided services related to improved housing, employment, sanitation, and domestic problems, and offered English language classes. In particular, they protested the practice of foot binding and critiqued stereotypes of Chinese and Chinese American women (96–100). Asserting their place in the public sphere, these early Chinese American feminists reshaped gender relations in their communities.

Asian American feminists were also instrumental in the Asian American movement of the late 1960s and 1970s in the United States. William Wei identifies the emergence of this "second wave" of Asian American feminism as stemming from dissatisfaction with the sexism in the Asian American movement. Becoming more and more aware of their "second-class" status within the Asian American movement, women became increasingly intolerant of sexist jokes and assumptions that their sexual favors were "just compensation" for Asian American men, who had been feminized by American racism and forced to live in bachelor communities because of exclusionary laws (Wei 75–76). Rather than viewing Asian American feminist movement as simply a part of the larger, mainstream women's liberation movement, he argues that in actuality, it was "independent and parallel" (73). In fact, he states,

> As a predominantly European American phenomenon grappling with the "feminine mystique," that is, the belief that a woman's role should be that of a housewife-mother, and advocating employment outside the house as a solution to it, the women's liberation movement initially seemed irrelevant to Asian American women whose self-image and self-esteem came from attachment to family. And, whether they wanted to or not, many of them were already working outside the home, usually in low-wage occupations in a racially stratified labor market, to supplement the family income. The tendency of European American feminists to "polarize the sexes, encourage narcissism, and deprecate individual obligation to others" alienated Asian American women who identified closely with their ethnic community. (73)

Like other women of color, Asian American feminists were critical of the mainstream feminist movement's lack of attention to race and ethnicity, as well as the movement toward separatism. Thus, Wei argues, they formed their own consciousness-raising groups, study groups, and organizations in the 1960s, and by the late 1970s had established national organizations and publications structured around feminist principles of group participation and consensus.[7]

Literary and artistic production have been key components of the emerging Asian American feminist movement. Kingston, in particular with her text, *The Woman Warrior*, introduced many of the themes of Asian American feminist thought to a wide readership. Unquestionably the most well-known text by an Asian American woman writer, according to Wei, *The Woman Warrior* has had an immense effect on Asian American feminist writings and actions. Hong Kingston's analyses of the effects of racism and sexism on Asian American women and her exploration of the relationship between an Asian immigrant mother and her American-born daughter resonate in almost all of the texts I have discussed in this book.

Additionally, many of the authors in this study construct narratives of female heroism. Appropriating the motif of heroism for female national subjects, the writers in *Tell This Silence* depict mythical and historical women warriors, including Fa Mu Lan, Aunt Emily, Yu Guan Soon, Induk, Yan, and the narrators themselves. They suggest critical linkages between women and national agendas, offering challenges to the historical records that have rarely recognized Asian American women's agency and public forms of resistance to not only sexism but racism, imperialism, and colonization. To do so, they rely on what Robyn Wiegman has termed a "disloyal" feminism. Building on Wiegman's analysis, Lee suggests a specifically Asian American feminism—a "feminism past innocence"— that "does not aspire to be the sole or ascendant macropolitical framework . . . [and that is] always alert to what it has excluded, [and] feels uncomfortable posing itself as the definitive counternarrative to broad (yet implicitly male) 'collective' narratives to save the world" (145). This feminism "both acknowledges that it is not outside power (that it cannot disavow how it works through dominance and exclusions) and yet still forwards its tactics and interventions—its alternative epistemologies—as necessary, even while not definitive, correctives to the History of Universal Man" (Lee 146). As such, the Asian American feminist practice suggested by Lee is always partial and aware of its own limitations. Unlike the totalizing histories critiqued by the authors of this study, these Asian American women writers propose recognition of multiple subject positions and discursive and political practices.

Through participation in public discourse, literary and artistic production, and direct-action strategies, Asian American women have often engaged this noninnocent feminism. That they have not necessarily always been heard or taken seriously is one of the premises of this project. To challenge the boundaries of feminism, Asian American women writers have developed multiple strategies of resistance, and one such strategy, as I argue, is silence. Such a strategy, in the texts discussed in *Tell This Silence*, raises many questions regarding the relationship of gender to race and nation. Additionally, silence introduces questions about feminism and poscolonialism. Who counts as truly feminist? What are feminist issues? Who decides, and who benefits? In her work *The Shock of Arrival: Reflections on Postcolonial Experience*, Meena Alexander reflects on language's relationships to migrancy and postcolonial memory. Considering the role of feminism for South Asian women in the United States, she writes: "And how will our goddess speak? In many tongues, in babble, too, I think, mimicking the broken words that surround her, here, now, in America. . . . It is as if the continuous pressure of violence, always already localized, had forged itself into a second language—an Otherness more radical than any the woman writer had been forced previously to feel—and through this anguishing, potentially fatal medium, she must voice her passions, reconfigure her world" (84). Silence as a strategy exists alongside a general silencing of Asian American women, and for this reason, it must be analyzed carefully so as not to be perceived simply as the internalization of oppression on the part of Asian American women. As a refusal to participate in their own erasure, silence may also signify, for Asian American women, a powerful means of unsaying.

notes

1. Introduction

1. Here, I rely on the term "national belonging" rather than nationality to draw attention to the fact that an individual may identify with a particular nationality (e.g., Asian Americans are, of course, Americans), yet he or she may not feel a sense of belonging. The social and political climate of the United States creates a problematic context for Asian Americans, for whom nationality and national belonging are not necessarily always the same thing.

2. My discussion of The Woman Warrior is not comprehensive and does not include a comprehensive review of the literature. In fact, because of the great number of critical essays and texts about The Woman Warrior—nearly two hundred published sources and several dozens of unpublished dissertations and theses— such a project is beyond the scope of this research. Rather, I offer this discussion as a kind of "microanalysis," demonstrating my methods and some of the themes to be addressed in subsequent chapters. Also, because Kingston's text is perhaps one of the best known and most frequently studied texts in Asian American literature, occupying a central space within the emerging "canon" of Asian American texts, it offers a unique vantage point from which to explore the issue of silence, an issue that I argue has relevance for most writings by Asian Pacific American women. For a discussion of the politics surrounding canonization and

Asian American literature, see Susan Koshy, "The Fiction of Asian American Literature," *The Yale Journal of Criticism* 9 (1996): 315–346.

3. See also Benedict Anderson, *Imagined Communities: Reflections on the Origin and Spread of Nationalism* (London: Verso, 1991).

4. Beverly Guy-Sheftall, Keynote Lecture, Women of Color Across the Women's Studies Curriculum Conference, Marquette University, Milwaukee, Wisconsin, March 15, 1996. Notably, however, the term "women of color" implies a binary framework for race only because it is so often conflated with African American women rather than used to mean all women of color (including Latina, Chicana, Native American, Pacific Islander, Asian American, and Arab American women).

5. For discussion of the problematic appropriation of Canadian texts such as *Obasan* by Asian American critics, see Meng Yu Marie Lo, "Fields of Recognition: Reading Asian Canadian Literature in Asian America." Ph.D. diss., Department of Rhetoric, University of California–Berkeley, 2001.

6. For example, Lisa Lowe points out the distinction between early Chinese immigrants to the United States in the 1850s, who were primarily poor laborers from the Canton province, with men outnumbering women by ten to one, and more recent Chinese immigrants who come to the United States from Taiwan, Hong Kong, the People's Republic, or from other parts of the Chinese diaspora, including Malaysia and Singapore. Recent Chinese immigrants are heterogeneous in class backgrounds and education and labor skills as well. See Lowe, *Immigrant Acts: On Asian American Cultural Politics* (Durham: Duke University Press, 1996) 66.

7. For more on this, see Naheed Islam, "In the Belly of the Multicultural Beast I Am Named South Asian," *Our Feet Walk the Sky*, ed. the Women of South Asian Descent Collective (San Francisco: Aunt Lute Books, 1993). She suggests that current usages of "South Asian" have become interchangeable with "Indian," particularly within academic and literary circles, where "South Asian" has recently gained currency, rendering many other groups of people invisible both within these circles and more generally.

8. See, for example, Elena Tajima Creef's "Notes from a Fragmented Daughter," in Anzaldúa, 1990: 82–84; Susan Ito, "Hambun-Hambun," in E. Kim, 1997: 128–132; and Juliana Pegues/Pei Lu Fung, "White Rice: Searching for Identity," in Lim-Hing, 1994: 25–36.

9. For discussion of the ways in which such themes are articulated and contested within recent Asian American literary criticism, see Viet Thanh Nguyen, *Race and Resistance: Literature and Politics in Asian America* (New York: Oxford University Press, 2002).

10. Here, following Tejaswini Niranjana's careful rearticulation of "trope," I hope to indicate, as she does, a "metaphorizing that includes a displacement as well as a re-figuring" (5).

11. See, for example, Robin Morgan, ed., *Sisterhood Is Powerful: An Anthology of Writings from the Women's Liberation Movement* (New York: Vintage, 1970); Toni Cade

Bambara, ed., *The Black Woman: An Anthology* (New York: Mentor, 1970); Amy Tachiki et al., eds., *Roots: An Asian American Reader* (UCLA Asian American Studies Center, 1971); Stokely Carmichael and Charles Hamilton, eds., *Black Power: The Politics of Liberation in America* (New York: Random House, 1967); George Breitman, ed., *By Any Means Necessary: Speeches, Interviews, and a Letter by Malcolm X* (New York: Merit, 1970); Michele Wallace, *Black Macho and the Myth of the Superwoman* (New York: The Dial Press, 1978); Glenn Omatsu, "The 'Four Prisons' and the Movements of Liberation: Asian American Activism from the 1960s to the 1990s," *The State of Asian America: Activism and Resistance in the 1990s*, ed. Karin Aguilar-San Juan (Boston: South End Press, 1994), 19–70; and Julia Penelope and Susan J. Wolfe, eds., *The Original Coming Out Stories* (Freedom: The Crossing Press, 1980), in which the notion of "coming out" represents a significant form of "breaking silence" and finding a voice.

12. Here, I rely on Sandra Lee Bartky's definition of "cultural domination," in which she suggests that all parts of our culture—including our language, institutions, art, and literature—are male-dominated and structured in such a way as to oppress women. See Bartky, *Femininity and Domination: Studies in the Phenomenology of Oppression* (New York: Routledge, 1990) 25.

13. Interestingly enough, this discourse has been engaged by scholars in a variety of different disciplines. For example, Giddings, Higginbotham, and Hine are all historians, specializing in African American women's history. Paula Giddings wrote the groundbreaking work *When and Where I Enter: The Impact of Black Women on Race and Sex in America* (New York: Bantam Books, 1984) as well as "The Last Taboo," *Race-ing Justice, Engendering Power: Essays on Anita Hill, Clarence Thomas, and the Construction of Social Reality*, ed. Toni Morrison (New York: Pantheon 1992), an essay about the Clarence Thomas/Anita Hill exchange that explores silences within the black community on issues of sexuality. Darlene Clark Hine has been involved in the huge publishing project of a sixteen-volume series about black women in U.S. history. She coined the term "culture of dissemblance" in her essay about black women, silences, and sexual violence, "Rape and the Inner Lives of Black Women in the Middle West: Preliminary Thoughts on the Culture of Dissemblance," *Unequal Sisters: A Multicultural Reader in U.S. Women's History*, ed. Vicki Ruiz and Ellen Carol DuBois (New York: Routledge, 1990) 292–297. Higginbotham addresses theoretical issues concerning race, sexuality, and historiography in essays such as "African-American Women's History and the Metalanguage of Race," published in *Signs* 17.2 (1992): 251–274 and "Beyond the Sound of Silence: Afro-American Women in History," *Gender and History* 1.1 (1989): 50–67. Meanwhile, bell hooks is a professor of English and a well-known cultural critic. Patricia Hill Collins, author of *Black Feminist Thought: Knowledge, Consciousness, and the Politics of Empowerment* (London: HarperCollins 1990), is a sociologist. Audre Lorde, poet, writer, essayist, and activist, was a professor of English whose work crossed disciplines such as women's studies, African American studies, English, history, and philosophy.

14. Silence, like masking, implies a "true" or "real" voice (or self) that can

be known if only the subject will speak (or remove the mask). Significantly, Ya-mamoto suggests that her argument is simultaneously grounded in two contra-dictory impulses—the notion that "identity is a highly contingent and constructed category" and that "for all the language of postmodern subjectivity, there re-mains a place for the self, that which is often rather condescendingly referred to as the product of a backwards humanism" (3). Following her lead, I suggest that locating identity, even while recognizing such location(s) as highly con-structed, contingent, and contested, is also imperative to the political projects of many people of color in the United States, for whom identity has never as-sumed the natural humanistic status as a given as it has for those of dominant racial and ethnic groups.

15. Here, I do not mean to posit a split between "writers of color" and "les-bian and gay writers," reinforcing the binary I am attempting to critique. Of course writers such as Gloria Anzaldúa, Audre Lorde, Cherríe Moraga, and Bar-bara Smith write as lesbians of color, along with many others. I do think, how-ever, that much of what has been regarded as queer history and theory within the academy has been white-centered and has paid scant attention to issues of race. For a particularly nuanced approach to issues of silence in queer history, see Yolanda Chavez Leyva's essay "Listening to the Silences in Latina/Chicana Lesbian History," in Trujillo, *Living Chicana Theory*. Recognizing the multiple and complex meanings of silence for Chicana and Latina lesbians, Leyva writes: "For lesbianas Latinas, silence has been an enigma, a survival strategy, a wall which confines us, the space that protects us" (427).

16. See Duberman et al., "Introduction," especially pp. 2–3.

17. For example, although the Stonewall riots of 1969 are generally regarded as the beginning of not only an organized gay liberation movement but also a gay community in the United States, both D'Emilio and Chauncey argue for a much more complex historical analysis, taking into account the bar communi-ties and other subcultures of periods prior to Stonewall. See John D'Emilio, *Sex-ual Politics, Sexual Communities: The Making of a Homosexual Minority in the United States, 1940–1970* (Chicago: University of Chicago Press, 1983); and George Chauncey, *Gay New York: Gender, Culture, and the Making of the Gay Male World, 1890–1940* (New York: Basic Books, 1994). In his introduction, D'Emilio writes about "a curious inconsistency . . . between the rhetoric of the gay liberation movement and the reality of its achievements. On the one hand, activists in the early 1970s repeat-edly stressed, in their writing and their public comments, the intertwining themes of silence, invisibility, and isolation. Gay men and lesbians, the argu-ment ran, were invisible to society and to each other. . . . A vast silence sur-rounded the topic of homosexuality, perpetuating both invisibility and isolation. On the other hand, gay liberationists exhibited a remarkable capacity to mobi-lize their allegedly hidden, isolated constituency, and the movement grew with amazing rapidity" (1–2). Also, Elizabeth Lapovsky Kennedy and Madeline D. Davis, in their work *Boots of Leather, Slippers of Gold: The History of a Lesbian Community* (New York: Routledge, 1993), discuss a flourishing lesbian community in Buf-

falo, New York, from the 1930s to the 1950s, centered around bars and house parties. They refer to "butch" and "fem" constructions of identity, sexuality, and community as "pre-political forms of resistance" (190).

18. See, for example, Deborah McDowell, "'It's Not Safe. Not Safe at All': Sexuality in Nella Larsen's *Passing*," *The Lesbian and Gay Studies Reader*, ed. Henry Abelove, Michele Aina Barale, and David M. Halperin (New York: Routledge, 1993) 616–625; Bonnie Zimmerman, "What Has Never Been: An Overview of Lesbian Feminist Criticism," *The New Feminist Criticism: Literature and Theory*, ed. Elaine Showalter (New York: Pantheon, 1985) 200–224 and *The Safe Sea of Women: Lesbian Fiction 1969–1989* (Boston: Beacon Press, 1990); and Teresa de Lauretis, "Sexual Indifference and Lesbian Representation," also in *The Lesbian and Gay Studies Reader*, 141–158.

19. In her text, *Are Girls Necessary? Lesbian Writing and Modern Histories*, Abraham distinguishes between the "lesbian novel" and "lesbian writing." The lesbian novel, she suggests, is one of those texts "written, presented, and read as representations of lesbianism by lesbian, gay, and heterosexual writers and readers" (xiii). Compare this to lesbian writing, the "much larger body of lesbian-authored fiction—as well as poetry, drama, essays, journals, and so on—that is not 'about' female couples" (xiii).

20. Abraham also suggests that the concept of coding "provided the basis for an unproductive critical opposition between realist and modernist writing . . . [which] furthered the naturalization of the formula lesbian novel. . . . The critical emphasis on coding turns formal innovation into a defensive choice, a deliberately obscurantist gesture whose only function is to conceal taboo meanings" (25–26).

21. For discussion of the politics of speech acts, see Judith Butler, *Excitable Speech: A Politics of the Performative* (New York: Routledge, 1997).

22. See Patricia Hill Collins, *Black Feminist Thought: Knowledge, Consciousness, and the Politics of Empowerment* (New York: Routledge, 1990), especially chapter 4, "Mammies, Matriarchs, and Other Controlling Images," in which she discusses the social, political, economic, and cultural consequences of binary thinking.

23. See, for example, Peggy Kamuf, "Writing Like a Woman," *Women and Language in Literature and Society*, eds. Sally McConnell-Ginet, et al. (New York: Praeger, 1980) 284–299; Jonathan Culler, "Reading as a Woman" in his book, *On Deconstruction: Theory and Criticism after Structuralism* (Ithaca: Cornell University Press, 1982) 43–64; Robert Scholes, "Reading Like a Man," *Men and Feminism*, ed. Alice Jardine and Paul Smith (New York: Methuen, 1987) 204–218; Tania Modleski, "Feminism and the Power of Interpretation: Some Critical Readings," *Feminist Studies/ Critical Studies*, ed. Teresa de Lauretis (Bloomington: Indiana University Press, 1986): 121–138; and Diana Fuss, "Reading Like a Feminist" in *Essentially Speaking: Feminism, Nature, and Difference* (New York: Routledge, 1989) 23–37.

24. Please note: in my discussion of Kingston's *The Woman Warrior*, I use "Maxine" when referring explicitly to the narrator, or protagonist, of the text and "Kingston" when referring to its author. Because the text is largely autobiographical, this practice may seem confusing. However, I acknowledge, as King-

ston herself suggests, that her memoirs are based not only on fact but on memory and imagination as well, reflecting the complicated relationship between history and fiction.

25. Here, note the linkage between silence and Maxine's school experience in the United States. In these paintings, she explains, the black paint represented a stage curtain, and the painting was "the moment before the curtain parted or rose" (165). They were, to Maxine, "so black and full of possibilities" (165), suggesting the need to be seen and/or known. Also, as Kingston herself suggests, this image of the black curtains "probably had its literal source in the blackout curtains of World War II, a war that not only threatened the United States but had for several years before the American entry devastated the Hong family's Chinese homeland" (Simmons 8–9). And, as Cheung argues, the experiences of Japanese Americans during World War II most certainly had significant repercussions for other East Asian Americans (90–91). Because Japanese Americans were interned against their will for the duration of the war, viewed as a threat to United States national security, the status of other Americans of Asian descent also became tenuous. Cheung notes that for Maxine, this desire to assimilate into American culture as fully as possible is effected by her outright rejection of all things Chinese—Chinese language, Chinese school, new Chinese immigrants, even her own family (91).

26. See Yung, p. 334, fn. 15, in which she explains Wong's transition to first-person narration in her second autobiography, No Chinese Stranger.

27. For more discussion on the experiences of students of color in university women's studies classes, see my essay, "Decentering Whiteness: Resisting Racism in the Women's Studies Classroom," Race in the College Classroom: Pedagogy and Politics, ed. Bonnie TuSmith and Maureen T. Reddy (New Brunswick: Rutgers University Press, 2002), 40–50. See also Shirley Geok-lin Lim and Maria Herrera-Sobek, eds. Power, Race, and Gender in Academe: Strangers in the Tower? (New York: Modern Language Association, 2000).

28. Cheung suggests that Kingston "emphasizes the difficulty of conveying reality by pointing out the omissions in received information and the lapses or discrepancies in her own memory" (11). To Cheung, memory is significantly related to history, particularly the "lost," distorted, and undocumented histories of Asian Americans.

29. In her conclusion to The Woman Warrior, Kingston offers a significant "talk-story" of her own, "A Song for a Barbarian Reed Pipe," based in part on one of her mother's stories. "The beginning is hers," she writes, "the ending, mine" (206). In this narrative, she mythologizes her mother's experiences as a first-generation Chinese immigrant woman in the United States. Ts'ai Yen, a Chinese poetess of ancient times, found herself captive in a land of foreigners—barbarians—who did not speak her language or understand her. Her own children adapted the ways of the barbarians; they did not speak Chinese nor did they seem to care to learn. When this poetess finally told her story, however, her children "did not laugh, but eventually sang along when she left her tent to sit

by the winter campfires, ringed by barbarians" (209). This story, Kingston writes, "translated well" (209).

30. Judy Yung provides an illuminating example in her discussion of her own family history. In her introduction to *Unbound Feet*, she explains that during her research on Chinese American women's history, she discovered that her own family name, Yung, was in fact the result of a business transaction. In 1921, her father borrowed money to purchase the name, Yung Hin Sen, the "paper son" of Yung Ung, in order to enter the United States. Whether there actually was a son in China named Yung Hin Sen or Yung Ung simply created a son in order to sell his name and family status, is unclear. For Yung, however, the discovery that her own family name and genealogy were affected—indeed constructed—by such a historical process serves to further illustrate her arguments about the particular details of Chinese American immigration to the United States (3).

31. Incidentally, while the narrative implies a parallel between "America" and "enjoyment," neither is fully possible in the childhood documented by *The Woman Warrior*.

32. While lies to outside authority figures are justified, even enforced within her family, lies to parents represent betrayals. For example, recalling an exchange with her mother during a visit home as an adult, Kingston narrates: "'I'll be back again soon,' I said. 'You know that I come back. I think of you when I'm not here.' [Her mother replies:] 'Yes, I know you. I know you now. I've always known you. You're the one with the charming words. You have never come back. "I'll be back on Turkeyday," you said. Huh.' I shut my teeth together, vocal cords cut, they hurt so. I would not speak words to give her pain. All her children gnash their teeth" (101). This silence, deployed to protect her mother, causes Kingston herself pain. Her "charming words," to her mother, represent lies and abandonment.

33. In the second chapter of *The Woman Warrior*, entitled "White Tigers," Kingston relates the tale of Fa Mu Lan, the mythical Chinese woman warrior who was said to avenge her village by passing as a man in battle and leading her people to victory. To become the woman warrior, the narrator must first train for fifteen years—the span of her childhood—with an old man and woman on mountainous, dangerous terrain. She must learn to go hungry, to battle those who would do her harm, to run from that which she cannot confront, and to "be quiet" (23). Most of all, she must learn to "make [her] mind large, as the universe is large, so that there is room for paradoxes" (29). This training, incidentally, resonates with Kingston's own training to survive in the United States. As an impoverished Chinese American daughter of immigrants, she, too, must learn to go hungry, to know when to fight and when to flee, to be quiet —fully aware of the multiple meanings of her silence—and to understand contradictions. However, as my student Kristin Goodman points out, the parallels end there. While the mythical subject of "White Tigers" is trained to conquer enemies and save her entire village, young Maxine recounts her American life as

"slum grubby," not glorious (51). A "disappointment" to her parents, she is unable to figure out what is her village (45). Also, while Fa Mu Lan passes into heroism largely through gender transgression, young Maxine is caught within the constraints of American (white) femininity.

34. See, for example, Cheung, 88; Feng, 127; Kim, 1981:153; Simmons, 97. See especially Sau-ling Wong's discussion of this girl as Maxine's "racial shadow."

35. Silence, for young Maxine, is also equated with ignorance and stupidity. When she confronts her mother toward the end of the text, she exclaims, "It's your fault I talk weird. The only reason I flunked kindergarten was because you couldn't teach me English, and you gave me a zero IQ" (201). Incidentally, Cheung points out that it is not simply the other girl's silence that makes her despicable to Maxine but also her "China doll haircut" (173). Kingston writes, "If she had had little bound feet, the toes twisted under the balls, I would have jumped up and landed on them—crunch!—stomped on them with my iron shoes" (178). Thus, Cheung argues, Kingston is angry and disgusted not only at silence but at being Chinese. Her "gratuitous cruelty can be understood only in terms of Maxine's virulent self-contempt at being Chinese" (1993, 89). Sadly, at this point in the text, and in her life, Maxine "can become articulate in Western discourse only by parroting self-denigrating Western assumptions. Her tussle with her ethnic double represents a phase in the narrator's life when her racial self-hatred is most acute and her acceptance of white norms ostensibly complete" (Cheung, 1993, 90).

36. In particular, Asian American male writers such as Frank Chin have excoriated Kingston, calling her, according to Simmons, "a purveyor of 'white racist art,' [and] a latter-day 'Pocohontas,' selling out Chinese Americans to pander to white readers" (1).

37. As Cheung points out, critics have accused Kingston of "reinforcing racist stereotypes and of falsifying Chinese myths and history" (1993, 77). Their criticism fails to grasp her artistry and the critical implications of her text, overlooking the ways in which she "resists the opposition of fact and imagination in the face of received falsehood and historical silence" (77).

38. To say that silence has been chosen, however, is misleading. The very notion of choice, especially "free" choice is problematic in a culture in which choices are limited for some groups of people.

2. What Makes an American?

1. I discuss some of the controversy over The Woman Warrior in chapter 4. For more information, see Sau-ling Cynthia Wong, ed., Maxine Hong Kingston's The Woman Warrior: A Case Book.

2. Unless, of course such actions or events involved the vilification of Asian Americans, as occurred during World War II with Japanese Americans who were incarcerated in internment camps (a history I discuss in my next chapter).

3. For discussion on exclusionary practices within definitions of "Asian Amer-

ican" that also limit understandings of Asian American history, see Elaine H. Kim, "Beyond Railroads and Internment: Comments on the Past, Present, and Future of Asian American Studies," *Privileging Positions: The Sites of Asian American Studies*, ed., Gary Y. Okihiro, Marilyn Alquizola, Dorothy Fujita Rony, and K. Scott Wong (Pullman: Washington State University, 1995) 11–19; and Lisa Lowe, "Heterogeneity, Hybridity, Multiplicity: Asian American Differences," *Immigrant Acts: On Asian American Cultural Politics* (Durham: Duke University Press, 1996) 60–83.

4. For complex discussions of whiteness and white privilege, see Ruth Frankenberg, *White Women, Race Matters: The Social Construction of Whiteness* (Minneapolis: University of Minessota Press, 1993); Paul Kivel, *Uprooting Racism: How White People Can Work for Social Justice* (Philadelphia: New Society Publishers, 1996); Peggy McIntosh, "White Privilege and Male Privilege: A Personal Account of Coming to See Correspondences through Work in Women's Studies," *Race, Class, and Gender: An Anthology*, ed. Margaret Andersen and Patricia Hill Collins, 3rd ed. (Belmont: Wadsworth Press, 1998); George Lipsitz, *The Possessive Investment in Whiteness: How White People Profit from Identity Politics* (Philadelphia: Temple University Press, 1998); Paula Rothenberg, ed., *White Privilege: Essential Readings on the Other Side of Racism* (New York: Worth Publishers, 2002).

5. At the time of this writing, there are more than fifty essays regarding *China Men*. For the purposes of this project, I refer to only a fraction of such citations, fully aware that there is, of course, much more to say about both texts.

6. I focus on the history of Chinese immigrants in the U.S. because, as Chu points out, the Chinese community represented the largest group affected by the immigration exclusion laws and subsequent discriminatory practices (29).

7. Similarly, Virginia Yans-McLaughlin argues that global immigration must be recognized, first and foremost, as "a form of labor recruitment in an international labor market," including the movement of free individuals, slaves, contract laborers, braceros, or guest workers (6). See her introduction to her edited volume *Immigration Reconsidered: History, Sociology, and Politics* (New York: Oxford University Press, 1990) 3–18.

8. Of course, the experiences of Asian immigrants were widely diverse. By generalizing to some degree, I do not intend to characterize their experiences as monolithic. However, I do emphasize the fact that historians have identified certain shared themes in the social history of Asian immigration, especially in their treatment by white Americans.

9. This "dual wage" system, however, is regionally based. In the U.S. South, racism against African Americans and the legacy of slavery led to a wage system that exploited African Americans while paying their white counterparts considerably higher wages. In parts of the Northeast, immigrants from southern and eastern Europe experienced harsh treatment and low wages compared to dominant white laborers. In Texas and the Southwest, Mexicans and Mexican Americans faced economic and cultural discrimination. See Evelyn Nakano Glenn, "From Servitude to Service Work: Historical Continuities in the Racial Division of Paid Reproductive Labor," *Unequal Sisters: A Multi-Cultural Reader in U.S. Women's His-*

tory, ed. Vicki L. Ruiz and Ellen Carol DuBois (New York: Routledge, 1994) 405–435; Maldwyn Allen Jones, *American Immigration*, 2nd ed. (Chicago: University of Chicago Press, 1992); David M. Reimers, *Still the Golden Door: The Third World Comes to America* (New York: Columbia University Press, 1985); and Virginia Yans-McLaughlin, ed., *Immigration Reconsidered: History, Sociology, and Politics* (New York: Oxford University Press, 1990).

10. The Chinese translation of "coolie," according to Amott and Matthaei, is "bitter labor" (196).

11. Amott and Matthaei point out that the United States' takeover of the Philippines was met with a great deal of resistance on the part of Filipinos/as. They write, "U.S. troops devised excruciating tortures, massacred entire village populations, and burned and forcibly relocated others in their attempt to subjugate the islands. By 1902, the independence movement had been crushed, and a Sedition Law imposed the death penalty or long imprisonment on anyone advocating independence, even by peaceful means. The economy was in a shambles" (236). By destroying the local economy of the Philippines, and by employing heavy recruitment tactics for laborers, the United States played a direct role in the immigration of large numbers of Filipinos/as to the U.S. mainland to work for meager wages while suffering exploitation and racial discrimination.

12. In fact, this pitting of Asian immigrants against one another (as well as historical conflicts among Asian nations) has served to further destabilize notions of Asians as homogeneous in the United States. However, the distinctions that Asian Americans of various national or ethnic backgrounds have drawn themselves consistently conflict with the dominant American perception that all Asians are somehow the same. I argue that this process of coming together (e.g., mobilizing around critical issues) and pulling apart (into discrete, autonomous cultural groups) during particular historical moments and/or crises characterizes Asian American cultural politics in the twentieth century.

13. See also Lisa Lowe, 1997, in which she discusses the ways in which Asian immigrant women's work experiences in the United States are shaped by global politics and Western expansionism in Asia. Asian immigrant women, she suggests, are most vulnerable to economic exploitation when their countries of origin are economically disadvantaged in relation to the United States (271).

14. As Patricia Chu writes, "exclusion," in Asian American studies, "refers specifically to the laws restricting Asian immigration and naturalization but more broadly to the whole range of discriminatory practices designed to prevent Asians from identifying themselves as Americans" (29).

15. Similarly, Carole Sheffield argues that patterns of bigotry have dominated U.S. history, involving brutal acts of violence against those defined as "other" within American culture. While Sheffield argues that hate crimes are often spontaneous and unorganized, she also suggests that such violence was and continues to be "institutionally organized and sanctioned" by our government and that, in fact, our government and its agents have often been the perpetrators of

such violence. See Sheffield, "Hate-Violence," *Race, Class, and Gender in the United States: An Integrated Study*, ed. Paula S. Rothenberg, 3rd ed. (New York: St. Martin's Press, 1995) 432–441.

16. In 1870, the San Francisco Board of Supervisors legislated that every three months, laundries using one horse for their delivery wagons were charged $2, laundries using two horses were liable for $4, and laundries that did not use any horses owed $15. As Chan states, "Since it was the Chinese who did not use horses, the spirit of the law discriminated against them, even though its letter ostensibly did not" (46).

17. For example, he notes the following juxtaposition: "Though the Chinese were filling and leveeing the San Joaquin Delta for thirteen cents a square yard, building the richest agricultural land in the world, they were prohibited from owning land or real estate" (Kingston, 1977, 153).

18. While some readers may view works like those of Sucheng Chan and Ronald Takaki as "official histories," juxtaposed against the "unofficial history" represented by Kingston's narrative, I consider all of these writings as oppositional, partial histories attempting to speak to—and *against*—the dominant official histories that have for so long excluded Asian Americans.

19. See Nakano Glenn's essay "Split Household, Small Producer and Dual Wage Earner: An Analysis of Chinese-American Family Strategies," *The Journal of Marriage and the Family* (February 1983): 35–46, for a discussion of the historical and sociological impacts of such a family system.

20. Here, I rely on the term "prostitution" rather than more current terms like "sex work" or "sex tourism" primarily because prostitution refers more to the specific historical period under consideration and because sex work connotes a set of ideologies and discursive practices that are beyond the scope of this study. For discussion of the politics of recent militarized prostitution and global sex tourism, see Cynthia Enloe, *Bananas, Beaches, and Bases: Making Feminist Sense of International Politics* (Berkeley: University of California Press, 1990); Katharine H. S. Moon, *Sex Among Allies: Military Prostitution in U.S.-Korea Relations* (New York: Columbia University Press, 1997); and Kamala Kempadoo and Jo Doezema, eds., *Global Sex Workers: Rights, Resistance, and Redefinition* (New York: Routledge, 1998).

21. While anti-Chinese prejudice and anti-miscegenation attitudes flourished during the years before, it was in 1880 that California's Civil Code institutionalized the prohibition of a marriage license to a white person and a "Negro, Mulatto, or Mongolian." See Yung, *Unbound Feet*, 29.

22. According to Yung, Ah Toy arrived in the United States from Hong Kong in 1849 and "soon became infamous as the most successful Chinese courtesan in [San Francisco]. . . . Within a year or two of her arrival she became a madam —owner of a number of Chinese prostitutes" (33). Ah Toy was also reported to be a well-known and influential public figure in the city. As Yung states, her experiences, while rare, offer a complicated history of race, gender, and class relations within Chinese immigrant history and suggest that "when given the op-

portunity, Chinese women promoted themselves from the rank of oppressed to oppressor, preying on younger women in a vicious cycle of traffic and procurement" (34).

23. Amott and Matthaei suggest that the "sale of one's children, especially daughters, was common among destitute families in China. Daughters were seen as expendable since they left their parents' homes upon marriage and, as a Chinese proverb put it, 'Eighteen gifted daughters are not equal to one lame son'" (202). However, they state, many girls sold into prostitution remained loyal to their parents, sending money home regularly. While such practices could potentially reinforce negative stereotypes about Chinese culture, it is crucial to view this treatment within the context of global relations, noting processes of imperialism, colonialism, and globalization, for example.

24. For example, Yung documents the fact that many white "patrons" were attracted to Chinese prostitutes because they considered them exotic and because they had heard rumors that Chinese women's vaginas "ran 'east-west' instead of 'north-south'" (28). Such a stereotype was also employed against Vietnamese women during the Vietnam War, according to Susan Jeffords, to encourage the mass military rapes of Vietnamese women by U.S. soldiers. See Jeffords, *The Remasculinization of America: Gender and the Vietnam War* (Bloomington: Indiana University Press, 1989) 65.

25. The Page Law was passed by Congress in 1875, and according to Yung, it was induced by public sentiment opposing the Chinese. The law forbade "the entry of 'Oriental' contract laborers, prostitutes, and criminals" (32). As Chan states, citing George Peffer, the law reduced the number of Chinese women entering the United States but not Chinese men, and it paved the way for the 1882 Chinese Exclusion Act (54).

26. Chan suggests, for example, that laundry work became especially significant for Chinese men (and in Chinese American history) because it was one of the few occupations open to them in California in the late 1800s and early 1900s. She writes, "Large numbers of Chinese eventually became laundrymen, not because washing clothes was a traditional male occupation in China, but because there were very few women—and consequently virtually no washerwomen of any ethnic group—in gold-rush California" (33). Also, King-Kok Cheung (1990) writes that Asian American men have "been confronted with a history of inequality and of painful 'emasculation,'" forced to do what was considered "women's work," and then negatively stereotyped accordingly.

27. Li Ju-Chen, *Flowers in the Mirror*, trans. Lin Tai-yi (Berkeley: University of California Press, 1965). (See Cheung, 1993, 102.)

28. Incidentally, both *China Men* and *The Woman Warrior* open with tales of gender transgression. In *The Woman Warrior*, Kingston's aunt, the "no name woman," has crossed sexual and gender boundaries by becoming pregnant while her husband is away—gone to the Gold Mountain. In *China Men*, Tang Ao is entrapped in the Land of Women. Goellnicht writes, "Just as the no-name aunt is forced into a position of powerlessness and silence, both physically and linguistically

(for her indiscretions, she is driven to suicide and denied a name) by the traditions of Chinese patriarchy that deny her existence once she has transgressed its laws, so too Tang Ao the sojourner finds himself forced into a position of powerlessness and silence by the Laws of the Ruling Fathers (the white majority)" (1992, 193). Yet, *The Woman Warrior* also includes the narrative of Fa Mu Lan, a "woman warrior" who passed as a man in order to save her village. Whereas her gender crossing—from female to male—offers the possibility of her heroism, Tang Ao's transformation to femininity is marked, in the words of Goellnicht, as a "demotion" (192). Also, Kingston's presentation of the legend of Tang Ao as "history" and "fact" enacts, in Cheung's analysis, a parody of sorts, whereby Kingston's narrative offers a challenge to the historical construction of Chinese men in (and, I might add, erasure from) U.S. history. See Cheung, 1993, 103.

29. For more information about this particular form of resistance, see Lucy E. Salyer, *Laws Harsh as Tigers: Chinese Immigrants and the Shaping of Modern Immigration Law* (Chapel Hill: University of North Carolina Press, 1995).

30. See Takaki, 1989, chapter 4 ("Raising Cane: The World of Plantation Hawaii"), pp. 132–176.

31. Indeed, as Linton suggests, most silences in *China Men* are distressing to Kingston. Linton writes, "Even when speech is exacted at a terrible price, it is valorized" (41). Commenting on the "black" cousin in China who demands money for a bicycle, Linton traces the Chinese grandfather who must have returned to China with a Hawaiian wife—a "black" woman who "jabbered like a monkey" (86). Presumably, the Chinese around her did not understand her language, and the narrator, having received a demand from this woman's descendant, is surprised by his "articulateness" (86). The point, Linton suggests, is that "any immigrant, exiled in a foreign land, is effectively silenced. The newcomer may 'jabber' but no one hears, and the risk is that he or she will give up and fall silent. A willingness to make demands, even unreasonable ones, is better than abject silence" (43).

32. I begin by discussing the racial theories of Omi and Winant because their text is one of the most comprehensive examinations of race in the United States to date, and their development of the model of "racial formation" provides insight into how race and racial ideology function to maintain dominance and subordination—two key themes in my analyses of Asian American women's writings.

33. Similarly, Amott and Matthaei trace a history of racism in the United States in which the religion-based viewpoint that people of color were not descendants of Adam and Eve, as were white people, gave way to scientific theories arguing that race is biological, that people of color are inherently inferior, and that racial inequality is therefore natural. They write, "The different social and economic practices of societies of color were viewed by whites in the nineteenth century as 'savage,' in need of the 'civilizing' influence of white domination" (17).

34. For example, while the authors argue that "there is nothing inherently white about racism" (72) and that people of color can also display racist behavior, they do make a distinction between racism (creating and reproducing structures of domination based on essentialist categories of race) and the ways in which people of color often come together for support, common interests, and even survival (the "strategic essentialism" mentioned above). See Omi and Winant, pp. 69–76.

35. I rely on racial theories by Higginbotham, Yamato, and Sethi, in particular, because all three writers address the ways in which race—and racism—interact with other categories of identity and because they attempt to disrupt the conventional black/white racial opposition. Higginbotham, for example, links race to gender, class, and sexuality in her analysis of African American women's history. Yamato attempts to break away from a simple dualistic racial framework in her discussion of forms of racism. And Sethi examines the forms of racism that are specifically aimed at Asians in the United States.

36. For discussion of internalized racism and what they term "cross-racial hostility," often referred to as "horizontal racism," see Virginia R. Harris and Trinity A. Ordona, "Developing Unity Among Women of Color: Crossing the Barriers of Internalized Racism and Cross-Racial Hostility," ed. Gloria Anzaldúa, (San Francisco: Aunt Lute Books, 1990) 300–316.

37. See Helen Zia's article, "Violence in Our Communities: 'Where Are the Asian Women?'" *Making More Waves*, ed. Elaine H. Kim, et al., for a feminist theoretical framework for understanding violence against Asian American women.

38. As Yamamoto suggests, for people of color who have been positioned along the intermediary spaces, other binaries come to construct meaning: West/East, North/South, domestic/foreign, and citizen/native. Non-normative categories in each binary always occupy sites "ranging from relative undervisibility to structural invisibility" (63).

39. The Naturalization Law of 1790 was rescinded with the Walter-McCarran Act of 1952, which stated, according to Takaki, that "the right of a person to become a naturalized citizen of the United States shall not be denied or abridged because of race. . . ." See Takaki, 1987, 28. For more discussion of racial politics behind the McCarran Act (also known as the Immigration and Naturalization Act of 1952), see David M. Reimers, *Still the Golden Door: The Third World Comes to America* (New York: Columbia University Press, 1985).

3. "White Sound" and Silences from Stone

1. See also Mirikitani's earlier collection of poems, *Shedding Silence* (selections from which are included in this more recent text), which also comments on the internment of Japanese Americans.

2. For years after the internment, Japanese Americans were reluctant to discuss what had been done to them. Because of feelings of intense shame and humiliation, many remained silent about their experiences in the camps. Until the

1970s, it seemed that the internment had been all but erased from history. A number of Japanese Americans, however, have been vocal and have fought for reparations and redress. In 1976, President Gerald Ford rescinded Executive Order 9066, and in 1980, Congress created the Commission on Wartime Relocation and Internment of Civilians (CWRIC), a project established to research the internment and recommend remedies. The CWRIC determined that the incarceration of Japanese Americans was the result of racism, war hysteria, and a failure of the nation's leadership. The commission heard twenty days' of testimony, from more than 750 witnesses, and uncovered documents proving that representatives of the U.S. government had lied and suppressed evidence in the Supreme Court cases of the only three Japanese Americans who filed cases protesting internment at the actual time of their relocation, Fred Korematsu, Gordon Hirabayashi, and Minoru Yasui. Thus, in 1983, the three men reopened their cases, charging the U.S. government with misconduct. Forty years after the fact, the cases were retried, and after five years, each of the men won. Judges ruled that the government had distorted facts because of racism and stated that the internment of Japanese Americans in concentration camps was unconstitutional. At the same time, in 1988, CWRIC released its report and recommended redress payments of $20,000 to all survivors of the camps. Also in 1988, President Ronald Reagan signed H.R. 442, the Civil Liberties Act, into law. See Hatamiya's text, in which she discusses the establishment of the CWRIC Act, the passage of the Civil Liberties Act, and the significance of the redress movement for Japanese Americans and all Americans. Also, see Brimner, 85–91.

3. On December 7, 1941, approximately fifteen hundred Issei aliens were arrested by the FBI, based on accusations of disloyalty. According to Donna K. Nagata, virtually all the leaders of Japanese American communities were taken, with no explanation. See Nagata, 6.

4. As a number of authors have pointed out, the United States was also at war with Italy and Germany. However, individuals of Italian and German ethnicity living in the United States were not forcibly removed to camps, suggesting a distinct fear of the Japanese, a "yellow peril." Nagata suggests also that while Italian and German Americans, who were more numerous and politically powerful than Japanese Americans, were viewed as racially similar to the dominant group of the United States, Japanese Americans were perceived as "treacherous, racially inferior, and unassimilable," therefore easily excluded (6).

5. Nagata cites cases of violence against Japanese Americans. She writes: "Between the December 7 attack on Pearl Harbor and February 15, 1942, five ethnic Japanese were murdered. In addition, 25 serious crimes including rape, shootings, and robbery were reported. More violence against ethnic Japanese continued after the signing of Executive Order 9066. These figures almost certainly represent a fraction of actual anti-Japanese acts because many instances went unreported. Yet, the CWRIC final report (1982) notes that protection from vigilantes would not be sufficient reason for mass evacuation, since keeping the peace is a civil, not a military, matter. In addition, such 'protection' would not

necessitate ordering the public from their homes and incarcerating them for such a lengthy period of time" (4).

6. When the Civilian Exclusion Order No. 5 was posted, under orders by the Western Defense Command and the Wartime Civil Control Administration, heads of households were required by law to register all members of their families and to report to control stations for further instructions. Many families were given no more than forty-eight hours' notice before their evacuation. They had to liquidate their property and possessions and pack only what they could carry. As documented by a number of historians, many Japanese Americans destroyed any possessions that might be construed as suspicious—personal letters written in Japanese, photographs, family heirlooms, and documents. Most lost their property or were exploited by their non-Japanese neighbors who offered them pittances or nothing at all as payment. For more on the tremendous economic losses suffered by Japanese Americans during internment, see Nagata, chapter 2, "The Consequences of Injustice," 17–35, as well as Brimner and Matsumoto. As Nagata points out, non-Japanese spouses of Japanese Americans were also interned if they chose to remain with their partners and/or families (9).

7. While I refer to the 1992 edition of *Camp Notes*, published by Kitchen Table Women of Color Press, please note that a new edition was published in 1998 by Rutgers University Press, entitled *Camp Notes and Other Writings*.

8. Along with feelings of extreme shame, anger, confusion, and anxiety, interned Japanese also felt a sense of resignation (Matsumoto 439). As historians suggest, many Japanese Americans cooperated not only because they were in a state of disbelief but also because they wished to demonstrate their loyalty to the United States. A common refrain, *Shikata ga nai*, translated as "it cannot be helped" or "it must be done" (Matsumoto 439; Brimner 38).

9. Both *enryo* and another term, *gaman*, are Japanese terms that indicate an etiquette structure and are associated with proper behavior. *Enryo* can be translated as deference, reserve, diffidence, modesty, reticence, and humility. According to Akemi Kikumura, "one of the main manifestations of *enryo* was the conscious use of silence as a safe or neutral response to an embarrassing or ambiguous situation" (Cheung, 1993, 31–32). *Gaman* translates to mean the "internalization . . . and suppression of anger and emotion" (Cheung, 1993, 32) as well as "stoic silence."

10. However, as I discuss later in this chapter, Japanese American men did not have access to the power structure of the United States. As men of color, they, too, faced extreme forms of oppression, exploitation, and discrimination linked to racism and colonialism. In fact, the internment severely dislocated their traditional authority within patriarchal Japanese family structures.

11. See the report of the National Japanese American Historical Society (NJAHS), *Due Process: Americans of Japanese Ancestry and the United States Constitution* (1995), 48.

12. Nagata reports that at the camp in Jerome, Arkansas, there were only seven doctors to care for ten thousand people. Several camps reported epidemics of typhoid, tuberculosis, and dysentery (10–11).

13. A number of internees were able to leave the camps for short periods of time or permanently. College students were granted leave to continue their studies (although they faced severe obstacles attempting to gain admission to any colleges in the United States at that time), and the government allowed internees to leave the camps in order to harvest crops for neighboring farmers in need of cheap labor. While many of the internees who left the camps to work on farms were exploited and cheated by their employers, most concluded that the temporary freedom from the camps made their experiences worthwhile (Matsumoto 441).

14. See also Nagata, who provides the following example: While women were able to earn the same wages as men, the Commission on Wartime Relocation and Internment of Civilians placed a strict limit on earnings for all workers (male and female, of all ages). Camp inmates could earn up to $19 a month, regardless of profession, education, or experience. Compare this figure to the $167 a month a white War Relocation Authority librarian might earn in the camps during the same period (11).

15. Tule Lake was a high-security concentration camp for prisoners of war, where they were confined after other internees had been freed. In 1943, because of pressures to form a Nisei combat team, President Roosevelt and the U.S. government decided to evaluate the loyalty of Japanese Americans with a questionnaire. Two questions, numbers 27 and 28, created conflicts for the internees: "Are you willing to serve in the armed forces of the United States on combat duty, wherever ordered?" and "Will you swear unqualified allegiance to the United States of America and faithfully defend the United States from any and all attacks by foreign and domestic forces, and forswear any form of allegiance or obedience to the Japanese emperor, or any other foreign government, power or organization?" (cited in Nagata, 12, and Brimner, 59). To be considered loyal to the United States, internees were expected—in fact, required—to answer yes to both questions. Anyone who answered "no" to these questions was removed to Tule Lake, often ensuring their separation from family and community members. For the Issei, these questions were especially problematic. Most of them were too old to fight in the armed services, and furthermore, they were excluded from U.S. citizenship. Renouncing their Japanese citizenship would make them citizens of no country. Nisei wondered if they were being tricked—was renunciation of any allegiance to Japan an admission that such an allegiance had once existed? Would answering "yes" get them into more trouble? (Nagata 12; Brimner 59; Hatamiya 20–21). As Brimner and Nagata point out, families were divided over the issue, as were Japanese American organizations. Most of the internees who answered "no" did so not because of loyalty conflicts but because they were angry that their own government had incarcerated them and resisted in the only way they knew how. Approximately eight thousand people answered "no," were labeled "disloyals," and sent to Tule Lake, where they joined Japanese Americans who wished to repatriate or expatriate to Japan (Nagata 12). For more information on the experiences of those who answered "no" to the

questionnaire, see Michi Weglyn, *Years of Infamy: The Untold Story of American's Concentration Camps.*

16. Many young Japanese American men and women, eager to leave the camps and prove their loyalty to the United States, enlisted in military service. According to Brimner, approximately thirty-three thousand Nisei left the camps or arrived from other parts of the country to serve in the military during World War II. Nisei soldiers formed the 442nd Battalion. Other Nisei, before the bombing of Pearl Harbor, had already formed the 100th Battalion in Hawaii. Facing a great deal of racism and distrust and still classified as enemy aliens, members of the 100th-442nd Battalion attempted to prove their loyalty in battle in Italy. They engaged in several extremely difficult battles and emerged from the war the most decorated regiment in U.S. Army history, having earned 9,486 Purple Hearts, with more than six hundred soldiers killed in action (Brimner 65–68). Yet, upon their return to the United States, Japanese American soldiers still found themselves the victims of state-sanctioned racism, harassment, and violence, much like Yamada's narrator in "Cincinnati."

17. Similarly, Marian Yee, in her review of *Camp Notes*, writes that only when Yamada identifies with the man, "another victim of prejudice," "can she release the pain and the anger suppressed for so long" (246).

18. See also King-Kok Cheung's discussion of *gaman*, 1993, 31–32.

19. However, many Japanese Americans *did* resist the internment, often attempting to achieve justice through court proceedings, including Minoru Yasui, Fred Korematsu, and Gordon Hirabayashi, all of whom questioned the constitutionality of what the U.S. government was doing, and all of whom lost. Yet they raised significant questions about what was happening to them, opening doors to more resistance efforts. See Brimner. Also, as Yamamoto points out, among the resisters was a young Nisei woman (214). In addition, Yamada's "reference to Kitty Genovese alludes to a more local instance of social apathy as well as registers [her] critique of simplistic forms of liberating rhetoric that assume social protest, like cries for help, will be answered by knights 'in shining armor'" (Yamamoto 214).

20. Cheng Lok Chua points out that Asians in Canada were denied the right to vote until 1947.

21. For more discussion of the ways in which Japanese Canadians were racialized in ways distinct from Japanese Americans, see Meng Yu Marie Lo, "Fields of Recognition: Reading Asian Canadian Literature in Asian America." Ph.D. diss., Department of Rhetoric, University of California–Berkeley, 2001.

22. Of course, *Obasan* is not an Asian *American* text, per se, but an Asian Canadian novel. As such, it addresses a history specific to Japanese Canadian dispersal to be distinguished from what Japanese Americans experienced. Meng Yu Marie Lo discusses this point in her dissertation, "Fields of Recognition: Reading Asian Canadian Literature in Asian America," suggesting that Asian American literary critics have subsumed Asian Canadian texts under the rubric, "Asian

American," while simultaneously erasing the specific contexts of the production of such texts, thereby enacting a kind of imperialist appropriation. While many of us continue to discuss *Obasan* and other Asian Canadian texts in relation to "Asian American Studies," I want to note here the problematic assumptions underlying such a move and suggest future discussion about the geographical and sociopolitical boundaries between Canada and the United States. I argue for some understanding of the shared construction of racial identity and strategies of resistance among Asians in North America, even as I heed the words of Lo, who writes, "given the fact that 'borders' were both the means and justification behind the racist logic that led to internment, national borders must not be uncritically erased under the rubric of a pan-Asian coalition" (36).

23. *Obasan* means "aunt" in Japanese, but it also means "woman." As Cheung suggests, relying on Gayle Fujita's argument, the title implicitly "acknowledges the connectedness of all women's lives—Naomi, her mother, her two aunts" (1993, 130).

24. See, for example, A. Lynne Magnusson, "Language and Longing in Joy Kogawa's *Obasan*," *Canadian Literature/Litterature Canadienne* 116 (Spring, 1988): 58–66; Eleanor Ty, "Struggling with the Powerful M(Other): Identity and Sexuality in Kogawa's *Obasan* and Kinkaid's *Lucy*," *International Fiction Review* 20.2 (1993): 120–126; and Shirley Geok-lin Lim, "Japanese American Women's Life Stories: Maternality in Monica Sone's *Nisei Daughter* and Joy Kogawa's *Obasan*," *Feminist Studies* 16.2 (1990): 288–312.

25. See, for example, Shirley Geok-lin Lim, "Japanese American Women's Life Stories: Maternality in Monica Sone's *Nisei Daughter* and Joy Kogawa's *Obasan*," *Feminist Studies* 16.2 (1990): 289–312; and Robin Potter, "Moral—In Whose Sense? Joy Kogawa's *Obasan* and Julia Kristeva's *Powers of Horror*," *Studies in Canadian Literature* 15.1 (1990): 117–139.

26. See, for example, Gary Willis, "Speaking the Silence: Joy Kogawa's *Obasan*," *Studies in Canadian Literature* 12.2 (1987): 239–249; Gayle Fujita, "'To Attend the Sound of Stone': The Sensibility of Silence in *Obasan*," in MELUS 12.3 (1985): 33–42; B. A. St. Andrews, "Reclaiming a Canadian Heritage: Kogawa's *Obasan*," *International Fiction Review* 13.1 (1986): 29–31; Lynn Thiesmeyer, "Joy Kogawa's *Obasan*: Unsilencing the Silence of America's Concentration Camps," *Journal of the Faculty of the Humanities* (Japan Women's University) 41 (1991): 63–80; Arnold Davidson, *Writing Against the Silence: Joy Kogawa's Obasan* (Toronto: ECW, 1993); and Erika Gottlieb, "The Riddle of Concentric Worlds in *Obasan*," *Canadian Literature* 109 (1986): 34–53.

27. In some ways, Obasan's silence on this matter also seems to suggest her active refusal to remember the details of the past with regard to Naomi's mother's disappearance and death.

28. Yamamoto suggests that the Grand Inquisitor, like Old Man Gower, also resonates with "the abuse of masculine, hegemonic power" (194).

1. Subsequent editions have been published by Third Woman Press (1995, 1999) and the University of California Press (2001).

2. Until recently, most of Cha's work was unpublished and available only at the Art Museum and Pacific Film Archive, University of California–Berkeley, housed in an archive/study center established in her name. In 2001, however, an exhibition of Cha's work, entitled *The Dream of the Audience: Theresa Hak Kyung Cha (1951–1982)* was organized by the University of California–Berkeley Art Museum and has traveled since then to several locations. For more information, see the exhibition catalogue, *The Dream of the Audience: Theresa Hak Kyung Cha (1951–1982)*, edited by Constance M. Lewallen (Berkeley: University of California Press, 2001).

3. Also, I begin with biographical information about Cha in the section of this project focused on the theme of displacement because many critics who have discussed displacement within *Dictée* have attempted to relate it to Cha's own history and background.

4. In our attention to "difference," however, it is important to recognize the different forms that difference may take. As Dana Takagi argues in her discussion of the relationships between sexuality and race within Asian America, "not all differences are created equally" (24). See Takagi, "Maiden Voyage: Excursion into Sexuality and Identity Politics in Asian America," *Asian American Sexualities: Dimensions of the Gay and Lesbian Experience*, ed., Russell Leong (New York: Routledge), 1996: 21–35.

5. For more on the rhetoric of "claiming America," see Rachel Lee, Laura Hyun Yi Kang (2002), and Shu-Mei Shih.

6. For example, Carlos Bulosan's *America Is In the Heart* (1943); Jade Snow Wong's *Fifth Chinese Daughter* (1945); John Okada's *No-No Boy* (1957); Maxine Hong Kingston's *The Woman Warrior* (1976); and Shawn Hsu Wong's *Homebase* (1979).

7. For more discussion of Chin's criticism of works by Kingston and others, see Patricia Chu's second chapter, in which she analyzes what she refers to as Chin's "authenticity thesis" (65). Also see Kang 2002, 54–60.

8. See also Frank Chin and Jeffery Paul Chan, "Racist Love," published in *Seeing Through Shuck*, edited by Richard Kostelanetz (New York: Ballantine), 1972.

9. Incidentally, the other writer who has been heavily critiqued by Chin is David Henry Hwang, whose writing includes explorations of gender transgressions and homosexuality.

10. From 1961 to 1979, South Korea was controlled by Park Chung-hee's military dictatorship, which initiated intense industrial modernization, increased urbanization, and an export-oriented economy. According to Takaki, the government played a large role in the acceleration of industrialization in Korea by prohibiting strikes and creating a surplus of workers (1989).

11. From an artist's statement viewed by the author at the Berkeley Art Museum Archive, presumed by Rinder to be from 1978 (see Rinder, 1990, 14).

Also cited by Rinder in "The Plurality of Entrances, the Opening of Networks, the Infinity of Languages," *The Dream of the Audience: Theresa Kyung Cha (1951–1982)*, ed. Constance Lewallen (Berkeley: University of California Press, 2001), 15–31.

12. See Susan Wolf for more description and discussion of this particular performance art piece.

13. For example, Cheung discusses "rhetorical," "attentive," and "provocative" silences.

14. See Kim's preface to *Writing Self, Writing Nation: Essays on Theresa Hak Kyung Cha's Dictée*, ed. Kim and Norma Alarcon (Berkeley: Third Woman Press, 1994) x.

15. Similarly, Miriam Ching Yoon Louie asserts minjung consciousness as rooted in oppression, in particular "the lives, culture, and struggles of the *minjung* —the locked out, the exploited, the downtrodden, the have-nots" (121). Minjung feminism is therefore rooted in women's suffering, based on gender and class oppression, and intricately tied to struggles against colonialism.

16. See both Shelley Sunn Wong and Eun Kyung Min.

17. Huston Smith, as cited in Rinder, 1990, 7.

18. Of course, as Elaine Kim points out, Huo Hyung Soon is in fact Cha's mother, and some readers of *Dictée* "apparently do not realize that Korean women generally do not assume their husbands' names (a practice that does not signify their autonomy but rather delineates them as outsiders to their husbands' families, to which their children belong). Although a Westerner might expect the mother's name to be 'Cha,' it is in fact Huo, her natal surname" (1994, 27).

19. See Spivak's introduction to Derrida, *Of Grammatology*, xiv.

20. Theresa Hak Kyung Cha, *It Is Almost That*, Worth Ryder Gallery, University of California–Berkeley, 1977 (cited in Rinder, 1990); and included in Lewallen's exhibition catalog, *The Dream of the Audience*, 20.

21. Lewallen, *The Dream of the Audience*, 3, 29.

22. In his essay "Looking for My Penis," Richard Fung is concerned with the politicized representations of Asian American men in gay male video porn, arguing that such images are directly tied to issues of power, inter- and intraracial relationships, and internalized racism and shame.

23. For example, Sohn Ki-jung, a Korean athlete, won a gold medal in the 1936 Olympics (disproving Hitler's claims of the Aryan "master race"), but because Korea was colonized by Japan at the time, he was forced to wear a Japanese uniform and thus, to the rest of the world, was simply Japanese. Likewise, although a Korean invented gunpowder, because of Korea's unequal relationship to China, gunpowder is now commonly believed to have been a Chinese invention (Kim, 1994, 8–9).

24. For example, see Monique Wittig, "One Is Not Born a Woman," *The Straight Mind and Other Essays* (Boston: Beacon Press, 1992) 9–20, in which she writes that "lesbianism provides for the moment the only social form in which we can live freely . . . [and] is the only concept I know of which is beyond the categories of sex (woman and man)" (20). See also Gloria Anzaldúa, *Borderlands*,

in which she establishes a cultural space—*la frontera*—in which *los atravesados* live: "the squint-eyed, the peverse, the queer, the troublesome, the mongrel, the mulato [sic], the half-breed, the half dead; in short, those who cross over, pass over, or go through the confines of the 'normal'" (3). Yet the new mestiza of this frontera adapts by developing "a tolerance for contradictions, a tolerance for ambiguity. . . . Not only does she sustain contradictions, she turns the ambivalence into something else" (79). The mestiza consciousness, then, though a source of pain, is our strength and our future. Anzaldúa writes: "As a *mestiza*, I have no country, my homeland cast me out; yet all countries are mine because I am every woman's sister or potential lover" (80), reminiscent of Virginia Woolf's statement: "As a woman, I have no country. As a woman I want no country. As a woman my country is the whole world," in *Three Guineas* (New York: Harcourt Brace Jovanovich, 1938) 109. See also Audre Lorde's biomythography, *Zami: A New Spelling of My Name* (Freedom: The Crossing Press, 1982), in which she creates a space and a location, writing: "It was a while before we came to realize that our place was the very house of difference rather than the security of any one particular difference. . . . It was years before we learned to use the strength that daily surviving can bring" (226). Teresa de Lauretis describes the "space off" as a site of liminality, in *Technologies of Gender: Essays on Theory, Film, and Fiction* (Bloomington: Indiana University Press, 1987). And finally, Chela Sandoval relies of similar premises in her essay "U.S. Third World Feminism: The Theory and Method of Oppositional Consciousness in the Postmodern World," *Genders* 10 (Spring, 1991), 1–24.

25. As Priscilla Wald notes, this passage is one of few in the text in which Cha actually uses the personal pronouns "I," "me," and "my." To me, her use of such pronouns suggests a resistance and refusal to be unnamed and/or misnamed as other than how she identifies, and signifies her insistence, once again, on the specificities of her identity and positionality.

5. Silence and Public Discourse

1. Even while Asian American women sometimes occupy radically different contexts than Asian women, racial and sexual stereotypes and myths, based as they are on imagined cultural traits and phenotype, rarely distinguish between them. See JeeYeun Lee, 116.

2. See Chandra Talpade Mohanty, "Under Western Eyes: Feminist Scholarship and Colonial Discourses," *Third World Women and the Politics of Feminism*, eds. Chandra Talpade Mohanty, Ann Russo, and Lourdes Torres (Bloomington: Indiana University Press, 1991) 51–80.

3. See Kamala Kempadoo's essay "Women of Color and the Global Sex Trade: Transnational Feminist Perspectives," *Meridians: Feminism, Race, Transnationalism* 1.2 (2002): 28–51; Tracy Lai, "Asian American Women: Not For Sale," *Race, Class, and Gender: An Anthology*, eds. Margaret L. Andersen and Patricia Hill Collins, 3rd ed. (Belmont: Wadsworth Publishing Company, 1998) 163–171; Sonia Shah, ed.,

Dragon Ladies: Asian American Feminists Breathe Fire (Boston: South End Press, 1997); Asian Women United of California, eds., *Making Waves: An Anthology of Writings by and about Asian American Women* (Boston: Beacon Press, 1989); Elaine H. Kim, Lilia V. Villanueva, and Asian Women United of California, eds., *Making More Waves: New Writing by Asian American Women* (Boston: Beacon Press, 1997); Yayori Matsui, *Women's Asia* (London: Zed Press, 1989); Jessica Hagedorn, "Asian Women in Film: No Joy, No Luck," *Ms. Magazine* (January/February 1994): 74–79; Patricia Hill Collins, *Black Feminist Thought: Knowledge, Consciousness, and the Politics of Empowerment* (London: HarperCollins, 1990), 169; Laurie Bell, ed., *Good Girls/Bad Girls: Feminists and Sex Trade Workers Face to Face* (Toronto: Seal Press, 1987) 161.

4. For discussion of the meanings and ideological dominance of "either/or dichotomous thinking" and binary oppositions in Western systems of knowledge, see both Collins and Mohanty.

5. I realize the disjunctive nature of identifying Beccah's race as "Korean" and "white," two unequal terms of categorization for racial/ethnic group membership. However, the specific ethnicity of Beccah's father is never identified in the novel—all we know is that he was a white missionary working in Korea. Perhaps Keller participates in a restructuring of race relations, turning on its head the conventional method of racial identification based on what Omi and Winant refer to as the "ethnicity model," whereby white Americans of European descent describe themselves in ever more complex ways, based on ethnic and religious group identification, while the dominant racial discourse of the United States continues to refer to "Africa" and "Asia" (and African Americans and Asian Americans), for example, without attention to national, cultural, regional, or linguistic identification.

6. Interestingly, in both *The Woman Warrior* and *Comfort Woman*, the narrators' mothers are "shamans" who communicate—and do battle—with ghosts.

7. To avoid confusion, I refer to the character of Soon Hyo as "Akiko" when discussing time periods of the novel during which this is how she is known by other characters and as "Soon Hyo" after her real name has been divulged. In general, I refer to her as Soon Hyo. At times, to make explicit her dual identity, I refer to her as Akiko/Soon Hyo.

8. I draw this information from the following sources: Dai Sil Kim-Gibson, "They Defiled My Body, Not My Spirit: The Story of a Korean Comfort Woman, Chung Seo Woon," *Dragon Ladies*, ed. Sonia Shah; George Hicks, *The Comfort Women: Japan's Brutal Regime of Enforced Prostitution in the Second World War*; and Hyunah Yang, "Re-membering the Korean Military Comfort Women: Nationalism, Sexuality, and Silencing," *Dangerous Women: Gender and Korean Nationalism*, ed., Elaine H. Kim and Chungmoo Choi. As Kim-Gibson suggests, the very term "comfort woman" is a euphemism and therefore problematic. Thus, I use it, as she does, "advisedly." Other euphemistic terms, like "recreation camps," function much like some of the terminology surrounding the U.S. concentration camps of World War II and therefore deserve more discussion and criticism.

9. As Yang points out, however, the Japanese government is not the only

government to virtually erase the history of the comfort women. She argues that Korea has participated in silencing this history from the official memory and history of the nation, writing, "I think it is important for Koreans to analyze the silence about the Military Comfort Women not just in relation to Japanese government actions and international policies, but also in relation to South Korean society itself" (127).

10. See Yang, in which she discusses a letter, written in 1992, by a Korean man who claims that the history of Japanese colonization and comfort women "amounts to an act in which the Japanese throw their dirty sperm bucket into our Korean people's face" (130). She exposes the underlying assumptions at work, which include the belief that since Korean women have been victimized and humiliated by the Japanese, all Koreans have been victimized and humiliated by the Japanese, and that men are the ones responsible for both the victimization (Japanese men) and protection (Korean men) of Korean women. She writes: "This reader's letter thus exemplifies how males become the only subjects involved in questions of nation and sexuality. This reveals the fictitious nature of the nationalist belief in a unified Korean body, since the body is constituted and sustained by non-homogeneity. . . . The nation becomes gendered, and women's sexuality becomes nationalized. Nation is equated with the male subject position, and women's sexuality is reified as property of the masculine nation. In this sense, the discourse is neither *about* nor *for* the (Military Comfort) women. Women occupy a position in which they are neither subject nor even object. Rather, they are misplaced as the material or the ground for 'men's talk'" (130). Thus, the history of comfort women moves from a history that involves Korean women and Japanese men to one that involves the relations between Korean men and Japanese men. Korean nationalism is constituted as a male prerogative.

11. My use of quotation marks around the word "heroic" is not to suggest that these women were not, in fact, heroic but to address Cha's—and Keller's—reworking of the very terms of the discourse surrounding what heroism is. If heroism is defined as solely a male prerogative, then clearly these women cannot be considered heroic. However, if we critique the (masculinist) nationalist language and ideology surrounding heroism, as these writers do, then we must reevaluate women's places within the movement, as well as the definition of heroism.

12. The "outsider within" refers to Collins's elaboration of marginality for African American women, a condition of both belonging and not belonging. See Collins, *Black Feminist Thought*.

13. Here I refer again to Darlene Clark Hine's elaboration of dissemblance, whereby she suggests that dissemblance is a strategy for survival used by black women in their attempts to protect themselves from sexual violence and abuse. Similarly, Cindy Patton describes another protective strategy used by oppressed groups of people—dissimulation. In her text *Inventing AIDS* (New York: Routledge, 1990), Patton discusses the ways in which research subjects in HIV/AIDS

vaccine test trials, exploited by researchers' stereotypes and lack of ethics (in this case non-Western research subjects), may dissimulate (or "lie strategically"). She argues that once the "truth" of the research subjects' statements is called into question, the Western researchers (and ethics) lose control over their so-called subjects. She writes: "Western ethics loses control at precisely the moment African subjects articulate their own social and ethical categories; Western discourse cannot speak its own language and that of the 'Other' without giving up its claim to be the totalizing, metaethical discourse" (85–86). Thus, while dissemblance and dissimulation operate as strategies for survival for dominated groups and may include forms of multiple narration or doublespeak, the dominant group cannot claim to speak both for its own interests and that of the "other" without losing grasp of its totalizing, dominating discourse. To speak from two or more places at once functions differently, depending on the locales from which one speaks.

14. Incidentally, Sulsulham, a city referred to as being in North Korea, translates to mean "loneliness." I credit my student Byung Koo for pointing this out to me.

15. See Lisa Rofel, "Liberation Nostalgia and a Yearning for Modernity," *Engendering China: Women, Culture, and the State*, ed. Christina Gilmartin, et al. (Cambridge: Harvard University Press, 1994); Lydia Liu, "Invention and Intervention: The Female Tradition in Modern Chinese Literature," *Gender Politics in Modern China: Feminism and Writing*, ed. Tani Barlow (Durham: Duke University Press, 1993).

16. Again, the motif of heroism. Such a theme seems particularly significant in light of recent discussions within the United States, as discussed in the previous chapter, specifically among Chinese American male and female writers and literary critics (e.g., Maxine Hong Kingston, Amy Tan, Frank Chin, and Shawn Wong, among others), linking Chinese heroism to both masculinity and nationalism. Also, because heroism has been a term of contestation among nations, especially since much of Western imperialism and expansion into Asia depended upon ideologies that "feminized" Asian nations, Min's reclamation of the term enacts both a conscious resistance to Western imperialism and a reworking of gender norms and prescriptions.

17. Rey Chow also discusses the "de-gendering" of Chinese women in relation to the Tiananmen Square massacre of June 4, 1989. Asked how to "read" the events of China in terms of gender, Chow responds that "at the moment of shock Chinese people are degendered and become simply 'Chinese.' To ask how we can use gender to 'read' a political crisis such as the present one is to insist on the universal and timeless sufficiency of an analytical category, and to forget the historicity that accompanies all categorical explanatory power" (82). Thus, she asks instead, "What do the events in China tell us about gender as a category, especially as it relates to the so-called Third World? What are gender's limits, where does it work, and where does it not work?" (82).

18. While Abraham discusses modernist lesbian writings by Western women, I rely on her framework, in part, because a number of the conventions and de-

vices she analyzes are employed by Min in the writing of her memoirs. Whether this is so because of the hegemonic nature of such formulaic devices when it comes to lesbian writing, an intentional attempt on Min's part to reinscribe a conventional narrative with new meaning, especially as the formulas have applied, for the most part, to white, Western women's writings, or is simply purely coincidental is open to speculation. However, Min's reworking of such strategies, as I explore in this section, raises significant questions about the representation of lesbian or same-sex desire, specifically in China during the Cultural Revolution. For more discussion of formulaic devices used in lesbian narratives, specifically in "coming out" narratives during the 1970s and 1980s in the United States, see Biddy Martin, "Lesbian Identity and Autobiographical Difference[s]," published in *The Lesbian and Gay Studies Reader,* ed. Henry Abelove, Mchele Aina Barale, and David M. Halperin.

19. My use of quotation marks here refers to Abraham's discussion of the distinctions between "lesbian novels" (about lesbians, but not necessarily always produced by or for lesbians) and "lesbian writing" (writings by lesbians, not necessarily about lesbianism), distinctions that invoke the highly contested terrain surrounding questions about what constitutes lesbian literature. See Abraham, preface, xii–xiv.

20. Here, Chow writes specifically of the violence of the Tiananmen Square massacre.

21. U.S. publishers and reviewers of *Red Azalea* have tended to rely on such orientalist assumptions. Pantheon Books publicized the text as "the most powerfully erotic and moving autobiography to emerge from modern China" and "unlike anything so far published in the West." Advertised as such, *Red Azalea* becomes a new and exotic form of sexual titillation offered up to Western audience. That the erotic components of the text center, first and foremost, on sexual dynamics between two women is rendered acceptable in such a context. Whether such an autobiography, published in the West by a white, Western woman would have received the same quality of praise allotted to Min is questionable. My point is not to suggest that Min's book is not powerful, erotic, or engaging but rather that her depiction of same-sex love is naturalized, for American readers, within a context that is always already perceived as foreign, exotic, and highly sensualized. In short, the Asian "other," in relation to Western culture, is always already understood to be sexually deviant within a history of orientalist discourse and appropriation. Thus, Min's work is reduced to mere sensationalism, a text that demonstrates not only how oppressive they are "over there" but also the extremes individuals are forced to go to attain and sustain sexual and/or romantic relationships with others in such oppressive contexts (e.g., homosexuality). Incidentally, reviewers mention Min's affair with Yan only in terms of their segregation, in the labor camp, from men.

22. In fact, as Somerson points out, his excessive femininity is reminiscent of Little Green's performance of femininity (110). While the Supervisor's actual

gender is left ambiguous, I use male pronouns when referring to "him" here simply because Min does.

23. Interestingly, Yan and the Supervisor, the narrator's two lovers in *Red Azalea*, both exert a considerable amount of power over her, suggesting that in this context, gender transgressions are more acceptable among those with relative power.

6. Conclusion

1. For example, Patricia Hill Collins prefaced the first edition of *Black Feminist Thought* (1990) with the suggestion that the text represented her struggle to claim her voice. Breaking silence was conceptualized as the proper first step in asserting a black feminist framework for theory. However, ten years later, in her preface to the second edition, Collins writes: "I am in another place now. I remain less preoccupied with coming to voice because I know now how quickly voice can be taken away. My concern now lies in finding effective ways to use the voice that I have claimed while I have it" (2000, xiii). Recognizing the ways in which free speech is rarely ever or always free from some groups of people in the United States, Collins places less emphasis on simply coming to voice, and more on employing the voice she has claimed, suggesting multiple ways of saying.

2. See Luce Irigaray, *The Sex Which Is Not One*, trans. Catherine Porter with Carolyn Burke (Ithaca: Cornell University Press, 1985).

3. On this topic, see Mitsuye Yamada, "Invisibility is an Unnatural Disaster" and "Asian Pacific American Women and Feminism," both in *This Bridge Called My Back: Radical Writings by Women of Color*; and Audre Lorde, "The Master's Tools Will Never Dismantle the Master's House," *Sister Outsider: Essays and Speeches* (Freedom: Crossing Press, 1984).

4. Again, see Yamada, 1984.

5. See for example, Judy Yung, *Unbound Feet: A Social History of Chinese Women in San Francisco* (Berkeley: University of California Press, 1995); and Sonia Shah, *Dragon Ladies: Asian American Feminists Breathe Fire* (Boston: South End Press, 1997).

6. This has not necessarily been an easy task, however. As Trinh points out, a woman of color who is also a feminist always faces accusations of at least three possible "betrayals": "she can be accused of betraying either man (the 'man-hater'), or her community ('people of color should stay together to fight racism'), or woman herself ('you should fight first on the woman's side')" (1989, 104).

7. For instance, the Los Angeles Women's Center was established in the early 1970s to provide outreach programs and services to local Asian American women; the *Asian Women* journal was established in 1970s at the University of California–Berkeley; Asian Women United was founded in 1975 in San Francisco; the Organization of Asian American Women began as a feminist theory study group in New York City in 1976; the Organization of Pan Asian American Women began

meeting in Washington, D.C., in 1976 to discuss national policy issues affecting Asian American women; the Pacific Asian American Women Writers-West was established in 1978 as a group of writers and artists; in southern California, a group of Asian American women writers founded Unbound Feet in 1978; the New York Asian Women's Center opened in 1984 to combat domestic violence in Asian American families; and Asian Immigrant Women Advocates in Oakland, California, and the Chinese chapter of the Coalition of Labor Union Women in New York City were both established in the early 1980s to serve low-income immigrant women in garment, hotel, and restaurant industries. See Wei, 78–87. See also Sonia Shah, "Presenting the Blue Goddess: Toward a National Pan-Asian Feminist Agenda," *The State of Asian America: Activism and Resistance in the 1990s*, ed. Karin Aguilar-San Juan (Boston: South End Press, 1994) 147–158.

bibliography

Abraham, Julie. *Are Girls Necessary? Lesbian Writing and Modern Histories.* New York: Routledge, 1996.

Adachi, Ken. *The Enemy That Never Was: A History of the Japanese Canadians.* Toronto: McClelland and Stweart, 1976.

Aguilar-San Juan, Karin. "Foreword: Breathing Fire, Confronting Power, and Other Necessary Acts of Resistance." *Dragon Ladies: Asian American Feminists Breathe Fire.* Ed. Sonia Shah. Boston: South End Press, 1997. ix–xi.

Alexander, Meena. *The Shock of Arrival: Reflections on Postcolonial Experience.* Boston: South End Press, 1996.

Amott, Teresa L., and Julie A. Matthaei. *Race, Gender, and Work: A Multicultural Economic History of Women in the United States.* Boston: South End Press, 1991.

Anderson, Benedict. *Imagined Communities: Reflections on the Origin and Spread of Nationalism.* London: Verso, 1991.

Anzaldúa, Gloria. *Borderlands/La Frontera: The New Mestiza.* San Francisco: Aunt Lute Books, 1987.

———. "Speaking in Tongues: A Letter to Third World Women Writers." *This Bridge Called My Back: Writings by Radical Women of Color.* Eds. Cherríe Moraga and Gloria Anzaldúa. New York: Kitchen Table Women of Color Press, 1981. 165–173.

———, ed. *Making Face, Making Soul / Haciendo Caras: Creative and Critical Perspectives by Feminists of Color.* San Francisco: Aunt Lute Books, 1990.

Bambara, Toni Cade, ed. *The Black Woman: An Anthology.* New York: Mentor, 1970.

Bammer, Angelika, ed. *Displacements: Cultural Identities in Question.* Bloomington: Indiana University Press, 1994.

Bartky, Sandra Lee. *Femininity and Domination: Studies in the Phenomenology of Oppression.* New York: Routledge, 1990.

Bhana, Hershini. "How to Articulate the Inarticulable I, II, and III." *Making More Waves: New Writing by Asian American Women.* Eds. Elaine H. Kim, Lilia V. Villanueva, and Asian Women United of California. Boston: Beacon Press, 1997. 174–176.

Bow, Leslie. *Betrayal and Other Acts of Subversion: Feminism, Sexual Politics, Asian American Women's Literature.* Princeton: Princeton University Press, 2001.

Breitman, George, ed. *By Any Means Necessary: Speeches, Interviews, and a Letter by Malcolm X.* New York: Merit, 1970.

Brimner, Larry Dane. *Voices from the Camps: Internment of Japanese Americans during World War II.* New York: Franklin Watts, 1994.

Brooks, Higginbotham, Evelyn. "African-American Women's History and the Metalanguage of Race." *Signs: Journal of Women in Culture and Society* 17.2 (1992): 251–274.

Butler, Judith. *Bodies That Matter: On the Discursive Limits of "Sex."* New York: Routledge, 1993.

———. *Excitable Speech: A Politics of the Performative.* New York: Routledge, 1997.

Carmichael, Stokely, and Charles Hamilton, eds. *Black Power: The Politics of Liberation in America.* New York: Random House, 1967.

Cha, Theresa Hak Kyung. "Audience Distant Relatives." *The Solar Cavern* 1–2 (1978); and *The Little Word Machine Publication* 10–11 (1978).

———. *Dictée.* New York: Tanam Press, 1982. Berkeley: Third Woman Press, 1995.

Chan, Sucheng. *Asian Americans: An Interpretive History.* Boston: Twayne Publishers, 1991.

———. "European and Asian Immigration into the United States in Comparative Perspective, 1820s to 1920s." *Immigration Reconsidered: History, Sociology, and Politics.* Ed. Virginia Yans-McLaughlin. New York: Oxford University Press, 1990. 37–75.

Chang, Juliana. "'Transform This Nothingness': Theresa Hak Kyung Cha's *Dictée*." *Critical Mass: A Journal of Asian American Cultural Criticism* 1.1 (1993): 75–82.

Chauncey, George. *Gay New York: Gender, Culture, and the Making of the Gay Male World, 1890–1940.* New York: Basic Books, 1994.

Chen, Xiaomei. "Growing Up With Posters in the Maoist Era." *Picturing Power in the People's Republic of China.* Eds. Harriet Evans and Stephanie Donald. New York: Rowman and Littlefield, 1999. 101–122.

Cheung, King-Kok. *Articulate Silences: Hisaye Yamamoto, Maxine Hong Kingston, Joy Kogawa.* Ithaca: Cornell University Press, 1993.

————. "The Woman Warrior versus the Chinaman Pacific: Must a Chinese American Critic Choose Between Feminism and Heroism?" *Conflicts in Feminism*. Eds. Marianne Hirsch and Evelyn Fox Keller. New York: Routledge, 1990. 234–251.

Chin, Frank. "Come All Ye Asian American Writers of the Real and the Fake." *The Big Aiiieeeee! An Anthology of Chinese American and Japanese American Literature*. Eds. Jeffery Paul Chan, Frank Chin, Lawson Fusao Inada, and Shawn Wong. New York: Penguin Books, 1991. 1–92.

Ching Yoon Louie, Miriam. "Minjung Feminism: Korean Women's Movement for Gender and Class Liberation." *Global Feminisms Since 1945: Rewriting Histories*. Ed. Bonnie G. Smith, New York: Routledge, 2000. 119–138.

Choi, Chungmoo. "The Minjung Culture Movement and the Construction of Popular Culture in Korea." *South Korea's Minjung Movement: The Culture and Politics of Dissidence*. Ed. Kenneth Wells. Honolulu: University of Hawaii Press, 1995. 105–118.

————. "Nationalism and Construction of Gender in Korea." *Dangerous Women: Gender and Korean Nationalism*. Eds. Elaine H. Kim and Chungmoo Choi. New York: Routledge, 1998. 9–31.

Chow, Esther Ngan-Ling. "The Feminist Movement: Where Are All the Asian American Women?" *Making Waves: An Anthology of Writings by and about Asian American Women*. Ed. Asian Women United of California. Boston: Beacon Press, 1989. 362–377.

Chow, Rey. "Violence in the Other Country: China as Crisis, Spectacle, and Woman." *Third World Women and the Politics of Feminism*. Eds. Chandra Talpade Mohanty, Ann Russo, and Lourdes Torres. Bloomington: Indiana University Press, 1991. 81–100.

Chu, Patricia P. *Assimilating Asians: Gendered Strategies of Authorship in Asian America*. Durham: Duke University Press, 2000.

Chua, Cheng Lok. "Witnessing the Japanese Canadian Experience in World War II: Processual Structure, Symbolism, and Irony in Joy Kogawa's *Obasan*." *Reading the Literatures of Asian America*. Eds. Shirley Geok-lin Lim and Amy Ling. Philadelphia: Temple University Press, 1992. 97–108.

Collins, Partricia Hill. *Black Feminist Thought: Knowledge, Consciousness, and the Politics of Empowerment*. London: HarperCollins, 1990. New York: Routledge, 2000.

Creef, Elena Tajima. "Notes from a Fragmented Daughter." *Making Face, Making Soul / Haciendo Caras: Creative and Critical Perspectives by Feminists of Color*. San Francisco: Aunt Lute Books, 1990. 82–84.

Culler, Jonathon. *On Deconstruction: Theory and Criticism after Structuralism*. Ithaca: Cornell University Press, 1982.

de Lauretis, Teresa. "Sexual Indifference and Lesbian Representation." *The Lesbian and Gay Studies Reader*. Eds. Henry Abelove, Michele Aina Barale, and David M. Halperin. New York: Routledge, 1993. 141–158.

D'Emilio, John. *Sexual Politics, Sexual Communities: The Making of a Homosexual Minority in the United States, 1940–1970.* Chicago: University of Chicago Press, 1983.

Derrida, Jacques. *Of Grammatology.* Trans. Gayatri Chakravorty Spivak. Baltimore: Johns Hopkins University Press, 1974.

Dhairyam, Sagri. "Racing the Lesbian, Dodging White Critics." *The Lesbian Postmodern.* Ed. Laura Doan. New York: Columbia University Press, 1994. 26–46.

Duberman, Martin, Martha Vicinus, and George Chauncey, Jr., eds. *Hidden from History: Reclaiming the Gay and Lesbian Past.* New York: Meridian Books, 1989.

Espiritu, Yen Le. "Race, Class, and Gender in Asian American." *Making More Waves: New Writings by Asian American Women.* Eds. Elaine H. Kim, Lilia V. Villanueva, and Asian Women United of California. Boston: Beacon Press, 1997. 135–141.

Feng, Pin-chia. *The Female Bildungsroman by Toni Morrison and Maxine Hong Kingston: A Postmodern Reading.* New York: Peter Lang, 1998.

Foucault, Michel. *The History of Sexuality: An Introduction.* Trans. Robert Hurley. Vol. 1. New York: Random House, 1978.

Fung, Richard. "Looking for My Penis: The Eroticized Asian in Gay Video Porn." *Asian American Sexualities: Dimensions of the Gay and Lesbian Experience.* Ed. Russell Leong. New York: Routledge, 1996. 181–198.

———. "The Trouble with 'Asians.'" *Negotiating Lesbian and Gay Subjects.* Eds. Monica Dorenkamp and Richard Henke. New York: Routledge, 1995. 123–130.

Fuss, Diana. *Essentially Speaking: Feminism, Nature, and Difference.* New York: Routledge, 1989.

Giddings, Paula. *When and Where I Enter: The Impact of Black Women on Race and Sex in America.* New York: Bantam Books, 1984.

Glenn, Evelyn Nakano. "Split Household, Small Producer and Dual Wage Earner: An Analysis of Chinese-American Family Strategies." *The Journal of Marriage and the Family* (1983): 35–46.

Goellnicht, Donald C. "Father Land and/or Mother Tongue: The Divided Female Subject in Kogawa's *Obasan* and Hong Kingston's *The Woman Warrior.*" *Redefining Autobiography in Twentieth-Century Women's Fiction: An Essay Collection.* Eds. Janice Morgan and Colette T. Hall. New York: Garland Publishing, 1991. 119–134.

———. "Tang Ao in America: Male Subject Positions in *China Men.*" *Reading the Literatures of Asian America.* Eds. Shirley Geok-lin Lim and Amy Ling. Philadelphia: Temple University Press, 1992. 191–212.

Grewal, Gurleen. "Memory and Matrix of History: The Poetics of Loss and Recovery in Joy Kogawa's *Obasan* and Toni Morrison's *Beloved.*" *Memory and Cultural Politics: New Approaches to American Ethnic Literatures.* Eds. Amritjit Singh, Joseph T. Skerrett, Jr., and Robert E. Hogan. Boston: Northeastern University Press, 1996. 140–174.

Guy-Sheftall, Beverly. Keynote Lecture. Women of Color Across the Women's

Studies Curriculum Conference. Marquette University, Milwaukee, Wisconsin. March 15, 1996.

Halberstam, Judith. *Female Masculinity*. Durham: Duke University Press, 1998.

Hatamiya, Leslie. *Righting a Wrong: Japanese Americans and the Passage of the Civil Liberties Act of 1988*. Stanford: Stanford University Press, 1993.

Hattori, Tomo. "Psycholinguistic Orientalism in Criticism of *The Woman Warrior* and *Obasan*." *Other Sisterhoods: Literary Theory and U.S. Women of Color*. Ed. Sandra Kumamoto Stanley. Urbana: University of Illinois Press, 1998. 119–138.

Hedges, Elaine, and Shelley Fisher Fishkin, eds. *Listening to Silences: New Essays in Feminist Criticism*. New York: Oxford University Press, 1994.

Hicks, George. *The Comfort Women: Japan's Brutal Regime of Enforced Prostitution in the Second World War*. New York: W. W. Norton, 1994.

Higginbotham, Evelyn Brooks. "African-American Women's History and the Metalanguage of Race." *Signs: Journal of Women in Culture and Society* 17.2 (1992): 251–274.

Hine, Darlene Clark. "Rape and the Inner Lives of Black Women in the Middle West: Preliminary Thoughts on the Culture of Dissemblance." *Unequal Sisters: A Multicultural Reader in U.S. Women's History*. Eds. Vicki Ruiz and Ellen Carol DuBois. New York: Routledge, 1990. 292–297.

hooks, bell. *From Margin to Center*. Boston: South End Press, 1984.

———. *Talking Back: Thinking Feminist, Thinking Black*. Boston: South End Press, 1989.

Islam, Naheed. "In the Belly of the Multicultural Beast I Am Named South Asian." *Our Feet Walk the Sky: Women of the South Asian Diaspora*. Ed. the Women of South Asian Descent Collective. San Francisco: Aunt Lute Books, 1993. 242–245.

Ito, Susan. "Hambun-Hambun." *Making More Waves: New Writing by Asian American Women*. Eds. Elaine H. Kim, Lilia V. Villanueva, and Asian Women United of California. Boston: Beacon Press, 1997. 128–132.

JanMohamed, Abdul R. "Sexuality on/of the Racial Border: Foucault, Wright, and the Articulation of 'Racialized Sexuality.'" *Discourses of Sexuality: From Aristotle to AIDS*. Ed. Domna C. Stanton. Ann Arbor: University of Michigan Press, 1992. 94–116.

———. and David Lloyd. "Introduction." *Cultural Critique* 6 (1986): 5–12.

Jones, Manina. "The Avenues of Speech and Silence: Telling Difference in Joy Kogawa's *Obasan*." *Theory Between the Disciplines: Authority/Vision/Politics*. Eds. Martin Kreiswirth and Mark A. Cheetham. Ann Arbor: University of Michigan Press, 1990. 213–229.

Kamuf, Peggy. "Writing Like a Woman." *Women and Language in Literature and Society*. Eds. Sally McConnell-Ginet, Ruth Borker, and Nelly Furman. New York: Praeger, 1980. 284–299.

Kang, Laura Hyun Yi. *Compositional Subjects: Enfiguring Asian/American Women*. Durham: Duke University Press, 2002.

———. "The 'Liberatory Voice' of Theresa Hak Kyung Cha's *Dictée*." *Writing*

Self, Writing Nation: Essays on Theresa Hak Kyung Cha's Dictée. Eds. Elaine H. Kim and Norma Alarcon. Berkeley: Third Woman Press, 1994. 73–99.

Kauanui, J. Kehaulani, and Ju Hui "Judy" Han. "'Asian Pacific Islander': Issues of Representation and Responsibility." *The Very Inside: An Anthology of Writing by Asian and Pacific Islander Lesbian and Bisexual Women.* Ed. Sharon Lim-Hing. Toronto: Sister Vision Press, 1994. 377–379.

Keller, Nora Okja. *Comfort Woman.* New York: Viking Penguin, 1997.

Kennedy, Elizabeth Lapovsky, and Madeline D. Davis. *Boots of Leather, Slippers of Gold: The History of a Lesbian Community.* New York: Routledge, 1993.

Kim, Elaine H. "Beyond Railroads and Internment: Comments on the Past, Present, and Future of Asian American Studies." *Privileging Positions: The Sites of Asian American Studies.* Eds. Gary Y. Okihiro, Marilyn Alquizola, Dorothy Fujita Rony, and K. Scott Wong. Pullman: Washington State University Press, 1995. 11–19.

———. "Poised on the In-between: A Korean American's Reflections on Theresa Hak Kyung Cha's *Dictée.*" *Writing Self, Writing Nation: Essays on Theresa Hak Kyung Cha's Dictée.* Eds. Elaine H. Kim and Norma Alarcon. Berkeley: Third Woman Press, 1994. 3–30.

———. "Visions and Fierce Dreams: A Commentary on the Works of Maxine Hong Kingston." *Amerasia Journal* 8.2 (1981): 145–161.

———. Lilia Villanueva, and Asian Women United of California, eds. *Making More Waves: New Writing by Asian American Women.* Boston: Beacon Press, 1997.

Kim-Gibson, Dai Sil. "They Defiled My Body, Not My Spirit: The Story of a Korean Comfort Woman, Chung Seo Woon." *Making More Waves: New Writing by Asian American Women.* Eds. Elaine H. Kim, Lilia V. Villanueva, and Asian Women United of California. Boston: Beacon Press, 1997. 177–183.

Kingston, Maxine Hong. *China Men.* New York: Vintage Books, 1977.

———. "Cultural Mis-readings by American Reviewers." *Asian and Western Writers in Dialogue: New Cultural Identities.* Ed. Guy Amirthanayagam. London: Macmillan, 1982. 55–65.

———. *The Woman Warrior: Memoirs of a Girlhood Among Ghosts.* New York: Vintage Books, 1975.

Kogawa, Joy. *Obasan.* New York: Anchor Books, Doubleday, 1981.

Koshy, Susan. "The Fiction of Asian American Literature." *The Yale Journal of Criticism* 9 (1996): 315–346.

Le Thi Diem Thuy, "Shrapnel Shards on Blue Water." *The Very Inside: An Anthology of Writing by Asian and Pacific Islander Lesbian and Bisexual Women.* Ed. Sharon Lim-Hing. Toronto: Sister Vision Black Women and Women of Color Press, 1994. 2–4.

Lee, JeeYeun. "Why Suzie Wong Is Not a Lesbian: Asian and Asian American Lesbian and Bisexual Women and Femme/Butch/Gender Identities." *Queer Studies: A Lesbian, Gay, Bisexual, Transgender Anthology.* Eds. Brett Beemyn and Mickey Eliason. New York: New York University Press, 1996. 115–132.

Lee, Rachel. *The Americas of Asian American Literature: Gendered Fictions of Nation and Transnation.* Princeton: Princeton University Press, 1999.

Lew, Walter K. *Excerpts from: Dikth/Dikte For Dictée* (1982). Seoul: Yeul Eum Publishing, 1992.

Lewallen, Constance, ed. *The Dream of the Audience: Theresa Hak Kyung Cha* (1951–1982). Berkeley: University of California Press, 2001.

Leyva, Yolanda Chavez. "Listening to Silences in Latina/Chicana Lesbian History." *Living Chicana Theory.* Ed. Carla Trujillo. Berkeley: Third Woman Press, 1998. 429–434.

Lim-Hing, Sharon, ed. *The Very Inside: An Anthology of Writing by Asian and Pacific Islander Lesbian and Bisexual Women.* Toronto: Sister Vision Black Women and Women of Color Press, 1994.

Linton, Patricia. "'What Stories the Wind Would Tell': Representation and Appropriation in Maxine Hong Kingston's *China Men.*" *MELUS: The Journal of the Society for the Study of the Multi-Ethnic Literature of the United States* 19.4 (1994): 37–48.

Lo, Meng Yu Marie. "Fields of Recognition: Reading Asian Canadian Literature in Asian America." Ph.D. diss., Department of Rhetoric, University of California–Berkeley, 2001.

Lorde, Audre. *Sister Outsider: Essays and Speeches.* Freedom: Crossing Press, 1984.

Lowe, Lisa. *Immigrant Acts: On Asian American Cultural Politics.* Durham: Duke University Press, 1996.

———. "Unfaithful to the Original: The Subject of *Dictée.*" *Writing Self, Writing Nation: Essays on Theresa Hak Kyung Cha's Dictée.* Eds. Elaine H. Kim and Norma Alarcon. Berkeley: Third Woman Press, 1994. 35–69.

———. "Work, Immigration, Gender: Asian 'American' Women." *Making More Waves: New Writing by Asian American Women.* Eds. Elaine H. Kim, Lilia V. Villanueva, and Asian Women United of California. Boston: Beacon Press, 1997. 269–277.

Maclear, Kyo. "Not in So Many Words: Translating Silence Across 'Difference.'" *Fireweed: A Feminist Quarterly of Writing, Politics, Art, and Culture* 44–45 (1994): 6–11.

Martin, Biddy. "Lesbian Identity and Autobiographical Difference[s]." *The Lesbian and Gay Studies Reader.* Eds. Henry Abelove, Michele Aina Barale, and David M. Halperin. New York: Routledge, 1993. 274–293.

Matsumoto, Valerie. "Japanese American Women During World War II." *Unequal Sisters: A Multicultural Reader in U.S. Women's History.* Eds. Vicki L. Ruiz and Ellen Carol DuBois, 2nd ed. New York: Routledge, 1994. 436–449.

McDowell, Deborah. "'It's Not Safe. Not Safe at All': Sexuality in Nella Larsen's *Passing.*" *The Lesbian and Gay Studies Reader.* Eds. Henry Abelove, Michele Aina Barale, and David M. Halperin. New York: Routledge, 1993. 616–625.

McFarlane, Scott. "Covering *Obasan* and the Narrative of Internment." *Privileging Positions: The Sites of Asian American Studies.* Eds. Gary Y. Okihiro, Marilyn

Alquizola, Dorothy Fujita Rony, and K. Scott Wong. Pullman: Washington State University Press, 1995. 401–411.

Min, Anchee. *Red Azalea: Life and Love in China.* New York: Pantheon Books, 1994.

Min, Eun Kyung. "Reading the Figure of Dictation in Theresa Hak Kyung Cha's *Dictée.*" *Other Sisterhoods: Literary Theory and U.S. Women of Color.* Ed. Sandra Kumamoto Stanley. Urbana: University of Illinois Press, 1998. 309–324.

Mirikitani, Janice. *We, the Dangerous: New and Selected Poems.* Berkeley: Celestial Arts, 1995.

Modleski, Tania. "Feminism and the Power of Interpretation: Some Critical Readings." *Feminist Studies/Critical Studies.* Ed. Teresa de Lauretis. Bloomington: Indiana University Press, 1986. 121–138.

Mohanty, Chandra Talpade. "Cartographies of Struggle: Third World Women and the Politics of Feminism." In *Third World Women and the Politics of Feminism.* Ed. Chandra Talpade Mohanty, Ann Russo, and Lourdes Torres. Bloomington: Indiana University Press, 1991. 1–47.

———. "Under Western Eyes: Feminist Scholarship and Colonial Discourses." *Third World Women and the Politics of Feminism.* Eds. Chandra Talpade Mohanty, Ann Russo, and Lourdes Torres. Bloomington: Indiana University Press, 1991. 51–80.

Morgan, Robin, ed. *Sisterhood is Powerful: An Anthology of Writings from the Women's Liberation Movement.* New York: Vintage, 1970.

Nagata, Donna K. *Legacy of Injustice: Exploring the Cross-Generational Impact of the Japanese American Internment.* New York: Plenum Press, 1993.

Naples, Nancy A. "Changing the Terms: Community Activism, Globalization, and the Dilemmas of Transnational Feminism Praxis." *Women's Activism and Globalization: Linking Local Struggles and Transnational Politics.* Eds. Nancy A. Naples and Manisha Desai. New York: Routledge, 2002. 3–14.

Nguyen, Viet Thanh. *Race and Resistance: Literature and Politics in Asian America.* New York: Oxford University Press, 2002.

Niranjana, Tejaswini. *Siting Translation: History, Post-Structuralism, and the Colonial Context.* Berkeley: University of California Press, 1992.

Okihiro, Gary Y. *Margins and Mainstreams: Asians in American History and Culture.* Seattle: University of Washington Press, 1994.

Olsen, Tillie. *Silences.* New York: Delta/Seymour Lawrence, 1965.

Omatsu, Glenn. "The 'Four Prisons' and the Movement of Liberation: Asian American Activism from the 1960s to the 1990s." *The State of Asian America: Activism and Resistance in the 1990s.* Ed. Karin Aguilar-San Juan. Boston: South End Press, 1994. 19–70.

Omi, Michael, and Howard Winant. *Racial Formation in the United States: From the 1960s to the 1990.* 2d ed. New York: Routledge, 1994.

Palumbo-Liu, David. "The Politics of Memory: Remembering History in Alice Walker and Joy Kogawa." *Memory and Cultural Politics: New Approaches to American Ethnic Literatures.* Eds. Amritjit Singh, Joseph T. Skerrett, Jr., and Robert E. Hogan. Boston: Northeastern University Press, 1996. 211–226.

Pascoe, Peggy. "Gender Systems in Conflict: The Marriages of Mission-Educated Chinese American Women, 1874–1939." *Unequal Sisters: A Multicultural Reader in U.S. Women's History*. Eds. Vicki L. Ruiz and Ellen Carol DuBois. 2d ed. New York: Routledge, 1994. 139–156.

Pegues, Juliana, and Pei Lu Fung. "White Rice: Searching for Identity," *The Very Inside: An Anthology of Writing by Asian and Pacific Islander Lesbian and Bisexual Women*. Ed. Sharon Lim-Hing. Toronto: Sister Vision Black Women and Women of Color Press, 1994. 25–36.

Penelope, Julia, and Susan J. Wolfe, eds. *The Original Coming Out Stories*. Freedom: Crossing Press: 1980.

Pfaff, Timothy. "Talk with Mrs. Kingston." *Conversations with Maxine Hong Kingston*. Eds. Paul Skenazy and Tera Martin. Jackson: University Press of Mississippi, 1998. 14–20.

Quimby, Karin. "'This Is My Own, My Native Land': Construction of Identity and Landscape in Joy Kogawa's *Obasan*." *Cross-Addressing: Resistance Literature and Cultural Borders*. Ed. John C. Hawley. Albany: State University of New York Press, 1996. 257–273.

Rich, Adrienne. *On Lies, Secrets, and Silence: Selected Prose, 1966–1978*. New York: W. W. Norton, 1979.

Rinder, Lawrence. "The Plurality of Entrances, the Opening of Networks, the Infinity of Languages." *The Dream of the Audience: Theresa Hak Kyung Cha (1951–1982)*. Ed. Constance Lewallen. Berkeley: University of California Press, 2001. 15–31.

———. "The Theme of Displacement in the Art of Theresa Hak Kyung Cha and a Catalogue of the Artist's *Oeuvre*." Master's Thesis, Department of Art History, Hunter College, City University of New York, 1990.

Roth, Moira. "Theresa Hak Kyung Cha 1951–1982: A Narrative Chronology." *Writing Self, Writing Nation: Essays on Theresa Hak Kyung Cha's Dictée*. Eds. Elaine H. Kim and Norma Alarcon. Berkeley: Third Woman Press, 1994. 151–160.

Scholes, Robert. "Reading Like a Man." *Men and Feminism*. Ed. Alice Jardine and Paul Smith. New York: Methuen, 1987. 204–218.

Schweik, Susan. "A Needle With Mama's Voice: Mitsuye Yamada's *Camp Notes* and the American Canon of War Poetry." *Arms and the Woman: War, Gender, and Literary Representation*. Eds. Helen M. Cooper, Adrienne Auslander Munich, and Susan Merrill Squier. Chapel Hill: University of North Carolina Press, 1989. 225–243.

Scott, Joan W. "The Evidence of Experience." *The Lesbian and Gay Studies Reader*. Eds. Henry Abelove, Michèle Aina Barale, and David M. Halperin. New York: Routledge, 1993. 397–415.

Sethi, Rita Chaudhry. "Smells Like Racism: A Plan for Mobilizing against Anti-Asian Bias." *The State of Asian America: Activism and Resistance in the 1990s*. Ed. Karin Aguilar-San Juan. Boston: South End Press, 1994. 235–250.

Shih, Shu-Mei. "Nationalism and Korean American Women's Writing: Theresa Hak Kyung Cha's *Dictée*." *Speaking the Other Self: American Women Writers*.

Ed. Jeanne Campbell Reesman. Athens: University of Georgia Press, 1997. 144–162.

Simmons, Diane. *Maxine Hong Kingston.* New York: Twayne Publishers, 1999.

Skenazy, Paul, and Tera Martin. *Conversations with Maxine Hong Kingston.* Jackson: University Press of Mississippi, 1998.

Smith, Barbara. "Toward a Black Feminist Criticism." *The New Feminist Criticism and Theory.* Ed. Barbara Smith. New York: Pantheon Books, 1985. 168–185.

Somerson, Wendy. "Under the Mosquito Net: Space and Sexuality in *Red Azalea.*" *College Literature* 24.1 (1997): 98–115.

Tachiki, Amy, Eddie Wong, Franklin Odo, and Buck Wong, eds. *Roots: An Asian American Reader.* Los Angeles: UCLA Asian American Studies Center, 1971.

Takaki, Ronald. "Reflections on Racial Patterns in America." *From Different Shores: Perspectives on Race and Ethnicity in America.* Ed. Ronald Takaki. New York: Oxford University Press, 1987. 26–37.

———. *Strangers from a Different Shore: A History of Asian Americans.* New York: Penguin, 1989.

Tan, Amy. "Mother Tongue." *Under Western Eyes: Personal Essays from Asian America.* Ed. Garrett Hongo. New York: Anchor Books/Doubleday, 1995. 313–320.

Terry, Jennifer. "Theorizing Deviant Historiography." *Differences: A Journal of Feminist Cultural Studies* 3.2 (1991): 55–74.

Tetreault, Mary Ann. "Accountability or Justice? Rape as a War Crime." *Feminist Frontiers IV.* Eds. Laurel Richardson, Verta Taylor, and Nancy Whittier. New York: McGraw-Hill, 1997. 427–439.

Trinh T. Minh-ha. *Framer Framed.* New York: Routledge, 1992.

———. "Not You/Like You: Post-Colonial Women and the Interlocking Questions of Identity and Difference." *Making Face, Making Soul/Haciendo Caras: Creative and Critical Perspectives by Women of Color.* Ed. Gloria Anzaldúa. San Francisco: Aunt Lute Books, 1990. 371–375.

———. *Woman, Native, Other: Writing Postcoloniality and Feminism.* Bloomington: Indiana University Press, 1989.

Trujillo, Carla, ed. *Living Chicana Theory.* Berkeley: Third Woman Press, 1998.

Vance, Carole S. "Pleasure and Danger: Toward a Politics of Sexuality." *Pleasure and Danger: Exploring Female Sexuality.* Ed. Carole S. Vance. New York: Routledge and Kegan Paul, 1984. London: Pandora Press, 1992. 1–27.

Wald, Priscilla. *Constituting Americans: Cultural Anxiety and Narrative Form.* Durham: Duke University Press, 1995.

Wallace, Michele. *Black Macho and the Myth of the Superwoman.* New York: Dial Press, 1978.

Weglyn, Michi. *Years of Infamy: The Untold Story of America's Concentration Camps.* New York: William Morrow, 1976.

Wei, William. *The Asian American Movement.* Philadelphia: Temple University Press, 1993.

Wells, Kenneth, ed. *South Korea's Minjung Movement: The Culture and Politics of Dissidence.* Honolulu: University of Hawaii Press, 1995.

Wittig, Monique. *Les Guérillères*. Trans. David Le Vay. Boston: Beacon Press, 1969. London: Peter Owen, 1971.

———. *The Lesbian Body*. Trans. David Le Vay. Boston: Beacon Press, 1973. London: Peter Owen, 1975.

Wolf, Susan. "Theresa Cha: Recalling Telling Retelling." *Afterimage: A Publication of the Visual Studies Workshop* 14.1 (1986): 11–13.

Wong, Jade Snow. *Fifth Chinese Daughter*. New York: Harper and Bros., 1950.

———. *No Chinese Stranger*. New York: Harper and Row, 1975.

Wong, Sau-ling Cynthia. *Reading Asian American Literature: From Necessity to Extravagance*. Princeton: Princeton University Press, 1993.

———, ed., *Maxine Hong Kingston's The Woman Warrior: A Casebook*. New York: Oxford University Press, 1999.

Wong, Shelley Sunn. "Unnaming the Same: Theresa Hak Kyung Cha's *Dictée*." *Writing Self, Writing Nation: Essays on Theresa Hak Kyung Cha's Dictee*. Eds. Elaine H. Kim and Norma Alarcon. Berkeley: Third Woman Press, 1994. 103–140.

Woolf, Virginia. *A Room of One's Own*. New York: Harcourt Brace Jovanovich, 1929.

Xu, Wenying. "Agency via Guilt in Anchee Min's *Red Azalea*." MELUS: *The Journal of the Society for the Study of Multi-Ethnic Literatures of the U.S.* 25.3–4 (2000): 203–219.

Yamada, Mitsuye. "Asian Pacific American Women and Feminism." *This Bridge Called My Back: Writings By Radical Women of Color*. Eds. Cherríe Moraga and Gloria Anzaldúa, New York: Kitchen Table Women of Color Press, 1981. 71–75.

———. *Camp Notes and Other Poems*. N.p.: Shameless Hussy Press, 1976. New York: Kitchen Table Women of Color Press, 1992.

———. "Experiential Approaches to Teaching Joy Kogawa's *Obasan*." *Teaching American Ethnic Literatures: Nineteen Essays*. Eds. John R. Maitino and David R. Peck. Albuquerque: University of New Mexico Press, 1996. 293–311.

———. "Invisibility Is an Unnatural Disaster: Reflections of an Asian American Woman." *This Bridge Called My Back: Writings By Radical Women of Color*. Eds. Cherríe Moraga and Gloria Anzaldúa. New York: Kitchen Table Women of Color Press, 1981. 35–40.

Yamamoto, Traise. *Masking Selves, Making Subjects: Japanese American Women, Identity, and the Body*. Berkeley: University of California Press, 1999.

Yamato. Gloria. "Something About the Subject Makes It Hard to Name." *Making Face, Making Soul/Haciendo Caras: Creative and Critical Perspectives by Women of Color*. Ed. Gloria Anzaldúa, San Francisco: Aunt Lute Books, 1990. 20–24.

Yang, Hyunah. "Re-membering the Korean Military Comfort Women: Nationalism, Sexuality, and Silencing." *Dangerous Women: Gender and Korean Nationalism*. Ed. Elaine H. Kim and Chungmoo Choi. New York: Routledge, 1998. 123–139.

Yee, Marian. Review of *Camp Notes*, by Mitsuye Yamada. *The Forbidden Stitch: An Asian American Women's Anthology*. Eds. Shirley Geok-lin Lim and Mayumi Tsutakawa. Corvallis: Calyx Books, 1989. 243–247.

Yung, Judy. *Unbound Feet: A Social History of Chinese Women in San Francisco.* Berkeley: University of California Press, 1995.

Zimmerman, Bonnie. "What Has Never Been: An Overview of Lesbian Feminist Criticism." *The New Feminist Criticism: Literature and Theory.* Ed. Elaine Showalter. New York: Pantheon, 1985. 200–224.

———, ed. *The Safe Sea of Women: Lesbian Fiction 1969–1989.* Boston: Beacon Press, 1990.

index

Abraham, Julie, 13, 200, 202, 208, 251n18
Adachi, Ken, 102
"Agency via Guilt in Anchee Min's *Red Azalea*" (Xu), 195
Alexander, Meena, 225
American-feminine, 22–23
Amott, Teresa, 40–44, 46
Anzaldúa, Gloria, 5, 8–9, 11–12
Articulate Silences (Cheung), 19
Asian American women: and Christianity, 50–51, 176, 180; "degendering" of, 196; equated with national bodies, 179; excluded from immigration, 44, 50; and feminism, 56, 221–25; in internment camps, 91; invisibility of, 11; prostitution of, 47–51; sexuality of, 50, 173–74; stereotypes of, 49, 174, 252n21

Asian Americans: attacks on, 40–41, 102, 131–32, 241n5; "bachelor societies," 44; and discriminatory U.S. policy, 42; dominant view of, 6; enslavement of, 35, 48; exploitation of, 35–38; feminization of, 51–52, 179, 238n26; historical silence of, 71; internment of, 28, 75–128; invisibility of, 11, 33, 131; labor strikes, 35, 53–55; literary attacks on, 131–32; litigation on behalf of, 55, 244n19; nationalism, 56; as non-Americans, 216; politics of, 236n12; problematic use of term, 3–7, 33–34; self-employment, 38; sexism of, 132–33; as social construct, 4, 105; stereotypes of, 6, 19, 49; unionization of, 37. *See also* Chinese Americans; immigration; intern-

sciousness in, 178–79, 183, 191; sexuality in, 175, 177, 182, 192; silence in, 174–75, 180–83, 185, 190–92; speech in, 177; truth in, 176, 185, 188; and *The Woman Warrior*, 176, 249n6
comfort women, 177–78, 249n8, 250n10
Commission on Wartime Relocation and Internment of Civilians (CWRIC), 76–77, 241n2
Compositional Subjects (Kang), 71–72
concentration camps. *See* internment; Japanese Americans
Constituting Americans (Wald), 72
culture of dissemblance, 10

D'Emilio, John, 12
Dhairyam, Sagri, 15
dichotomous thinking, 3–4, 8, 15, 33; in *Camp Notes*, 86, 155, 162–63, 249n4; and racism, 240n35; in *Red Azalea*, 198–99, 202–03, 205, 210–12
dictation. *See* *Dictée*; translation
Dictée (Cha): and audience, 149–54; borderlands in, 164–67, 248n24; "broken" English in, 171; characters in, 140; colonization of Korea in, 136–37, 140–41, 143, 158; dictation in, 156–58; displacement in, 136–40, 144–45, 147–49, 152, 166–67; family in, 139–43, 149; female martyrs in, 140–44; frontispiece of, 137–38, 152; Korean identity in, 136, 142, 165; language in, 141–42, 144, 146–47, 158, 170; primary themes of, 136–39; resistance in, 146–48; silence in, 153–54, 159, 164, 170–71; textual inaccessibility of, 138, 151, 164; "third space" in, 162–64, 169, 219; translation in, 154–62, 170; and writing, 144

discourse: male forms of, 8; of silence, 14–15. *See also* silence
dispersal, 102–03. *See also* internment
displacement. See under *Dictée*
doublespeak, 103

either/or thinking. *See* dichotomous thinking
"Evidence of Experience, The" (Scott), 104
Executive Order 9066, 80–81, 241n2

female sexuality, 173
femininity, American, 22–23; and class, 196
feminism, xi, 220–25, 253n6
Fifth Chinese Daughter (Wong), 18
first-person. *See* subjectivity
Fishkin, Shelley Fisher, 16
Ford, Gerald, 241n2
Foucault, Michel, 14–15, 146, 218
Fung, Richard, 105, 150

Gentlemen's Agreement of 1907, 36, 46
Glenn, Evelyn Nakano, 45
Goellnicht, Donald, 43, 60, 115–17
"Gold Mountain," 34
Grewal, Gurleen, 120, 122, 125, 127
Guy-Sheftall, Beverly, 3, 228n4

Halberstam, Judith, ix
Hatamiya, Leslie, 81
Hattori, Tomo, 117–18
Hawaii Laborers' Assocation, 54
Hedges, Elaine, 16
heroism, 250n11, 251n16
heterosexual plot, 200, 202, 208
Hicks, George, 178
Higginbotham, Evelyn Brooks, 65–67
Hine, Darlene Clark, 9, 250n13
history: and counterhistory, 106–07; radical potential of, 209–10; re-

103; definition of, 245n23; familial disruption in, 109–10; historical figures in, 106; language in, 114, 119, 124; memory in, 106–10, 112–13; "Orientalism" in, 117–18; psychoanalytic interpretations of, 114–15; reconciliation in, 126; as revision of history, 104–05, 108–09, 111, 118; sexual abuse in, 115; silence in, 113, 116–28

transgressions in, 195–97, 199, 206–08, 251n17, 253n23; heterosexual plot of, 200, 202–03, 208, 251n18; lesbian sexuality in, 175, 197–98, 203, 252n21; sexuality as resistance in, 199, 202, 207, 209, 213; silence in, 174–75, 194, 198, 201, 207–08, 210–11

14; protective, 78, 122, 181, 190, 242n9; and racism, 2; as resistance, ix, 15, 19, 23–24, 28–29, 78, 146, 210; and sexuality, 9, 12, 174; and speech, ix, 14–15; stereotypes of, 216; and subjectivity, 23; as trope, 7. *See also* specific works

American women; sexuality; specific works

Wong, Jade Snow, 18

Wong, Shelley Sunn, 130–31, 133, 138, 141, 158–60

Woolf, Virginia, 16–18

World War II. See *Camp Notes; Comfort Woman*; internment; Japanese Americans; *Obasan*

writing: and liberation, 24; as resistance in *Dictée*, 144; and speech, 15, 170; and subjectivity, 17

Xu, Wenying, 195

Yamada, Mitsuye: and American identity, 95, 98, 100; and Canadian internment, 102–03; and feminism, 100–01, 132; internment experiences of, 81–82, 87–92; on *Obasan*, 115; and silence, 94, 98–101; and women's visibility, 11. *See also* specific works

Yamamoto, Traise: and masks, 10–11, 88, 95–96, 229n14; and works by Kogawa, 115, 126; and works by Mirikitani, 77, 81; and works by Yamada, 81, 93, 95

Yamato, Gloria, 67–68

Yang, Hyunah, 178–80

Yee, Marian, 97–98

Yung, Judy, 18, 20, 48–50